NICK CLOONEY

THE MOVIES THAT CHANGED US

Reflections on the Screen

ATRIA BOOKS

New York London Toronto Sydney Singapore

ATRIA BOOKS

1230 Avenue of the Americas
New York, NY 10020

ISBN: 0-7434-1043-2

First Atria Books hardcover printing November 2002

10 9 8 7 6 5 4 3 2 1

ATRIA BOOKS is a trademark of Simon & Schuster, Inc.

For information regarding special discounts for bulk purchases,
please contact Simon & Schuster Special Sales at 1-800-456-6798
or business@simonandschuster.com

Designed by Jaime Putorti

Printed in the U.S.A

For Nina

ACKNOWLEDGMENTS

Let me begin by thanking my late sister, Rosemary Clooney. Not only did she help me directly in preparing Chapter 16, but she shared with me a lifelong passion for the movies. For a time, her California home with her then-husband Jose Ferrer was something of a salon for filmmakers and musicmakers and I was always welcome to attend when I was in town.

This book is the brainchild of my friend Joanna Pulcini, a wonderful young woman who neglected to remind me that the idea would require about 75,000 words, one after the other. Another friend is my editor for Atria Books, a film buff who brought his own solid writing skills to the editing process with salutary effect, Mitchell Ivers.

While speaking of Atria Books, the enthusiasm of publisher Judith Curr, deputy publisher Karen Mender, and director of publicity Seale Ballenger has been encouraging. It is the assistant director, Louise Braverman, who has kept me busy on the phone and on the road.

Interviews I conducted long ago and others of much more recent vintage have been woven into the text. And so I am grateful first to the late Thomas Mitchell for his insights into *Stagecoach* and to the late, prolific director George Marshall for pointing me toward *Miracle of Morgan's Creek* as a pioneering breach in the wall of the "Code." After a long series of questions, Mr. Marshall asked, "What are you, kid, a reporter?" He knew me better than I knew myself.

For more recent interviews, I am grateful to director Steven Soderbergh; actor Ernest Borgnine; actress Janet Leigh; actress Louise Platt; actor Eddie Bracken; noted psychiatrist Dr. Milton Rosenbaum; Dr. Kenneth White, historian from Catholic University; Bill Pence and Jim Bedford of the Telluride Film Festival; Ed Rigaud, president of the Underground Railroad Museum; Ms. Blanche Chambers of Maysville, Kentucky; and nearly one hundred other interviews that were conducted without being quoted in the text but were invaluable as background. Pat Davis and George Callahan of American Movie Classics long ago set me on useful research paths.

It must be added that time spent as a fortunate teenager in conversations with actor-director Jose Ferrer, producer Irving "Dad" Asher, music doctor Roger Edens, writer Ketti Frings, actor Jim Backus, director Michael Curtiz, and the fine character actors Walter Abel, Ann Seymour, Ted de Corsia, and Royal Dano added incalculably to my store of notes and memories. And few can re-create early Hollywood with the verve of my brother-in-law, movie dancer Dante DiPaolo.

Jill Partin deciphered my manuscript with patience and good suggestions. My daughter, Ada, and son, George, were enthusiastic supporters. Above all, my wife kept me focused when other projects intervened.

While I am grateful for everyone's help, I want to make clear that all opinions and any errors are my responsibility.

Nick Clooney
Augusta, KY

CONTENTS

CONTENTS

INTRODUCTION

For every thousand movies that entertained us there was, perhaps, one that changed us.

Many find lists as invidious as comparisons, particularly in the arts. "Best" and "worst" are subjective terms and will not be used to describe any of the films outlined in this book.

Instead, you will see an effort to present evidence that, as a result of each of these motion pictures, the course of society—or, at a minimum, the course of movies themselves—was altered.

As America continues to adjust to a world made different by the thunder and fire of September 11, 2001, there has been a temptation to search deeply into every aspect of our lives, including popular culture, for clues to the roots of those disasters.

Some writers, including me, succumbed to that temptation in the weeks after the terrorist attacks, assigning a fraction of the blame to the video-game quality of many movies, which use astonishing special effects to seem to destroy our national institutions, bring down our towering buildings and attack our popular attractions, all in the name of entertainment. Surely, went this line of reasoning, these kinds of movie spectacles served to deaden the nerve endings of a generation of people around the world to this kind of atrocity, to somehow bring it within the ring of plausible actions to effect political change.

At least part of this reaction, it now seems clear, was born when so many of us actually saw on our television screens the second sleek jetliner slice cleanly through the splendid geometry of the remaining World Trade Center tower. The blow to our collective solar plexus came because this time we knew there were real people aboard that aircraft and real people sitting in those offices, and that they were dying as we watched.

For many, that chilling, indelible picture made cheap and vulgar the guilty pleasure we had derived from watching dozens of similar pictures created by Hollywood in an increasingly frantic effort to shock us into buying tickets. Could some trail be found that would connect the all-too-real attacks of September 11 and the superheated fantasies of high-tech disaster films? Some of us thought those dots could be connected.

It appears we were wrong. Far from using any part of American popular culture to provide a blueprint for mass murder, the attackers and their sponsors reviled it in every detail. Instead of embracing high-tech, they learned and used only the barest minimum necessary to complete their murderous mission. In philosophy, they are much closer to the Luddites of the nineteenth century, condemning advancing technology as immoral, than to the *Terminator* attitude of the twentieth century, embracing technology in an updated manic, fantasized fascism.

If, however, movies are not implicated in 2001's seminal event, that does not mean that they have not had an important role in other changes—both melancholy and incandescent—in the hundred years since their introduction.

The twenty chapters of this book and its epilogue will trace in reverse order much of the long road from the titillating arcade attraction of the early twentieth century to the acknowledged art form of today. It has been a long road with many detours. This book will chart some of those detours and argue that they were detours that changed things.

A preponderance of the titles found in this book come from a time often called the "golden era" of motion pictures. That is not because I believe that films of the 1930s, 1940s, and 1950s were better than those made earlier or later. That is an argument for another book.

In fact, many of the movies that most experts agree are the best will *not* be seen here. *Citizen Kane*, stunning achievement that it was, did not really change anything. Even today it stands alone in isolated splendor, one of a kind. *Gone With the Wind*, brilliantly filmed and performed, was essentially a revisiting of ground already plowed by *The Birth of a Nation* a generation earlier.

The premise here is that in order for a film to be seen as one that "changed" us, the content must be ahead of, or at least on top of, the curve of change. For that reason, a movie such as *Gentleman's Agreement* (1947) didn't make the cut. Although it was a powerful statement against anti-Semitism, it came *after* the world already knew about the Holocaust and where casual anti-Jewish bigotry could lead. The same movie made just a few years earlier might have, indeed, changed things.

To return to the question of why so many of the films described in this book came from the middle years of the twentieth century, the reason is *quantitative* rather than *qualitative*. In order to change anything in an important way, the films have to reach and affect large masses of people. By the last decades of the twentieth century, movies were no longer reaching the same large masses of our population as they had in the middle years of the century.

Numbers can make the eyes glaze over, but a few of them here might be interesting and make a point. In the decade of the 1920s, most of that a time of silent films, 31 percent of all the men, women, and children in the United States went to the movies every week. In the 1930s, that number skyrocketed to an astounding 73 percent, cutting across all age, ethnic and economic boundaries. Throughout the 1940s the percentage remained in the 60s and even after the advent of television in the 1950s, more than four out of ten of us headed for the neighborhood theaters every week.

In the 1960s, the number dropped to below 25 percent, then the bottom really fell out. No more than 9 percent of all Americans went to the movies weekly in the decades of the 1970s and 1980s, and that percentage has not changed substantially in more recent years.

So, for instance, a film such as *JFK*, which many educators feared would substitute revisionist theory for actual history in an entire generation—as did *The Birth of a Nation* eighty years earlier—does not appear to have had much impact, simply because only a minority of young people, and an even smaller fraction of those in middle years or older, have ever seen it.

That was not always so.

For thirty years, from the time sound was introduced into motion pictures in 1927 to the fracturing of the studio system in the mid-1950s and the emergence of television, movies were the dominant entertainment force in the world. And the Hollywood studios dominated the movies. Along the way, they also, almost as a by-product, overwhelmed the emerging community of Los Angeles, becoming for a time its major industry.

It is perhaps increasingly difficult to re-create for the younger reader the time in which movies ruled, but it is worth the effort.

The background influences were, in relatively quick succession: history's worst economic depression; history's most devastating war; and the nation's greatest period of affluence up to that time.

The engines driving our popular culture were the movies and radio, both of them heading us in a direction we all wanted to go. We were looking for consensus. We yearned to be defined as Americans. Not hyphenated Americans, but truly *sui generis*.

We hoped—believed—we were inventing a new person, this American found exclusively from sea to shining sea and nowhere else on earth.

That might seem so naive as to be almost like another world to latter-day Americans who have made a virtual religion of celebrating differences, but that is how it was. When one-time teenage refugee Henry Kissinger spoke of having as his goal wearing a V-neck sweater and argyle socks and losing his accent, he was speaking for many. Second-generation Americans refused to use the native Italian, German, Spanish, Yiddish, Russian, French, or a dozen other languages that were spoken in their homes. We took very seriously the *"Unum"* in *"E Pluribus Unum."* In a way probably not seen before or since, we wanted to be "indivisible." Our true language was slang and our sound track was swing.

Granted, this was all on what was, in retrospect, a superficial level. The deep cultural divides and long-held prejudices were still there, breaking out in occasional ugly pustules of violence and acrimony. But the urge was no less real for being superficial, a manifestation of our willingness to pay at least lip service to the aspirations outlined in our most cherished documents, the Declaration of Independence and the Constitution, with its Bill of Rights. At some level, the hope must have been that the form would evolve into reality. It didn't work out that way, but we didn't know that then.

Everything seemed possible, even when ruin impended at every turn.

Perhaps it is because all of our heroes and villains were bigger than life. On radio, they were whatever we imagined them. On the screen, they were thirty feet tall.

And what were these giants teaching us? Simplistic lessons that we took to heart, most of us, and believed at some level for the rest of our days: That we were to protect those weaker than we and defy those who were stronger. That if we were honest and worked hard, life would reward us. That when we got a bad break, the best way to deal with it was with stoicism, or a joke, or a song. That dreams could come true if you had the courage to pursue them. That America was always right, that she always won, and that God was always on her side. And that with enough kindness and understanding of human frailty, all endings could be happy.

Cynicism, always looming outside the theater, had difficulty getting a foothold among a population taught optimism by giants on the screen.

"Reality" films didn't stand much chance in those years. There was entirely too much reality just outside each door. Many recent observers marvel at how few movies of the 1930s, for instance, even make reference to the Depression. Those who lived through it, however, are not at all surprised. The Depression was the elephant in the living room, capable of crushing every living thing. Any reference was superfluous. So we were taught by our movies to dance and sing and laugh through hard times; all in all, a valuable lesson.

Certainly, we were taught other things as well. Many stereotypes, particularly black-white racial stereotypes, were reinforced, to society's detriment.

Still, even here, there were moments. There was one wartime action picture called *Crash Dive*, starring Tyrone Power, a native of the city in which I was living, Cincinnati, Ohio, so it had special significance. There were plenty of military heroics, so as an eight-year-old I was able to wade through the tiresome love triangle, which included Dana Andrews and Anne Baxter.

But tucked into this story was a surprise. There was the usual old salt, played by James Gleason, and the usual black mess steward, played by Ben Carter. In early scenes, Gleason verbally abused Carter, who was appropriately obsequious. But as the screenplay evolved, there was a dramatic change. By the time the battle climax was reached, Carter was an equal participant in the firefight. He had a helmet and a Thompson submachine gun, and he held off the enemy heroically while his comrades made their getaway. Did writer Jo Swerling and director Archie Mayo do that transformation deliberately? There is no one left to tell us.

It was a great surprise to see that characterization of a black man. My two sisters and I were born in Kentucky, and though our grandmother, who raised us, would never permit the slightest racist remark or epithet in our house, we were surrounded by institutional racism: The railroad station had two waiting rooms, two water fountains, and four rest rooms. At our own house of dreams, the beautiful Russell movie palace in Maysville, African Americans had to do their dreaming in the "colored balcony." We did not rail at these arrangements. They were simply the way things were.

Yet, *Crash Dive* was perhaps an opening wedge for a series of questions that led to the raising of our consciousness after the war. If a black man could be—or even play—a hero for his country, as Ben Carter did, all thirty feet of him, how could we now deny him rights he had fought for?

In a way, that rise in consciousness led to my greatest disappointment in the research for this book. The *Crash Dive* experience shows what Hollywood *could* have done had it set its considerable skills on the race question early on. In the end, it was sadly behind the curve, leading to the book's final chapter, "The Movie That Never Was."

Millions of us, sitting in the anonymous darkness every week—double feature, a short, a cartoon, and a newsreel—came out of each movie slightly changed. Perhaps it was something as simple as a crush on an impossibly attractive star. Perhaps it was a reinforcement of some attitude. Perhaps it was the changing of an opinion. Perhaps it was a melody or a dance routine. Perhaps it was only a different way of talking or combing your hair, or holding your cigarette, or crossing your legs.

After the movies lost their mass audience, there was a very big difference in the way Americans received their entertainment. For the baby boomers and each generation that followed, the heroes were not *larger* than life, they were *smaller* than life. Moreover, they were not the sole, overwhelming object of the viewer's attention, as they were in darkened theaters. There were telephone interruptions, conversations, the baby crying, the doorbell, and, above all, commercial breaks.

The principal medium of entertainment from the 1950s on has been smaller than the consumer and has delivered its product in short, disjointed chunks. It has been much harder to take seriously.

That seems a profound difference and one which may have contributed to the fragmentation of our culture and the return to an alienation from institutions that was prevalent in our nation's earliest years.

Is there empirical evidence? Not much. But, as Winston Churchill often said when his rational conclusions were contradicted by scientists laden with bothersome facts, "If that isn't true, it ought to be."

Whatever the psychological ramifications, it is clear that movies now must "narrowcast" their releases, targeting an ever-younger audience voracious for action, technology, explicit sex, and almost surreally graphic violence. After September 11, 2001, there was a temporary suspension, not only of the making of ultraviolent films, but of the release of many already made and even of the playing on television of some of the more recent fantasies of violence. That suspension is now just a memory.

It should also be noted that all through this contemporary period of feeding ever more primitive, violent, simplistic, and very nearly inarticulate movies to a specific audience, hundreds of brave and brilliant filmmakers are out there producing excellent fare and even the occasional masterpiece, often outside the studio system and, therefore, on the narrowest of economic margins. It is most often they who remind us of what we loved about that unique experience from the first time we sat down in a theater and someone dimmed the lights.

The fascination remains. The hope is stubborn. As opening titles roll, just before the first establishing shot, before we've heard a word of dialogue, our expectations are in equipoise with possibilities.

This could be a movie that changes us.

February 2002
Nick Clooney

1

SAVING PRIVATE RYAN

1998

DIRECTOR: STEVEN SPIELBERG
STARS: TOM HANKS, EDWARD BURNS, TOM SIZEMORE
RUNNING TIME: 2 HOURS, 49 MINUTES

Soon after D-Day, June 6, 1944, a U.S. Army captain is ordered to locate a Private Ryan, get him out of harm's way, and return him to the United States. His three brothers have been killed in combat, and his death, it is thought, would be a serious public relations disaster for the military in the wake of the deaths of the five Sullivan brothers earlier in the war. The captain takes his squad into Normandy to carry out his assignment, with predictable but still shocking results.

The now-famous opening sequence on Omaha Beach is only the first of the most harrowing battle scenes ever filmed.

Note: *Saving Private Ryan* is based on an actual episode in World War II.

Dreamworks (Courtesy of The Kobal Collection)

I t was late summer in the year 2000. Five people sat in a lounge just off the lobby of the Hotel Scribe, hard by L'Opera in Paris. Four of them had just returned from a daylong tour of Omaha Beach in Normandy. The fifth was a young French woman who worked as a tour guide.

"I'm not sure what I was supposed to feel. I don't think I felt anything." The woman speaking was in her early seventies. Her voice had the sharp, confident cadence of a midwestern country-club Republican. Her remarks, while directed at the whole group, seemed meant for her contemporary, a man of similar years and similar background.

But not, apparently, similar opinions. His face reddened. "You mean to tell me," he responded in a voice so soft that everyone had to strain to hear him, "that you could look on row after row of white crosses, look down on that beach from the dunes, actually walk on that beach, and not *feel* anything?"

The woman smiled faintly. She and the man who had just spoken were most decidedly *not* a couple. They had been thrown together in the willy-nilly fashion of a commercial tour. For the first week—in London—she had remained substantially anonymous. Then she learned she could strike sparks with the gentleman in question simply by saying something with which she knew he would disagree. Since then she had virtually stalked him, waiting for her moment. She was having a fine time.

Mr. Seventy-something was by now speechless with anger. He looked at the others, spluttering, a call for help in his eyes.

Two of those he faced *were* most definitely a couple. Now in their mid-sixties, they had been together for forty years. Their quick glance at one another said, "Here we go again."

The sixty-something man began in a conciliatory tone. "Well, I suppose the point is you're not *supposed* to feel anything, you do or you don't." A typical remark, because the man was cursed with a facility for seeing both sides of a dispute. This time, however, he paused. He no longer saw his companions, but a sort of computer screen cataloguing the events of this long day.

A train ride from Paris past familiar communities. Off the train at Caen, stubbornly held by the Germans for weeks after D-Day. Then onto a bus, a competent tour guide chanting names and numbers, now just as famous—and as sterile—as the French legends of Marshall Foch and Captain Dreyfuss and Jeanne d'Arc.

It was raining by the time the group reached the U.S. military cemetery above the famous beach, 176 acres that are American soil forever, bought by the dreams and hopes and fears and futures of American kids.

The nine thousand markers are neat, looking exactly like the pictures everyone had seen. More Stars of David than one might have thought, perhaps. Even the rain seemed unreal, soft and sad, like tears ordered from a special-effects service to fall just here, just now, not too hard, not too cold.

The sixty-something man and his wife walked the neat paths, talking softly about where they were when these men met the crucial, final, moment of their lives. He was ten, she was five. He remembered everything about that day, she very little.

"The war was trains to me," she said. "Bordering our farm was a train track. Train after train would go by and so many of them were troop trains. I would get as close as I was allowed to the tracks and wave. The windows on the trains were open and usually they weren't going very fast. Almost always some of those boys waved back.

"Daddy had a map in the kitchen, up on the wall, and he had little pins in it. He would listen to the radio and move the little pins. I never knew what the pins or the map meant.

"But I certainly knew about all those young men. Momma and Daddy made it clear to me that they were going to a place of terrible danger and that they were doing it to keep us safe.

"And now I can't help wondering if any of those boys on the trains that went by our little farm are . . ." She gestured in a 180 degree arc. "Here."

The rain was intermittent, but the thin stream of visitors was not. Most were old, some on canes and walkers, a few in wheelchairs. Occasionally, the older ones would be accompanied by a small knot of younger adults and some children. Family members, for the most part.

A woman limped off the path and into the grass. Soon she was among the crosses, staring intently first at a piece of paper in her hand, then at the markers. The piece of paper was de rigeur. A visitor who was looking for a particular gravesite would be handed directions to help find it.

In a few moments, the woman stopped. She was overweight, dressed in a light-colored pants suit. Her hair had lost the battle with the light drizzle and straggled over her ears. She bent to touch the top of a cross. After a moment, she knelt down heavily, using the cross for support. Her head bent forward and rested on her hand.

The group behind her looked away. The moment was private. Was it a brother, a friend, a lover, a husband? What was she mourning? The decayed remains of a shattered body that had been brought to this place so long ago? Her own young, slim, erect form standing consonant with his, making plans, dreaming of a life together?

All gone in the fire and smoke of a longest day on a beach called Omaha.

Some in the group felt an urgency to get down to the beach itself, to stand where *they* had stood. The bus negotiated a narrow road, then the narrow streets of Coleville-sur-Mer, then a beachside road, gray-green ocean to the left, beige and green dunes and bluffs to the right.

It could have been any beach, anywhere. There were cottages, a few restaurants, a small cluster of shops. It could have been any beach anywhere, but, of course, it wasn't.

The bus stopped at a parking lot a few yards from a marker. Of those alighting from the bus, half went to the marker, the other half to a nearby gift shop.

The marker had been put up by an engineering unit. There were several of them all up and down Omaha.

The tide was in, so the beach was much narrower than that long-ago morning. A curious thing happened. The group of Americans, who had previously taken in the sights in twos or threes or fours, split apart as on some silent command. Those who went to the beach went alone. Some walked far along the hardened sand, the sixty-something man among them. He strained to see and hear, to engrave the moment—for which he had waited fifty-six years—in his mind. The feel of the sand, its color, the sound of the gulls. He stood with his back to the dunes staring at the choppy sea. Empty now, except for a lone freighter. How was it that day when, as the morning mist rose, German soldiers saw that horizon—the very same horizon— filled from end to end with ships of every description.

He turned back toward the dunes. They were higher than he had imagined, but the image was all wrong. This concrete seawall, had it been there? He didn't remember it from the pictures. And the road. And, of course, all the houses. Then he had an idea. He crouched down. The seawall hid the road and the houses. Yes, that was how he thought it would look. Just the sand here and the bluff up there, with the pass over there and the heights of Pointe du Hoc farther over there. The cloudy skies muted the colors, casting the whole scene near his black-and-white memory.

Up until now, everything had been quite matter-of-fact, an exercise in historical recall, almost by rote. Then, unexpectedly, he felt hot tears in his eyes, overflowing, running down his cheeks. He was unused to and uncomfortable with tears, ashamed of them. He was glad he was alone.

So many young men in harm's way. So many individual acts of heroism here, and there, and over there, most of which were never chronicled.

Was it here, the sixty-something man thought, on this stretch of sand that the great war correspondent Ernie Pyle was walking on June 7, 1944, when he, in his immortal lines, wrote "I took a walk along the historic coast of Normandy in the country of France. It was a lovely day for strolling along the seashore. Men were sleeping on the sand, some of them were sleeping forever. Men were floating in the water, but they didn't know they were in the water, for they were dead." Was it right here, Ernie? he thought.

He had paused long enough for his embarrassing tears to dry, so he trudged back to the bus. A lively conversation was under way among the group waiting to board.

"I think it's disgraceful," said a woman, indicating a building across the street. "Look at that. L'Omaha Restaurant and Bar! It's disrespectful to the dead."

The man didn't get into it, though he disagreed. He thought the bar, the restaurant, the summer houses, the very ordinariness of it all was the whole point. Those long-ago soldiers were ordinary men who liked ordinary things. In a way, they were here because of their attachment to things they had come to think of as ordinary, many of which were threatened by the forces of evil arrayed on that powerful and unforgiving bluff.

The ride back on the bus and the train and finally a taxi to the lounge at the Hotel Scribe had been a time of sorting out emotions. In a way, he was reluctant to talk about it here, trivializing the experience by using it as a chip in a game of badinage between his two older companions.

So he fell silent and there was an awkward pause in the hotel lounge.

"I had not been there until last August." The fifth person in the group spoke in the careful sentences of those who have mastered a second language. She was French, not yet thirty, a student and a very good tour guide, smart, well-informed, and with a saving sense of humor. She was waiting to take a group for a dinner cruise on the river Seine that evening.

"You will have some difficulty, perhaps, understanding but for most French people, particularly young people, World War II is not our favorite war. Our country did not distinguish itself in the early days of the fighting. After the defeat, the majority of my countrymen adjusted to the occupation by the Germans. Most followed the orders of our leader, Pétain. Most thought of de Gaulle as a deluded dreamer, Britain as finished, America too distant to matter. As far as the Resistance was concerned, the most effective of them were Communists whom most Frenchman thought of as no better than the Nazis. To tell the truth, we also thought the Nazis were invincible, and that standing up to them only would get more and more innocent people killed.

"Whether we knew it or not our history lessons in school were slanted, I now believe, to emphasize the French—we did not call them 'Free French'—role in the defeat of Hitler. The part played by America and Britain was, I think, deliberately downgraded.

"When de Gaulle came to power he subtly encouraged this attitude. His purpose, I believe, was admirable. He wished to save us from a debilitating national inferiority complex.

"What changed all of that for me was a movie. *Saving Private Ryan*. It was incredible. It was not a film I would have seen on my own. I went with a group of students. We went, I believe, to poke holes in another piece of American propaganda, more self-aggrandizement.

"I was locked in my chair. It was like an epiphany. The thunderbolt that struck me was this: All that fire and steel and pain—and *none of those young American boys had to be there.* The French, yes, and the Poles and the Norwegians and Belgians and even the British, because they are part of Europe. But not the Americans.

"Those thousands of young American boys faced death not because they had to but because they thought it was the right thing to do. It is an amazing episode in history.

"It led me to rethink everything. I read facts that had been, I believe, hidden from me or shrugged off. I read numbers that had been left out when our professors told us of those times. I went to Omaha Beach, and to Utah and Sword and Gold and Juno. And to St. Mere Eglise.

"I still take pride in General Leclerc and the contribution of the French to the war, but it is a more realistic appreciation now. France had an honorable role in its own national salvation, just not a major one.

"*Saving Private Ryan* freed me from an anger I had not ever understood before, and many of the fellow students who saw it felt the same way. Isn't it interesting that a movie, a shadow on a screen, can do that?"

She looked at her watch, smiled briefly, and left to find her tour group. We were silent, digesting her words; *Saving Private Ryan* had changed her view of her country's history, and ours. Were there others in France who felt the same way?

She had called it "a shadow on a screen." There was a deep coincidence between our discussion and its location. The Scribe Hotel is the very place where the brothers Auguste and Louis

Lumière caused the sensation of 1895 by introducing the motion picture. The images were shown for months, right in this hotel, and within a very short time that same year, moving pictures were being featured in other countries, notably the United States.

It took a long time for this diversion to get—or, for that matter, deserve—respect. But respect would come.

In recent years, a lot of that respect would be earned by a man who was not born until three years after the watershed moments on Omaha Beach.

Steven Spielberg, like his colleague George Lucas, was a shy youngster who found expression in the world of film at a very early age. He was fascinated by home movies, started putting together screenplays with amateur actors when he was twelve, and at thirteen produced his first contest winner, a forty-minute documentary called *Escape to Nowhere*. Significantly, it was a war film.

Steven Spielberg has seen in World War II the defining period of the twentieth century and, perhaps, of much more than that.

Though his successes have shown an admirable range of subject matter and a phenomenal ability to make money, a clear thread of his work goes back to the first half of the decade of the 1940s: the entire *Raiders of the Lost Ark* series, his rare failure *1941*, *Empire of the Sun*, *Schindler's List*, and, in 1998, *Saving Private Ryan*.

There are those who believe that Steven Spielberg has deliberately undertaken a serious effort to let generations who were born long after World War II know how it was, what it meant, and why remembering it in detail is still important.

In the face of rampant revisionism, Spielberg seems determined to stem the tide of "antihistory."

From the mid-1960s through recent times, social commentators have noted a bias against history in many important enclaves of the academic community. The core of the bias begins with the perfectly accurate observation that many important people and forces were left out of most of mainstream history. But then, instead of correcting the problem by immediately ensuring that those people and forces will never again be voiceless, it progresses to the puzzling conclusion that the solution is to throw out what we *know* and replace it with that about which we can only *speculate*.

The result has been one full generation of Americans who are shockingly ignorant of the most rudimentary elements of their nation's history, leaving them vulnerable to those who would distort or bend the past to suit their own agenda for the future.

For many years now, films have been used to advance the cause of antihistory. Perhaps the first and, by any measure, the most successful of these was 1915's *The Birth of a Nation*. The damage done by that film to American society was so cataclysmic that Hollywood, by and large, left revisionism severely alone, except for innocuous biographical screenplays that sanitized their subjects shamelessly.

After the mid-1960s, however, film would reenter the arena of reinventing history. The example usually cited is Oliver Stone's *JFK*. Like *The Birth of a Nation*, it was an excellent film but very poor history. Ignoring thousands of hours of testimony from hundreds of witnesses and book after book of documentation, Mr. Stone chose to enshrine fantasy as fact, leaning on the weak reed of one ambitious politician and one newspaper interview from overseas to justify his conspiracy theory, condemning willy-nilly United States government agencies and the highest elected officials for the most heinous crimes imaginable. Only *The Wizard of Oz* asked more suspension of disbelief from its audiences than Oliver Stone's *JFK*.

Against this tide of shrill anti-Americanism, Steven Spielberg appeared determined to keep pristine at least one period of our national experience. His works were no less fictional than those of Stone and the others, but their purpose seemed at the opposite end of the pole. His attempt was nothing less than to illuminate the truth by use of parables. Not allegories. He used real people and events or at least based his stories on them. But it is clear his intent was to infuse a larger theme.

Has he been successful? Have Steven Spielberg's epic movies about World War II really "changed things"?

Frankly, it is too early to know. Any filmmaker these days faces the inevitability of numbers. His or her film, even if successful, and even including television plays and video rentals, will only reach a fraction of the general audience movies once commanded. This obviously limits the potential impact of any film after 1965.

On the other hand, those who do go to movies or rent videos are disproportionately young, exactly the audience Spielberg—and Stone—wanted to reach.

There is not yet, as far as I am aware, any empirical evidence about the effect *Private Ryan* or *Schindler's List* have had on the upcoming generation.

On the other hand, anecdotal evidence abounds. Inspired by the conversation in Paris, I conducted a survey of two hundred high school American history teachers. Though the poll has no pretensions to scientific accuracy, the results are interesting.

Here they are. A remarkable 53 percent of the questionnaires were returned. Most teachers had taken a great deal of time and care in their answers, for which I am grateful.

Of those who responded, more than 80 percent *had* used *Saving Private Ryan* in history or other classes in school. Many of the accompanying comments were enlightening. These excerpts are from teachers who used the film, or, at least, clips from it, in regularly scheduled schoolwork.

"*Private Ryan* has bolstered patriotism and a newfound respect for the elderly." "[Our students'] main question was why weren't more movies made about the black heroes of World

War II?" "Routine reference. Routine reaction." "Shocked."
"Somber." "Blood and gore gets 'em every time." "Keep in mind,
many children do not know fact from fantasy, so some respond
indecorously when they watch movies which confront true acts
of horror." "Awestruck. Could I have done what they did?" "We
don't show [it] because of parents' concerns, but most have seen
it and there are lively discussions." "Some simply don't believe
it." "[We] took 500 students to see *Private Ryan* [in the theater].
The teachers felt it had an [unprecedented] impact." "When *carefully used*, movies like this have a powerful impact." "I think it
is too long." "I showed it last year, but will not be showing it
this . . . it was so realistic it was actually disturbing to a couple of
my students." "A D-Day vet told me it was the most realistic
depiction of combat on film, so I show it." "[The students]
couldn't believe the D-Day section was real." "My students are
infinitely more involved after [watching the film.]"

"In one class a young man snickered and said 'Cool' when
the flamethrowers were in operation. Another kid turned
around and looked at him and said, 'You think that's cool?
What's wrong with you?' No more was said. It was all I could
have hoped for."

Speaking for those who do *not* elect to use the film, perhaps
this midwestern teacher distills their reasoning. "I do not use
movies because, 1. No non-documentary movie is historically
accurate. 2. Movies involve passive rather than active learning
on the part of the students. When the play button goes on the
minds go off. 3. I'm a better teacher for my students than any
movie producer."

The majority of teachers who responded disagree with his
conclusion that films have no role in teaching. As a point of
interest, on the form I sent out was a question about whether
any other commercial films were used in teaching history or
other subjects. A list of 96 titles resulted. The top ten—after
Saving Private Ryan—in order of preference were: 1. *Schindler's*

List. 2. *Glory*. 3. *The Last of the Mohicans*. 4. *Dances with Wolves*. 5. *1776*. 6. *All the President's Men*. 7. *Amistad*. 8. *Tora! Tora! Tora!* 9. *The Grapes of Wrath*. 10. *Mr. Smith Goes to Washington*. It was interesting to see that two classic-era movies made the cut.

For the record, the largest group of responses, 43 percent, came from suburban middle-class high schools. Just under 16 percent were from very affluent districts; 14 percent from rural, economically mixed areas; just over 14 percent from urban poor, racially mixed; and a bit more than 12 percent from predominately minority student bodies—for the most part, African American. Both Asian and Latino populations are clearly underrepresented in this sample and that should be taken into account.

It should also be noted that one quarter of the responses came from private schools and 14 percent were single-gender institutions.

So, *Saving Private Ryan* is having its chance, it would appear, to make an impression on young minds. It will be decades before we know how that impact plays out.

The colors are fast fading. The time will come—and it is not too distant—when those reading these words will inhabit a planet in which there is no living connection to that morning on Omaha Beach. Or other equally bloody and equally important mornings on the beaches of Tarawa, Anzio, Iwo Jima, Salerno, Okinawa, and a hundred more.

No living connection, either, with the unrelenting horror of Dachau, Auschwitz, Belsen, and a score of other camps whose names will live in infamy.

Will the first twenty minutes of Mr. Spielberg's *Saving Private Ryan* give that future disconnected moviegoer a sense of how it was for the boy-men of June 6, 1944?

Or of the grainy black-and-white degradation of men and women herded, naked and afraid, to be slaughtered by conquerors gone mad—encouraged in madness by leaders cloaked in evil—with power and unreasoning hatred?

Can a movie do that?

We know that this movie changed one young Frenchwoman and profoundly affected many American high school students. So far, that is all this chapter can claim with verifiable justification. *Saving Private Ryan*'s footprint is too fresh for more, though there are important straws in the wind.

Succeeding chapters will offer more mature evidence on the way "shadows on a screen" can change us.

2

STAR WARS

1977

DIRECTOR: GEORGE LUCAS

STARS: MARK HAMILL, HARRISON FORD, CARRIE FISHER

RUNNING TIME: 2 HOURS, 1 MINUTE

All of this happened "a long, long time ago, in a galaxy far away."

It is a galaxy ruled by the evil Grand Moff Tarkin and Darth Vader. Two robots, C-3PO and R2-D2, escape their clutches and land on a dry planet where they encounter Luke Skywalker. Soon Skywalker hears a plea from Princess Leia asking for rescue from the huge, wicked space station Death Star.

Promoted by the last of the good Knights of the Planetary Round Table, "The Jedis," Skywalker hires the mercenary space pilot Han Solo to take him to Death Star.

After many hair-raising adventures and help from "The Force," the source of positive energy in the universe, Skywalker effects the rescue.

There are a series of climactic moments, but the story ends, as it must, with the destruction of the Death Star and the triumph of "The Force."

Note: *Star Wars* was the first of nine proposed episodes to be filmed, but not first in proper order. That had to wait for 1999's *Star Wars Episode I: The Phantom Menace.*

Lucasfilm

In 1977, Japanese automakers announced that after much experimentation, they were now successfully employing seven thousand robots on their assembly lines. The news galvanized the world of manufacturing and sent major companies around the globe scrambling to catch up. The news was also seen as a body blow to labor unions.

That same year, thousands of miles away, the motion picture *Star Wars* burst on the Hollywood scene with precisely the same impact. Film backers' eyes lit up, filmmakers went back to their storyboards, and film actors pondered their future.

If there has been one consistent criticism of Hollywood films in the past twenty-five years it is that they rely too little on good stories and believable performances and too much on special effects and computer-generated gimmicks.

However well-grounded the criticism, it no longer matters. The successive and bewildering technical refinements have become as important to movies as the camera, and there is no turning back.

The direct and most influential antecedents of this generation of movies are one filmmaker, George Lucas, and one film, *Star Wars*—a motion picture so important that a missile defense system was named for it, a filmmaker so important that he sued the government to get them to stop using his title for the missile defense system.

In a business replete with iconoclasts, few makers of film have been as individualistic as George Lucas. His most repeated quote is "I'm an introvert. I don't want to be famous."

It is much too late for that. *Star Wars* put Mr. Lucas in a category few have reached. It is not that the movie brought to the screen any specific techniques that had not been used before in other films. It was that Mr. Lucas brought them all together for the first time, each honed and burnished to a dazzling perfection.

There can be no doubt that *Star Wars* was the culmination of one man's love for a special kind of American movie. George Lucas, born in 1944, didn't see the *Flash Gordon* serials on the *big* screen. He saw them on the *little* screen after Universal had sold the rights to TV. "I loved the Flash Gordon comic books. I loved the Universal series with Buster Crabbe."

He never forgot them, or his affection for special effects. They have been a constant thread through his career that even conservative observers would have to call, in a Hollywood publicist's term, "fabulous."

Mr. Lucas's Modesto, California, youth and adolescence would later be chronicled in his *American Graffiti*, the 1973 look at teenagers in this country just before the distorting influence of Vietnam.

There were two years of junior college, then a stint at the Cinema School at the University of Southern California. To show where his heart was, Lucas's prize-winning film there was the science-fiction entry *THX-1138: 4EB (ELECTRONIC LABYRINTH)*. The film world should have been paying attention. That awkward-appearing title was a harbinger of things to come.

At least one important filmmaker *did* pay attention to the young Mr. Lucas.

A major prize for Lucas's winning the 1965 Student Film Festival was the opportunity to be an observer as Francis Ford

fired an opening volley in 1958, followed by *Jason and the Argonauts* in 1963 in which we saw dueling skeletons matching man against animated models. He called this process Dynamation and its next generation Superdynamation. Mr. Harryhausen received a special Academy Award in 1992.

There were literally hundreds of other animators, most of whom were—and remained—anonymous, a substantial fraction of whom worked at one time or another for Walt Disney.

But it was not the fluid artistry or classic storytelling of *Snow White and the Seven Dwarfs* or *Bambi* that most attracted George Lucas. If there were to be legends, let them be born in the future. And if the owners of *Flash Gordon* would not let him use the character in his film—and, incredibly, they would not—he would create his own.

There were many who discouraged Lucas in his single-minded pursuit of his project, but there were champions, too. It was Alan Ladd Jr. who went to bat for Lucas at 20th Century Fox when the studios balked at the $8.5 million price tag for the film's budget.

Some of the best in the business were convinced that Lucas had a great contribution to make. Among them was the superlative cinematographer Haskell Wexler, no mean filmmaker himself. Wexler, like Lucas, had made films from the time he was a teenager. As he matured, his passion was for the larger arena of politics and civil rights, and much of his work reflected that. At a 1997 film festival on Long Island honoring *In the Heat of the Night*, on which Mr. Wexler was the cinematographer, he emphasized that aspect of his career to me when I moderated a panel of the film's principals. Pointing to director Norman Jewison, actors Rod Steiger and Lee Grant, as well as others sharing the stage with him, he said "These people didn't just make films to get rich or become famous. Each project had a purpose. It was our intention to help make things better and sometimes that meant spotlighting unpleasant truths. Often, those kinds of convictions can have adverse effects on careers but that did not deter these artists." His own brilliant film *Medium Cool* from 1969 symbolized his point of view. He directed, wrote, photographed, and coproduced this intensely personal drama set against the chaos of the 1968 Democratic Convention in Chicago. No stranger to big-budget Hollywood, Mr. Wexler is the last person—so far—to receive an Oscar for cinematography in a black-and-white film, *Who's Afraid of Virginia Woolf?* in 1966. He took home another Academy Award for *Bound for Glory* in 1976.

In other words, the praise and encouragement of Haskell Wexler made a great deal of difference in the professional life of George Lucas.

He plunged into his project with predictable energy and enthusiasm. Some who knew him at this time said George Lucas was born for this moment. He would direct the film, though some critics later insisted that Lucas was primary proof that certain kinds of movies are produced, not directed. In a way, he himself supported that point of view by turning directing chores over to Irving Kershner and Richard Marquand for the next two episodes, both of which are, unmistakably, Lucas films.

The production of *Star Wars* spanned a fair chunk of the globe. Some footage was shot in California's Death Valley, some in Tunisia, some in Guatemala, and much on ten sound stages in Great Britain.

The cast, which would become internationally famous, began the year 1977 modestly enough. Only one actor was well known, the redoubtable Alec Guinness, whose enthusiasm for the project began at a decidedly low ebb and diminished thereafter. In his book *My Name Escapes Me,* he doesn't trouble to disguise his distaste for all things *Star Wars.* He returned photographs of his Ben Obi-Wan Kenobi character unautographed and detested the unending packages of plastic *Star Wars* toys and figurines sent to him. Though he appeared in the first three films, he told interviewers in 1995 he would not appear in any more sequels "even if asked."

Mark Hamill, as Luke Skywalker, was actually making his big screen debut. Carrie Fisher, Princess Leia, had little more film experience, with only an appearance in *Shampoo* to her credit. Harrison Ford—Han Solo—had, on the other hand, been making feature films for more than ten years. And Peter Cushing was one of the most familiar faces of all to fans of "horror" films as he brought Grand Moff Tarkin to life.

It is a measure of the lasting impact of *Star Wars* that a number of its character names are now used as generic terms to describe a particular kind of personality, and that people of all ages know what the speaker or writer means. "Darth Vader," "C-3PO," "R2-D2," and "Luke Skywalker" have all entered the language.

It would be no exaggeration, however, to say that John Dykstra, a man whose name few know, would have the greatest impact on the audience and on the film industry for years to come. It was he who, encouraged by George Lucas, developed a computer-assisted camera that would produce effects in numbers and in quality never seen before.

Star Wars struck like a hurricane. At first, audiences assumed it was a children's movie. But parents, having taken their youngsters to see it, came back wide-eyed and awestruck, spreading the *Star Wars* gospel. A man in his mid-thirties, a blue-collar worker from Queens, was interviewed on New York television news and said, "It's an honest-to-God movie. No sex, no murder, no rape. I've seen it sixteen times. Yeah, I know, I am crazy. So, I'm going back again."

That man put his finger on an interesting phenomenon, exemplified, perhaps, by *Star Wars* in a degree not seen before and superseded only by *Titanic* years later: audience recidivism—the same people returning time after time to see one movie. It was not new. Many had seen *Gone With the Wind* multiple times, but the economic realities of the 1930s and 1940s put a limit on that number, usually fairly low.

No such encumbrance existed in the late 1970s. It was still rare for adults, such as our worker from Queens, to go back to the box office more than once. But, it was by no means out of the ordinary for teens and subteens to go back day after day, sometimes for weeks, often learning the dialogue by heart. The return visits swelled the movie's receipts, but sometimes misled statisticians as to the number of people who had actually seen a given film. Two thirteen-year-olds seeing *Star Wars* twenty times each does not equal forty people seeing *Star Wars*, though Hollywood is slow to make that distinction.

No matter. *Star Wars* was a smash.

The world of 1977 was still gripped by the Cold War. Jimmy Carter was in the White House, and spiraling oil prices would, by the end of the year, put inflation at a frightening 11 percent. The Dow Jones Industrial Average kept pace, rising to a dizzying 999 before falling back.

It was the year that singing icons of two very different Americas, Bing Crosby and Elvis Presley, died. It was a year that an odd language, which always began with the frantic greeting "Breaker, Breaker!" was abroad in the land. It was citizens band radio but, for a time, it seemed to be more. Perhaps CBs would prove to be a connection for the essentially isolated community of automobile commuters and over-the-road travelers.

It was a year that a man whose history contained a serious flirtation with Nazi Germany would become an international hero. By an act of very nearly unbelievable personal courage, Egypt's Anwar Sadat traveled to what was one day earlier the center for the hated enemy to be fought to the death no matter what the cost. He went to Israel. He said to Israelis regarding the struggles between Israel and Egypt, "Ring the bells for your sons. Tell them those wars were the last of wars and the end of sorrows."

Israel's Menachen Begin, himself often described as a former terrorist against the British, then went to Egypt and expressed similar sentiments. For a moment anything seemed possible.

In America's Middle West and East, the worst winter in decades raged, helping to boost the rating of the most-watched television series of all time, *Roots*.

This was the United States that greeted *Star Wars*. It is now easy to see that the film's success was inevitable, but no such crystal ball was available for the executives at 20th Century Fox, nor, for that matter, for George Lucas himself. They were on pins and needles as they sent their innovative effort into the commercial market. No one had to tell them that innovative films often failed spectacularly.

Instead, tens of millions of dollars began to pour in every week. Most critics were ecstatic. The $10 million investment returned $100 million, then an unheard of $200 million. *Star Wars* marketing began and was an unprecedented hit from the first.

From coast to coast, as traditional religious clergy trembled, "May the Force be with you" became a mantra.

It remained to be seen what traditional Hollywood would have to say about all of this. On the one hand, the movie establishment worshiped success. On the other hand, it was suspicious of newcomers and particularly of new technology that might upset the status quo. George Lucas and his *Star Wars* technology seemed to threaten the biggest revolution since sound.

Nonetheless, the Academy of Motion Picture Arts and Sciences nominated *Star Wars* for awards in an impressive ten categories, including several of the "glamour" awards, such as Best Picture, Best Writer, and Best Director.

For those who called the Screen Actors Guild home, however, there was an ominous portent. For the most-nominated film of 1977, only one *actor* was nominated, and that was Alec Guinness, whose stature in the business virtually guaranteed a nomination in a major film.

There were other straws in the wind. After the astounding success of the film, those who made such decisions invited R2-D2, C-3PO, and Darth Vader to be the first non-humans to leave their imprints in the courtyard of what was for years known as Graumann's Chinese Theatre since Roy Rogers's horse, Trigger, had done it thirty years earlier.

Nor was that all. At the Academy Awards telecast from the Dorothy Chandler Pavilion on March 28, 1978, the second presenting team, for the Special Achievement Awards, consisted of Mark Hamill, R2-D2 and C-3PO. If Hollywood had not yet completely surrendered to the technological future, it was clearly in serious negotiations.

And yet, if anyone remembers the 1977 awards at all, it is not the robots and technology that comes to mind. It is an all-too-human actress and the volatile politics of the moment.

After a suitable interval for a monologue from the inevitable Bob Hope, the first award of the night was presented by John Travolta, the surprise nominee for Best Actor for his role in *Saturday Night Fever*. He was to present the statuette for Best Supporting Actress. And therein lies a story.

Among the five nominees was Vanessa Redgrave for *Julia*. The film was a remarkable—and true—outline of one woman's struggle against the horrors of Nazi Germany. And yet Miss Redgrave had become anathema to many in the Jewish community in the United States and abroad for her passionate embrace of the cause of the Palestinians in the Middle East. Many were furious at her for being in the film at all. There were vocal protestors at the Academy Awards as she entered the theater.

As fate and talent would have it, she was the winner. Much to the chagrin of the Academy, Miss Redgrave did not back off from her cause as she accepted the Oscar. She paid tribute to the Academy for not being intimidated by threats from "a small bunch of Zionist hoodlums." For a moment, everything else in the movie world, including looming revolutionary technology, was forgotten. There was a gasp and scattered boos.

The audience was still buzzing as the show continued. Immediately, the team of Mark Hamill, R2-D2, and C-3PO presented the Special Achievement awards, which included among the winners Ben Burtt for creating the robot voices for *Star Wars*, including those of R2-D2 and C-3PO.

One category later, two denizens of classic Hollywood, William Holden and Barbara Stanwyck, were on stage to give the Oscar for Best Sound. Once again there was a very human moment when Bill Holden paid tribute to his copresenter, saying she had saved his career when he was about to be sacked from his first starring role in *Golden Boy* in 1939.

The gesture was poignant, after which both stars went about the business of passing the torch to the new wave. America was discovering on that March night how collegial the new technology was. The Best Sound award went to *Star Wars* and an unwieldy four winners, Don MacDougall, Ray West, Bob Minkler, and Derek Ball.

The next category, Visual Effects, made the point even more emphatically. Again *Star Wars* won, and again a small army of winners trooped to the stage. John Stears, John Dykstra, Richard Edlund, Grant McCune, and Robert Blalack each got a golden statuette.

And *Star Wars* was three for three.

It was Greer Garson—*Mrs. Miniver* herself—and Henry Winkler who presented the awards for Art/Set Decoration. Another win for *Star Wars* and another cavalry charge. John Barry, Norman Reynolds, Leslie Dilley, and Roger Christian.

Supporting Actor. The brilliant Brits Michael Caine and Maggie Smith opened the envelope, and most wondered if the winner would be their countryman, Alec Guinness, for *Star Wars*, the only actor nominated from the film. By contrast, *Julia* and *The Turning Point* had *four* actors each nominated. The *Star Wars* sweep hit a speed bump. The winner was Jason Robards for *Julia*.

When Natalie Wood announced that the winner for Costume Design was John Mollo for *Star Wars*, the juggernaut seemed back on track. Hollywood insiders began to smell a record number of Oscars when John Williams got the Original Score award for his memorable theme, handed to him by two men who knew their way around film music, Johnny Green and Henry Mancini.

Film Editing was the next category in which *Star Wars* was nominated. Could they keep the momentum going? They could. The Academy Award went to Paul Hirsch, Richard Chew, and Marcia Lucas, George Lucas's wife.

Perhaps we should pause here for a moment and wonder what might have been going through Mr. Lucas's mind just then. Of the seven categories for which his movie had been nominated, he had six wins. It was already a staggering achievement. There were only three more to go, but they were the three big ones. Writer, Director—and the Best Picture of the year.

Cicely Tyson and King Vidor gave the Best Director award to Woody Allen for *Annie Hall*. Paddy Chayefsky gave the Writing award to Woody Allen for *Annie Hall*. Jack Nicholson gave the Best Picture award to producer Charles Joffe for *Annie Hall*.

If the triumph of an angst-filled romance between two achingly human beings over robots and aliens and laser-beam sword fights seemed satisfying to some, it proved to be an illusion.

The computer and all its descendents have taken over Hollywood, for good or ill. George Lucas was—and is—in the middle of it all. His *Indiana Jones* fantasies in collaboration with Steven Spielberg made more money than the gross national product of medium-size countries. His *Empire Strikes Back* in 1980, *Return of the Jedi* in 1983, their rerelease along with the original *Star Wars Episode Four: A New Hope* in 1997, all of them preceding *Star Wars Episode I: The Phantom Menace* in 1999, shattered records for revenue.

And we saw the inevitable; completely computer-generated characters, such as Jar Jar Binks.

The Lucas businesses, such as Lucasfilm, Skywalker Ranch, and Industrial Light and Magic, remain on the cutting edge of audio and video in their accelerating incarnations.

The technology shot fired in 1977 was heard round the world, its echoes felt still in blockbusters from *Independence Day* to *Twister* to *Titanic* to *Perfect Storm*.

Star Wars changed the way we make movies.

3

TAXI DRIVER

1976

DIRECTOR: MARTIN SCORSESE
STARS: ROBERT DE NIRO, JODIE
FOSTER, CYBILL SHEPHERD
RUNNING TIME: 113 MINUTES

A taxi driver in New York City keeps a diary, condemning all the ugliness he sees, and he sees only ugliness. Except for a teenage prostitute, whom he decides to free from those who degrade her. He buys weapons, goes into training, murders her pimp and several other lowlifes. Instead of being tried for the homicides, he is lionized by New Yorkers as a hero, a poster boy for a wave of twisted vigilantism.

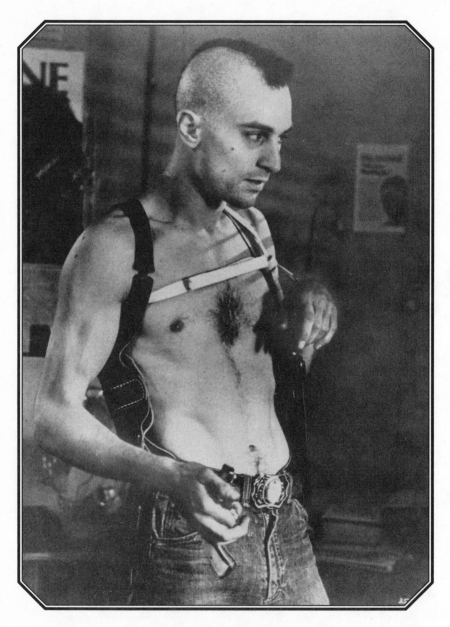

Columbia (Courtesy of The Kobal Collection)

W as a movie responsible for the assassination attempt on President Ronald Reagan?

It is a provocative question that routinely calls up every defense Hollywood can muster, but it deserves an answer. Here is the story and, perhaps, the smoking gun.

It was not quite 11:30 A.M. in Los Angeles. The marine layer was still burning off, the sun gamely battling the remaining haze and the temperature starting its climb to the mid-70s.

In toney hotels and homes of privilege, famous faces were confronting mirrors, rehearsing words and gestures, trying on expensive finery. Some had even begun the laborious process of applying makeup, preparing for the biggest night of the year that, for many of them, would actually begin in mid-afternoon. Television networks made rigid demands.

It was to be the night of the Academy Awards, Monday, March 30, 1981. Though it had been many decades since movies were the leading industry in Los Angeles, films and those who made them remained the vibrant soul of the Big Orange, so intense interest radiated from the Dorothy Chandler Pavilion out to Compton and Agoura and Laguna and back downtown again. That night, the whole world would be watching Hollywood.

Johnny Carson, who would be master of ceremonies for the third year in a row, went over his monologue one more time.

Lucy Arnaz kept repeating the troublesome lyrics to the production number with which she would open the show. It was a musical obituary, really, saluting movie greats who had died since the last Academy Award telecast, including Mae West and Alfred Hitchcock.

One person who didn't need to worry about rehearsal was the president of the United States. Ronald Reagan had already taped his introductory remarks in the White House several days earlier.

President Reagan was, of course, no stranger to Oscar nights. Himself a product of the vanished "studio system," he had been the star of a nominated documentary, *Mr. Gardenia Jones,* all the way back in 1942, when many in Hollywood and around the nation still pronounced his last name "Ree-gan." He had often attended the event as president of the Screen Actors Guild and during his terms as governor of California from 1967 to 1974.

One newcomer to the celebration, however, was Robert DeNiro. He had been nominated before, and had won before, a Supporting Actor Oscar for his role in *The Godfather, Part II,* but this year's collaboration with his friend the director Martin Scorsese—*Raging Bull,* the wrenching portrait of fighter Jake La Motta—had finally been motivation enough to drag him from his beloved New York to southern California. At that moment he was still adjusting to the time change, checking on the accessories for his tux, and trying to decide whether to have lunch or not. It might be a long time until dinner.

Meantime, 2,311 miles away, the sun that would finally win its battle against the California haze was having no such luck in Washington, D.C., despite a three-hour start. It was a wet, gray, chilly Monday, and President Reagan had just completed a gray and chilly task.

It was an after-lunch speech to the Building Trades Council of the AFL/CIO. He asked this poker-faced audience to support his tax and budget-cut proposals, a speech that, with superficial changes to suit individual audiences, he had given many times. He got his laughs at the expected places, but applause on his policy points was subdued.

He had hoped for more. His solid victory over Jimmy Carter the previous fall had come with the support of "Reagan Democrats," many of whom were union members. On the other hand, union leaders were not always on the same page with their rank and file on this issue and saw bleak days ahead for organized labor under Reagan. Union leaders dominated that meeting room.

Still, at least the president had not wasted anyone's time. He had not left the White House until 1:45, waving a cheery thumbs-up to his secretary, Helene Van Damm. Now it was only 2:20 and he was already finished with the speech and heading back to the Oval Office for an afternoon of meetings and briefings.

He had commented to a visitor that he hoped that night's Academy Award telecast would not drag on as it sometimes did. There was no question of his missing the broadcast. He had never lost his fascination with the movie business and always referred to himself as a movie fan. Some even thought his interest bordered on obsession, but, if so, it was only with a certain kind of film. It was not at all unusual for the president and his wife, Nancy, to watch three, and even four, movies over a weekend. Though some would be recent, most would come from the period of the 1930s through the 1950s. If they were more contemporary, they would be of the "uplifting" or "feel-good" variety, and might come in for a word of presidential praise for those involved in the productions.

On the way to the side exit at the Washington Hilton, the president reminded his aide Michael Deaver of the inaugural ball he had attended at that very hotel seventy days earlier. It was there, as Reagan later confided to biographer Edmund Morris, that he tweaked his formal white tie in the mirror, turned to his family, leaped in the air, clicked his heels, and said, "I'm the president of the United States!"

By the time the presidential entourage reached the side door, it was 2:25 P.M. Fewer than fifty feet away, the armored limousines purred in readiness. There was the usual knot of reporters, photographers, and just passersby outside hoping to get a look at the president. Reagan smiled and waved, as he always did. He thought he caught a glimpse of something unusual. A blond youth, crouched in a firing position. He didn't see the pistol, but it was there. John Hinckley Jr. fired it six times in less than two seconds. Bullets struck four men, including the president, though neither he nor anyone else knew it at that moment.

President Reagan was pushed into his limousine by White House Chief of Security Jerry Parr, who then jumped in himself, covering the president's body with his own. Reagan felt a sharp pain and saw blood coming out of his mouth. "I think you've broken a rib, Jerry," he said.

Parr, deeply concerned at the bleeding from the president's mouth, made an immediate decision to divert the limousine to George Washington University Hospital, where they arrived in under five minutes. The president was getting weaker by the second.

When they pulled up at the emergency room door, the president waved Parr away and started walking on his own. The distance was little more than ten feet. Parr did not dispute the decision. On the off-chance news cameras were around, he wanted them to record the president walking into the hospital on his own.

It was a gritty performance for the old actor. As soon as he was inside the doors, he sagged to the floor; his eyes rolling upward as he momentarily lost consciousness. At that moment, because of the massive loss of blood that the Devastator bullet (made to explode on impact) had caused, Ronald Reagan was dying.

Back at the scene of the shooting, the chaos had given way to numb shock. Three other victims had already been whisked away to hospitals; a District of Columbia policeman with a bullet near the spine was put into an ambulance. For Secret Service man Timothy McCarthy, a legend was already forming. He was the man who "took one in the chest to protect the president." McCarthy, as one of the presidential party, was sped to the hospital in another of the limousines. So was the most severely injured of all, Press Secretary James Brady, a "fuzzy-warm bear of a guy," whose blood and brains were clearly visible to horrified bystanders after one of the bullets exploded in his head.

Within minutes, the powerful apparatus of government began to produce a profile of the would-be killer they had in custody. John Hinckley Jr. was the young scion of a prominent Colorado family. No criminal record, but very soon it was clear he had been a walking time bomb.

As Secretary of the Treasury, Donald Regan presided over the Secret Service. Almost immediately, Regan's sources began to fill in the blanks. Hinckley was a resident of Colorado, but he carried two IDs, one from Texas Tech University in Lubbock and another from an institution in Denver. He also had cards from two psychiatrists, one from Texas and the other from Colorado. With regard to the weapon, it was a "German-made, Florida assembled .22 pistol—very cheap, a Saturday night special. It had been sold to Hinckley by a Dallas pawnshop."

Dallas. Once again a haunting connection to violence against the presidency by that star-crossed city.

From William French Smith at the FBI, more information filtered in: Hinckley had "the same psychological profile as Arthur Bremer," the troubled young man who had shot George Wallace in 1972. It appeared that Hinckley had stalked President Jimmy Carter during the 1980 presidential campaign, but no one had put him on a "watch" list.

As various law enforcement agencies and psychologists

examined him, there was one thing on which all could agree. Hinckley was a "disturbed man who was obsessed with movies and movie stars." Not the kind of movies shown in the White House every weekend. Dark movies, brutal themes, violence triumphant, sleaze encroaching on every crevice of the story. These were the stuff that John Hinckley Jr.'s twisted dreams were made of.

In his autobiography, Ronald Reagan summarized what happened. "I learned Hinckley had gone to a movie, *Taxi Driver*, and fallen in love with an actress in the picture [Jodie Foster], and then began trailing her around the country, hoping to meet her so he could tell her how he felt."

Failing to make connection, Hinckley decided to get a gun and emulate a scene in the movie where a deranged taxi driver, portrayed by Robert De Niro, shoots several people to save a twelve-year-old street whore, portrayed by Jodie Foster.

Crossing the line from fantasy to reality, Hinckley decided to shoot someone prominent, thus somehow demonstrating his love for Jodie Foster. He first stalked Jimmy Carter, trying to find a moment when the president might be vulnerable. But, as Ronald Reagan succinctly put it, "He never got the chance so he shot me instead." Clearly, John Hinckley Jr.'s troubles went back a long way. But the direct line of action leading to 2:25 P.M. March 30, 1981, can be traced with precision to one source: *Taxi Driver*, 1976, written by movie-obsessed Paul Schrader, directed and bull-dogged to the screen by movie-obsessed Martin Scorsese. It was the darkest major movie brought to the screen up to its moment. It was not just its violence that set it apart, though it cradled, caressed, celebrated violence in breakthrough ways. It was the unrelenting despair of its story, its absence of any moments of absolution, its portrait of New York as an unredeemable cesspool of depravity, that left audiences breathless and sent critics to their dictionaries. Obviously, a new language would have to be developed if this was the emerging direction of mainstream filmmaking. Because, whatever else it was, *Taxi Driver* was brilliantly written, directed, and acted. What some saw as its threat to the arts and to society lay in that very brilliance.

Paul Schrader, the writer, did not see the world or movies as most did. In fact, he did not see a movie at all until he was eighteen years old. He was reared by parents who were deeply religious and very strict. No movies allowed. Schrader went away to divinity school, but was sidetracked at the seminary when he discovered films. He began to devour them wholesale. After graduation, he did not join the clergy, but instead went to UCLA and enrolled in its graduate film program.

This was 1968, when all values were questioned and every institution seemed to be crumbling. Paul Schrader's talent took him first to film criticism, then to editing the magazine *Cinema*, then to turning out screenplays, most of which were rejected. Unfortunately, this was also the period during which he began to descend into depression and alcoholism. In fact, it is told as Hollywood legend that he wrote *Taxi Driver*—inspired, in part, by vocalist Harry Chapin's record "Taxi"—in two fevered weeks while convalescing in a hospital.

It was this screenplay that would bring Schrader into the orbit of another movie-obsessed man on the rise, Martin Scorsese. Four years Schrader's senior, the son of Sicilian immigrants and raised in Little Italy, Scorsese would seem to have little in common with a writer from Calvinist stock in Grand Rapids, Michigan, but the differences were deceiving.

Like Schrader, Scorsese had a deeply spiritual streak. A sickly child, he had sparse real contact with his contemporaries, played no sports, had little street interaction with neighborhood gangs. His was the life of a young loner, and religion was so much a part of it that he actually entered the seminary just after the eighth grade. He dropped out after one year, seamlessly transforming his focus from Roman Catholic liturgy to the esoterica of films and filmmaking.

Later he would draw comparisons between pre-Vatican II Catholic churches—with their dark interiors, flickering candles, scent of incense, and murmured Latin phrases—and movie theaters, their lightless interiors brightened only by flickering frames against a screen. He found the two experiences equally spiritual, despite their obvious differences.

Martin Scorsese saw so many movies, absorbed them so completely, that it is tempting all these years later to conclude that he lived through them. Or, more precisely, constructed a life through them. He received a bachelor's degree in film from NYU in 1964 and a master's in 1966. He stayed on as an instructor there until 1970. All this time he had been making films, short films at first, which won awards, sharpened his skills, and whetted his appetite. He had talent, he had tireless energy, and he had found his life's work.

There was a detour or two. In 1972, Scorsese spent time flirting with television, and was caught up for a while with the CBS-TV news unit tracking the fading fortunes of Hubert Horatio Humphrey, the happy political warrior who had given Richard Nixon a scare in the final days of the 1968 presidential race.

But the small screen held no permanent attraction for Martin Scorsese. He wanted to make movies. He had, in fact, already drawn attention with his first feature-length film, *Who's That Knocking at My Door*, made in 1968 on a very low budget, but showing even then themes that would recur often in his subsequent movies: The streets of New York, conflicts caused by a strict Catholic upbringing, and troubled relationships. It also brought the director together with an actor who would become an indispensable member of his film repertory company, Harvey Keitel, a rugged ex-marine from Brooklyn, who made his film debut in *Who's That Knocking*.

Scorsese's next big screen director credit went to *Boxcar Bertha* in 1972, his first plunge into studio-connected films. It was an obvious derivative of *Bonnie and Clyde*, but that fact had its own significance in the evolution of Martin Scorsese's style. It will be remembered that Arthur Penn's 1967 *Bonnie and Clyde* had stunned audiences with the graphic violence of its conclusion. The storm of protest was muted by the fact that those two bodies jerking and dancing as they were ripped apart by tommy-gun bullets were, after all, two murderous criminals getting their just desserts. What Scorsese saw was the effectiveness of the bigger-than-life violence. Might not the violence be, he thought, in a way, even more effective if it were stripped of its moral and legal justification?

When he was growing up watching every movie he could, young Martin Scorsese liked all kinds of films and, apparently, remembered every one in detail, but the category that stuck with him longest was the one that came to be known as "film noir." Literally "dark" or "black films," they came into their own in the 1940s, usually featuring crime and corruption but, unlike gangster movies, both the villains and the heroes were cynical, and the stories were seamed with disillusionment and set in a sort of bleak realism, shadowy and moody. That influence would be evident in 1973's *Mean Streets*, a remarkable film about life and nickel-and-dime crime in Little Italy—a life Scorsese as a child watched from his tenement window. Harvey Keitel was back as a hood, but a new face had joined the Scorsese coterie. His name was Robert De Niro.

Another New Yorker with a dark view of life and the city, De Niro had trained with famous names such as Stella Adler and Lee Strasberg. His focus was stage work off-Broadway and, eventually, with touring companies. He was in his mid-twenties before he took on the medium of film and, at first was neither impressed nor impressive.

All that changed in 1973, when he gave a fine performance as a dying baseball player in *Bang the Drum Slowly*, a role Paul Newman had played fifteen years earlier in a television drama. That same year, De Niro and Scorsese joined forces for *Mean*

Streets. The connection has resulted in a rich lode of film history: *Taxi Driver, New York, New York, Raging Bull, The King of Comedy, Goodfellas, Cape Fear, Casino.* Not all of these were successful by any means, but all merit critical examination as serious collaborations by talented filmmakers.

Even that partial list gives insight into what has developed into the recognizable Scorsese style. In *New York, New York*, a musical drama, Scorsese manages to explore only the darkest corner of the Big Band era in America. In *The King of Comedy*, he illustrates only the sharp, depressing acute angles of comedy and of a comedian.

When he was asked to direct the remake of the 1962 thriller *Cape Fear*, he rejected the script three times. The new treatment paralleled the original story in which an abusive, deranged criminal, released from prison, attempts to wreak vengeance on the upstanding lawyer who had sent him up—and on his wife and daughter. The tension was between the aberrant, psychotic killer and the nice, ordinary, middle-class family. Scorsese would have none of it. When asked why, he said that he could easily understand the villain, but he had no way to relate to a nice family. He found them uninteresting and impossible to film. He was then urged to rewrite the script to fit his vision and he did, making the family dysfunctional and adulterous, and their young daughter, the innocent object of the villain's depraved lust in the first film, an ambivalent near-participant in a stark sexual encounter in Scorsese's version.

But *Taxi Driver* was the first time the Scorsese style seared full-blown across most American screens. No one had seen anything quite like it before. Here was Scorsese's beloved film noir given a splash of color and taken perhaps to its logical, despairing conclusion.

The reaction must have been satisfying to a man who had decided to make film his life. He carved out a niche that no one had dared to occupy. There were cries of anguish from those who felt film had a higher purpose than the exploitation of the worst violent excesses that could be devised from a distillation of a dozen police blotters. There were also cheers from those who saw the toppling of more barriers to absolute freedom in filmmaking.

No one could deny the talent of those who made the film. Robert De Niro's reviews were uniformly triumphant. He won the New York Film Critics' award as Best Actor.

As to the film itself, the response varied.

Pauline Kael saw it as "one of the few truly modern horror films." Roger Ebert thought it was "a brilliant nightmare." *Time* magazine found it "too heavy with sociologizing to be truly moving." Actor Burgess Meredith was not entirely impressed: "Brilliant, perhaps, but not a 'rooting' picture." He was doubtless thinking of the film in which he was costarring that year, *Rocky,* which definitely was a "rooting" picture.

Taxi Driver hadn't found many rooters in Hollywood when Scorsese went looking for a studio to finance it. He thought it would be clear sailing when Julia and Michael Phillips agreed to be producers. They had, after all, produced the huge commercial success *The Sting* just two years earlier.

The studios were not moved. So Martin Scorsese went back to the drawing board. He convinced all the actors to take minimum salaries, then slashed his own compensation and went to Columbia Pictures with a budget just under $2 million. David Begelman, the studio chief, snapped it up. "At that price, there was no way I could lose." He was right. The film made $12 million in its first release.

Every film runs into obstacles on its way to the big screen, but *Taxi Driver* seemed to have more than its share.

Scorsese recruited Bernard Herrmann to write the musical score, even though the extraordinary composer-conductor was then terminally ill. At sixty-four, Mr. Herrmann had made his mark in radio, the concert stage, opera, and most notably, motion pictures. After a long stint at CBS—where he met a young Orson Welles—he began his movie music career at the top. He wrote the score for *Citizen Kane*. After that he scored dozens of top productions for, among others, Orson Welles and Alfred Hitchcock, including the nerve-twisting music for *Psycho*.

As it turned out, Mr. Herrmann had not lost his impeccable sense of timing. He completed the recording sessions for *Taxi Driver*, said good night to his musicians, went home, and died in his sleep. Scorsese dedicated the film to his memory.

The biggest potential problem was posed by the smallest of the film's stars. Jodie Foster was 12 years old when she was offered the role of Iris Steensman, but was already a veteran actress, having begun her career at the age of three.

Still, this was quite a departure from the pictures she had made for Disney and others. She would, in fact, be portraying an underage street whore. To the California State Welfare Department, that sounded dangerously akin to child pornography, and they were prepared to block Miss Foster's participation.

They did not reckon with Jodie's mother, Brandy Foster. "I was determined to win," she said. "Here was some board trying to tell me what was too adult for my own daughter." She knew this role would propel her daughter into an entirely different category from the traditional child star, and she was certain Jodie could handle the adult theme. Still, the State of California was hard to convince. They insisted that Jodie undertake a battery of written and oral psychological tests lasting several hours to try to determine if permanent damage might result from the kind of material with which she would be working.

It is difficult to imagine that anyone the state could muster would be able to match Jodie Foster, even if she was only twelve years old. She had been reading since she was three, and continued to carry a full scholastic load at prestigious private schools even while working, eventually graduating as valedictorian of her class. Later, she would earn A's at Yale toward a literature degree while continuing her career full bore. She must have been quite an intimidating twelve-year-old.

That hurdle overcome, the filming went on, with Scorsese creating perhaps the most unattractive vigilante hero in film history. The De Niro character, Travis Bickle, is, in this distorted fantasy, lionized by New Yorkers for slaughtering in cold blood those who are only slightly more repulsive than he.

Mr. Scorsese looked at this ugly offspring and saw it only as "a continuation of *Mean Streets.* It's a film dealing with religious anxiety, guilt, and one man's attitude toward women—attitudes that were arrested at age thirteen."

It was all of that, but some moviegoers thought they saw more. It is fair to say that most critics thought they were seeing a breakthrough film with regard to theme, and they were sure a new filmmaking star had been born.

Others agreed that Scorsese was a moviemaker to be reckoned with, but were appalled at this particular film. Mainstream critic Leonard Maltin wrote, "This gory, cold-blooded story of a sick man's descent into violence is ugly and unredeeming." The editors of *Motion Picture Guide,* even ten years after its release, found *Taxi Driver* to be "so much trash, expensively arranged in Scorsese's unimaginative garbage cans."

No harsh words would matter if Mr. Scorsese's film would be recognized by the established dispensers of awards. And it was.

The Cannes Film Festival has long been the champion of the off-beat in cinema. Even here, there were dissenters. Of all people, Tennessee Williams (the breaker of so many rules in theater and film) found himself disgusted by the lurid violence, and he was president of the Cannes Festival Jury. Mr. Williams might have been surprised to learn that the depiction of violence could have been even worse: Observers from the studio, seeing the effusion of what appeared to be gallons of bright red blood, strongly suggested that the amount be reduced. Scorsese refused, but came to a compromise of sorts when he toned down the bright red color of the ersatz blood to a brown-red. It is said that is the reason some remember the film as being in black-and-white rather than color.

In the end, the opposition of Tennessee Williams did not matter. *Taxi Driver* received the Golden Palm in Cannes.

The Academy Award nominations also took note of what some were calling an avant-garde American film. There was a nomination for Bernard Herrmann's score, and for Jodie Foster as supporting actress. (Jodie's mother turned out to be right, this was only her first trip to the Oscar well. She would win ten years later for *The Accused*, win again for *Silence of the Lambs* in 1991, get another nomination for *Nell* in 1994, and become a respected director of major films.) There was a nomination for Robert De Niro as actor, and most significant of all, one for best picture of the year.

Conspicuously absent was a nomination for either the writer or director. In Martin Scorsese's case, it was hardly a surprise. If he had been a loner from childhood, he was clearly an outsider in Hollywood. Even his obvious love for the medium and his tireless work on film preservation did little to mitigate his bleak themes, his New York orientation, and his sometimes prickly pronouncements.

There would be no Academy Awards for *Taxi Driver*, but the nominations drew attention to every subsequent project mounted by Martin Scorsese.

There was something else. *Taxi Driver* became a fixture on the short list of movies being blamed for the undeniable increase in violence across America. Battle lines were drawn between religious groups, parents' organizations, and conservative politicians on one hand and filmmakers on the other. Fruitless debates went on endlessly as antagonists hunkered down in their positions.

Do movies instigate violence or only reflect it?

Polls showed that most Americans believed that movies with graphic, gratuitous violence *do* cause the young or the unbalanced to want to copy what they see on the screen. Many psychologists agreed. There were isolated, anecdotal cases that seem to give credence to their view. Certain violent acts seen at the movies would be copied exactly on Main Streets across the nation.

Still, as filmmakers pointed out, there was no real "smoking gun." There had been violence in America before there were movies, and plenty of it. Those arguing both points of view subsided, limp from the effort, but unconvinced.

Months went by, then years. *Taxi Driver* receded in public memory. But the time was approaching when that one movie—and one moviegoer—would make a difference.

John Hinckley Jr. paid for his ticket and sat down in the anonymous darkness to watch Martin Scorsese's *Taxi Driver*. What he saw was Jodie Foster in her character as Iris, the tiny prostitute who needed protection and got it from the demented taxi driver who simply shot everyone who hurt her.

Most moviegoers, at one time or another, leave a theater fantasizing about an actor, but John Hinckley Jr. was not most moviegoers. His "crush" became obsession, and his family had the money to indulge his wishes.

As previously noted, he actually trailed Miss Foster around the country. When his entreaties to meet her failed repeatedly, his fevered mind hatched a plan to get her attention. The taxi driver in the movie had risked everything for her by getting a gun and shooting someone. Hinckley would do the same, but on a grander scale. He would shoot a president.

And, on Monday, March 30, 1981, that is exactly what he did.

While Ronald Reagan lay dying, half his red blood supply already lost, word flashed around the world about the assassination attempt. Few knew how serious it was.

Among the first to get and react to the message were the organizers of the Academy Awards in Los Angeles. Most were already on hand anyway, caught in the vortex of final preparations for the ceremony. As minutes ticked by, there was hesitation. They watched each bulletin, concentrating on reports of Reagan's condition. Would he be all right? The first decision—unannounced—was that the event would be postponed. Before the requisite calls could be made, word from the hospital in Washington was better. The prognosis now was good.

In fact, quick work in the emergency room saved Ronald Reagan's life. The lead surgeon later reported it had taken him nearly forty minutes to get through the president's chest wall, so thick was the muscle mass. He had never seen a man of Reagan's age in that good a physical condition. He found the spent bullet within an inch of the heart. Unit after unit of blood was required, in the end nearly replacing his entire supply, but he was alive and had every prospect of recovery.

His quips had already become part of presidential lore, and remain so today. Each sounds like a line from a movie. To his distraught wife: "Honey, I forgot to duck." To his aide: "Who's minding the store?" And, most memorably, to the phalanx of green-clad doctors about to operate on him: "Please tell me you're Republicans."

In California, the bleachers outside the Dorothy Chandler Pavilion at the Los Angeles Music Center complex were already beginning to fill up. Seats would be at a premium within the hour. Caterers had arrived to begin work on the post-telecast parties.

The Academy had three options. Cancel the awards entirely, go on as scheduled, or postpone for an indeterminate time. The first was considered briefly. It would still be the choice if the president died. The second remained under active consideration for two hours, but with the continuing uncertainty, they arrived unanimously at the third alternative. Since Mr. Reagan seemed to be out of danger it was decided to postpone for twenty-four hours. The decision was not made until 2:00 P.M. Pacific time, so coordinators scrambled to get the word out to everyone involved while ABC made quick programming changes. Ironically, their job was made easier by the virtual wall-to-wall coverage of the assassination attempt.

By the time the awards show finally began on Tuesday, the whole nation knew about the connection between John Hinckley's shooting of the president and *Taxi Driver*. Fans shouted questions about it at Robert De Niro when he arrived with his wife in the obligatory limousine. The same for Martin Scorsese, who this time *was* nominated for Best Director, for *Raging Bull*. In fact, the film had eight nominations.

Johnny Carson set the tone right at the start of the telecast by giving everyone a positive report on the president's prognosis, then taking a good-natured swipe at him for federal cuts in funding for the arts. President Reagan's taped introduction was played, viewers were assured, at his insistence.

The ceremony plowed on in its now-familiar pattern, but with many references, of course, to the president. *Raging Bull* won only two Oscars, one for editing and the other for Robert De Niro as Best Actor. Once again, Martin Scorsese was passed over. Outspoken Harvey Keitel, Scorsese's long-time friend, was quoted as saying, "Maybe he got what he deserved—exclusion from the mediocre."

One thing his failure to get a statuette did spare him was the necessity of answering questions from reporters. Robert De Niro was not so lucky. He had read his acceptance speech—crediting Scorsese with preparing it—but then he was expected to attend the ritual backstage news conference. He arrived in a good mood, but it didn't last long.

De Niro was clearly surprised and increasingly upset by the tone and insistence of the questions. No one wanted to ask about *Raging Bull*. All questions dealt with the assassination attempt and the role of *Taxi Driver* in it. Did he know Hinckley?

Had Hinckley written him? How did he feel about that role now that it was implicated in the shooting of a president? "I don't know about that story. I don't want to discuss the matter." Did he feel a responsibility in the shooting? Should he apologize to President Reagan? Had he talked to Scorsese about it? Had he talked to Jodie Foster? Rattled, the actor said, "Look, I said what I wanted to say out there—that's it." And he left the stage—one newspaper reporting it as "stormed off the stage"—to join Scorsese and others for a post-Oscar party.

That was not the end of it, of course. From that day to this the subject comes up periodically for all the principals involved. The connection was too deep, the incident too close to the national bone.

There can be no doubt that the subject wears on everyone who had a part in the incident. Jodie Foster, far past that wise-beyond-her-years twelve-year old, attempts on occasion to discuss it rationally. Asked if the roles she has played, particularly 1988's *The Accused* in which she portrayed a provocative woman who is gang-raped, don't feed the destructive fantasies of unstable minds, responded, "I can't stop playing a victim just because of John Hinckley. Being a victim is unfortunately a big part of women's lives."

And, as Rap Brown once said, "Violence is as American as apple pie."

On the evidence, both have a point. But the evidence also shows that its graphic depiction on film for a quarter century has done nothing to excise the cancer from society, as some had hoped.

The assassination attempt and its association with *Taxi Driver* did, however, have a specific result that changed things in the United States.

Those who had been striving for tighter gun control laws had been drowning in the rising conservative tide and the powerful gun lobby was in the ascendant.

This incident changed all that, at least for a time. With the strong support of the wife and family of the fallen James S. Brady, and the occasional poignant speech by the badly injured man himself, the Brady Bill began a long torturous journey through the minefield of Congress. Even President Reagan himself, long an advocate of gun rights, was converted to the Brady Bill. In spite of that, the measure that under federal law requires a waiting period and background check for those who wish to purchase handguns was not signed into law until 1993, twelve years after Ronald Reagan was nearly killed by a cheap Saturday night special.

The year 1981 saw two additional assassination attempts of major world leaders: Egypt's Anwar Sadat was gunned down by Muslim fundamentalists who believed him a traitor to Islam because of his peace agreement with Israel. Pope John Paul II was shot at a public appearance in the Vatican. His assailant was a lone gunman, a Muslim, whose motive appeared to be religious as well. The pope survived.

Only the attempted assassination of Ronald Reagan can be said to have been written, directed, and starred in by the American motion picture industry. Is that a fair conclusion? That will be up to history, but the evidence appears convincing.

If there had been no *Taxi Driver*, would there have been no assassination attempt? No one can say for sure, but the possibility must be faced.

Should filmmakers ever be concerned about the consequences of their art on an audience? Cold as it may sound, many believe they should not. One role of art, goes this argument, is to stretch the borders of the freedom of the human mind beyond any current strictures. Only in that way does society progress.

It is a powerful argument.

But film is a powerful medium, and its effects for good or evil are difficult to measure.

There is a haunting image from *Taxi Driver*, more compelling, perhaps, than all the gore. Travis Bickle—Robert De Niro—is talking to his image in the mirror, as he descends into madness. He is alone.

"You talking to me? You talking to me? You talking to me? Well, who the hell else are you talking to? You talking to me? Well, I'm the only one here. Who the fuck do you think you're talking to?"

Who was the movie *Taxi Driver* talking to? It appears John Hinckley Jr. was sure it was talking to him.

On the other hand, a direct line from *Taxi Driver* to the Brady Bill makes it a movie that—at deeply troubling cost—changed things.

4

THE GRADUATE

1967

DIRECTOR: MIKE NICHOLS
STARS: ANNE BANCROFT, DUSTIN
HOFFMAN, KATHERINE ROSS
RUNNING TIME: 1 HOUR, 45 MINUTES

Graduating college student Ben Braddock is at loose ends. He quietly rejects the affluent life his parents have created, but he has no substitute in mind.

While without plans, he is seduced by Mrs. Robinson, the wife of his father's best friend. The desultory affair continues while Mr. Robinson, unaware of the betrayal, advises Ben to think "plastics" for his future.

Ben instead is beginning to see the Robinsons' daughter, Elaine, as his future. Mrs. Robinson explodes at the suggestion and sends her daughter away to college. Both Elaine and her father learn of the affair; Elaine quickly becomes engaged to another man and plans an immediate wedding.

Ben chases Elaine everywhere, refusing to give up, sure she loves him. The last series of scenes at the wedding have become classics. Ben and Elaine run away, she still in her wedding dress, and board a bus bound for the 1970s and . . . what?

Note: Watch for Richard Dreyfuss in a small role as a college student.

Embassy Pictures (Courtesy of The Kobal Collection)

M ike Nichols's casting of Dustin Hoffman in *The Graduate* was the seminal event in the defining of motion picture leading men in the last fifty years."

It was Steven Soderbergh speaking, the brilliant young Academy Award–winning director of *Traffic, sex, lies, and videotape, Kafka, King of the Hill, Out of Sight,* and *Erin Brockovich.* The conversation about *The Graduate* had sprung from an earlier exchange between me and a film critic.

There was a full house at the Gielgud Theatre in London's legendary West End on a late summer evening. The play was *The Graduate,* brought to the boards thirty-three years after the film's enormous success.

On that evening, the pace of the play was more stately than brisk. The sets seemed oddly oversized, diminishing the actors. Early in the run, movie star Kathleen Turner had galvanized the audience and the London press by removing all of her clothes during one of her scenes as Mrs. Robinson. Now, several months later, another audience thought they knew why. The play needed a jolt of energy, but Kathleen Turner was gone.

At a quiet moment in the second act, a film critic whispered to his companion, "If this hadn't been one of the best movies ever made, do you think this story we're watching would hold up?" On getting a negative response, he continued, "Too bad.

This is at best a tepid salute to a film powerful enough to kill romantic movies."

The phase hung in the air after the curtain came down and for days afterward. Had *The Graduate* been some kind of death knell for romance in the movies? Experts have long agreed that the groundbreaking 1967 romantic comedy had great impact on Hollywood, the clarion call from the baby-boom generation that things were going to be different from now on.

But declaring romance would be *different* was one thing. Declaring it *dead* was quite another. This would take some research.

Within the next few weeks, a random sampling of more than two thousand movies turned up a remarkable result. Of movies made before 1967, 36 percent had romance or romantic comedy as the central theme. Of movies made since 1967, that number is 11 percent. A startling turnaround in a relatively short period of time.

Why?

For an answer, it seemed appropriate to call on a filmmaker who was immersed in the arena *today*. Steven Soderbergh was only four years old when *The Graduate* premiered. Born in Atlanta, he grew up in Louisiana where his father was dean of the College of Education at LSU. For Steven, however, it was always the movies. After a film class, he skipped any other higher education aspirations and headed for California. Splitting his time between his home and where his heart was, Steven made short films and music videos. He wrote screenplays that began to get attention, and he has for more than a decade now been on the cutting edge of his profession.

Why so few romantic films now? Won't backers finance them?

"No, that's not it. Financing depends on stars. The cast drives everything, not the story. You can get almost anything made if you have the hot stars of the moment."

Then why the big difference in making that kind of film before and after The Graduate?

"Actually, I'm very surprised at that statistic you have, Nick. I suppose if I think back on it . . .yes, there were many more movies in the forties and fifties where the relationship between a man and a woman was the central focus of the story."

Specifically, why don't you make that kind of movie now?

"To tell you the truth, it is impossible for me to take that genre seriously.

"Besides, making that story work for today's audience is difficult. The movie audience is young and getting younger.

"They are so infected by the age of irony it is impossible for them to take a traditional romantic story seriously. What you would hear at critical moments, I think, would be a nervous titter.

"You see, the basic problem is that in today's social and cultural climate, what is the obstacle that would keep these two people from getting together? There has to be the obstacle—the conflict—to make the film work."

Mr. Soderbergh's point is well made. A generation ago—certainly two generations ago—there were any number of obstacles that could keep a couple apart. Different views on divorce, more rigid attitudes about sex, a deeper connection to religion, and an out-of-wedlock pregnancy was anathema. These constraints—obstacles—have by no means disappeared, but they clearly have weakened, particularly among the younger segment of the population.

"Let me return to casting," continued Mr. Soderbergh, "because it presents one other problem. The two characters would have to be mature enough for their relationship to have some dimension, some history. But today's audience might then find them too old to be interesting."

Yet some romances and, particularly, romantic comedies continue to be made. *Sleepless in Seattle* is always cited because of its enormous commercial success. The same with *When Harry Met Sally*.

"Yes, of course. Did you see *Dave?* I thought *Dave* was a good romantic comedy."

Still, the numbers point to an inescapable truth. The filmmaker who wishes to make a post-*Graduate* romantic movie has a fair-sized mountain to climb. A mountain built by director Mike Nichols, some would say. In 1967, Mr. Nichols was at the beginning of a hot streak such as few filmmakers ever realize. It had been a long road.

Michael Igor Peschkowsky, born in Berlin, was a seven-year-old refugee from Nazi Germany when he arrived in New York City. The streets were not paved with gold, but at least the family found safe haven. World War II was still raging when Mike's father, a physician, died. Mike was twelve.

With a survivor's drive and keen intelligence, Mike got through school winning scholarships, and, by the time he arrived at the prestigious University of Chicago, paying his way through with a bewildering number of jobs. He later reported that he had driven a delivery truck, and was a night desk clerk at a hotel, a janitor, and a mail clerk at the post office. In spite of his needing every spare minute and every spare dime just to survive, it was in Chicago that Mike Nichols found a new passion. He wanted to be an actor.

He knew that Lee Strasberg had been instrumental in founding a new acting school in New York that was attracting the best young dramatic talent in the country, so that's where he went.

It was to be a great disappointment to Mike that he didn't succeed as an actor, but nothing stopped him for long. He discovered in acting school a gift for improvisation, particularly interacting with others in sharp-edged comedy. There was in those days a cabaret in New York called The Compass. It was there that Mike and a small company of performers, which included Elaine May, Alan Arkin, and Barbara Harris, found their footing. Not too much time passed before Mike and Elaine May made comedy records that became—and remain—classics of their moment. Their coast-to-coast personal appearances were enormously successful for a couple of years, capped when they opened on Broadway in 1960 with *An Evening with Mike Nichols and Elaine May.* It was a triumph and ran for a year.

Even before Mike and Elaine became part of the culture of the late 1950s, Mike had pursued an interest in directing. He had an excellent rapport with performers, an eye for detail, and a solid grasp of what worked. An association with writer Neil Simon was fortuitous for both of them, and Mike Nichols soon had a reputation for the "golden touch." He was thought of as what a later generation would call "bullet proof," tearing off three Broadway hits in a row, *Barefoot in the Park, Luv,* and *The Odd Couple.*

That was the kind of success that attracted Hollywood, which, at bottom, has always believed in luck. "Success gets success" is a phrase as old as *The Great Train Robbery.*

Before long, Mike Nichols was negotiating to direct a film project very unlike his trademark comedies: Edward Albee's wrenching *Who's Afraid of Virginia Woolf?* Not only that, he was required to put this profane, downbeat story on film using the services of two movie stars, Elizabeth Taylor and Richard Burton, who, some said, had already become caricatures of their tabloid images.

Nichols's golden touch was intact. He pulled it off. *Virginia Woolf* was a critical success and, more important to the studio, a financial success. Now Mike had "juice," in Hollywood's view.

He would need it. The next project was a story defining a new kind of generation gap, from a novel by Charles Webb: children rejecting the hard-won prosperity of their parents.

No one could have predicted the forces that were coming together in 1967. The first wave of baby boomers was graduating from college. The fading—but influential—"beat" generation had planted seeds of doubt among the young about things such as consumerism. The Vietnam War was expanding, a popular—and young—president had been murdered, and the civil rights struggle was in its most militant phase.

This was the moment during which Mike Nichols began to organize the men and women who would make the romantic comedy of the generation.

Directors, both stage and film, have often said that their most important task is casting. "If you have done that right," my onetime brother-in-law, the outstanding stage director and fine actor José Ferrer, once said, "the rest is tweaking, cheerleading, and maintenance." It is, of course, a great deal more than that, but the exaggeration underscores the importance of choosing the right people to say the writer's words.

It is at this level that director Mike Nichols changed things. To play his leading man he chose Dustin Hoffman.

The problem was not simply that Dustin Hoffman was unknown. Money people were sometimes amenable to introducing an unknown in an important part. In fact, every young actor in Hollywood was sent to Nichols for an interview or a reading or a test. Among them was a thirty-year-old with a dozen or so film credits to his name, which was, incidentally, Jack Nicholson. Nicholson didn't get a callback.

Nor did any of the others. Nichols insisted on Dustin Hoffman. Few around the director understood why. By traditional standards, Hoffman was clearly wrong for the role.

Hoffman was the same age as Nicholson, thirty, in 1967. His had been a long, circular journey back to California. Born in Los Angeles, the son of a man who designed furniture, Hoffman's early ambition was in the field of music. His hope was to be a concert pianist and to that end he studied music at Santa Monica City College.

But not for long. A latent acting bug surfaced and bit hard.

He dropped out of the Santa Monica school and went to the nearby Pasadena Playhouse. By age nineteen, Hoffman was an actor.

For some time, however, it appeared he was the only one who thought so. He went to New York because he wanted a career on the stage instead of movies. But jobs were very hard to come by, and when they did come they didn't pay enough to live on. Years went by when most of Hoffman's income came from his work as a janitor, a desk clerk, even an attendant in a hospital mental ward. One famous legend has it that, for a long time, his only bed was a pallet on the kitchen floor of another struggling young actor, a fellow named Gene Hackman.

At this moment, if you please, a pause for a parenthetical aside. There seems to be an almost eerie parallel to the early careers of Mike Nichols and Dustin Hoffman: Both had real talent and endless drive, both wanted to be actors, and both went to the best available teachers, showed up at every audition, did a dozen menial jobs, and both were rejected time after time.

They could not get others to see what they knew in the deepest corners of their hearts: They were *actors* and, given the chance, they would prove it.

Mike never got the acting opportunity, but he became a world-class performer and, eventually, director. Is it possible that when he saw and then talked to this young man, he recognized him immediately? Is it too much of a stretch to imagine that he, empowered by his success, might give this actor the breakthrough role that would make his career? The kind of role Mike himself never got?

This is not to suggest that Mr. Nichols had only that kind of vindication on his mind. Far from it. It would appear that his thinking was much more strategic than that. Mike Nichols was on a mission to change movies, at least the ones he could affect.

He could certainly affect *The Graduate*. Dustin Hoffman had begun to get small, episodic roles on television and, sometimes, an extended job in summer stock. But it was not until 1965 that he landed an off-Broadway part, for which he got an Obie in 1966. That same year, he won a good part in the British farce *Eh?* That was where Mike Nichols saw him and decided, then and there, that Dustin Hoffman would be Benjamin Braddock.

Take a moment to recall the leading men in Hollywood's romantic comedies: Clark Gable in *It Happened One Night,* Cary Grant in *The Awful Truth,* William Powell in the *Thin Man* series, Robert Montgomery, Melvyn Douglas, right up through the era of Paul Newman and Robert Redford in such fare as *Barefoot in the Park.* A romantic comedy needed a romantic leading man, which meant a handsome movie star.

Obviously, Dustin Hoffman would be a departure from that tradition. Against all pressure, Nichols persevered with his leading man. He was approached for a trade-off, a compromise with commerce on his leading lady, which he flirted with for a while. A tentative offer to play the role of Mrs. Robinson was tendered to the All-American movie star Doris Day—about whom the irreverent Oscar Levant once said, "I knew Doris *before* she was a virgin." The offer never got to the formal stage because Doris Day said the role "offended my sense of values."

For that matter, the role of Mrs. Robinson would be a departure for actress Anne Bancroft, too. This, after all, was the Tony and Oscar-winning Annie Sullivan of *The Miracle Worker.* She was also, of course, one of the premier actresses of her generation, so if the part called for her to be a predatory older woman— she was in reality only six years older than Mr. Hoffman—Miss Bancroft would suggestively hike her skirt and expose a major-league pair of legs with the best of them.

It is easy now to forget that Anne Bancroft's career could have been lost in a shower of Hollywood gold dust, as so many were. But she displayed a grit every bit as tenacious as that of Mike Nichols or Dustin Hoffman.

Anna Maria Italiano was never going to be anything *but* an actress, even at age four in her home in the Bronx. She was dancing and performing at any opportunity. At nineteen she had second leads on live TV productions. She had already studied at the American Academy of Dramatic Arts and Actors Studios.

Then came the detour that almost destroyed her career: Hollywood came calling. The first offer seemed good. She had a third lead in an interesting thriller starring Richard Widmark and Marilyn Monroe called *Don't Bother to Knock*. At twenty-one, however, the young actress who had become Anne Marno, then Anne Bancroft, didn't understand about studio contracts.

For the next five years she would be assigned to such fare as *Treasure of the Golden Condor, Gorilla at Large, New York Confidential, The Naked Street, The Girl in Black Stockings*, the kind of "B" picture cul-de-sac from which few escape.

Anne went back to New York and reconnected with her theater roots. The very next year, 1958, she landed the plum role in *Two for the See Saw* opposite Henry Fonda. She was presented the Tony Award, and her professional world was full of promise again.

Among her greatest admirers through this period was Mike Nichols. They shared a passion for New York City that they have never lost. Though both have had major success in Hollywood since the mid-1960s, neither chooses to live there.

In fact, Nichols was quoted in a national magazine as saying that one of his ambitions for *The Graduate* was "to stop the Los Angelization of America."

Nichols and Bancroft also share outrageous senses of humor. In Miss Bancroft's case it is, perhaps, self-defense. She is, after all, married to Mel Brooks.

The Graduate exploded on thousands of screens in 1967, and before many weeks had gone by, the buzzword in young America was "plastics," the key to the future whispered to Benjamin Braddock at his graduation party.

There was also some laughter about an interview the film's ingénue, Katherine Ross, gave concerning her first impressions of her costar: "He looked about three feet tall, so dead serious, so unkempt, so humorless. I said to myself 'this is going to be a disaster.' Boy, was I wrong!"

The film had taken some heavy-handed joshing from the financial pages early on. "Godzilla Bankrolls Graduate" read one headline. The reference was to Embassy Pictures chief Joseph E. Levine, who had made a bundle buying Japanese and Italian films, such as *Godzilla* and *Hercules*, for very low prices, then spending substantial sums promoting them. The technique worked so well that by the 1960s Levine was able to back some big-budget Hollywood films like *The Carpetbaggers*, *Harlow*, and *The Oscar*. It was Embassy's money that Mike Nichols was now spending.

Mr. Levine would have no reason to complain, nor would he see derisive headlines in the newspapers again. *The Graduate* took in $40 million in its first run, and we must remember, that was $40 million in *1967*.

Some time after the film's release, director Mike Nichols was asked about the famous closing scene in which Katherine Ross leaves her fiancé at the altar and runs off with Dustin Hoffman, the two on a bus to nowhere, appearing to thumb their noses at their parents, their parents' entire generation, and society at large.

Mr. Nichols replied, "I think Benjamin and Elaine will end up exactly like their parents. That's what I was trying to say in that last scene."

At the time, it was a singularly unwelcome explanation to many. Virtually an entire generation thought they were seeing exactly the opposite; that a young couple was rejecting the materialism of their parents and launching a new life with new values.

Mr. Nichols's response back in 1967 might have been unsatisfactory as explanation, but as we now know, it was cruelly accurate as prophecy.

But what of the central point, the one made by the London movie critic? Did *The Graduate* kill romantic movies? The evidence seems clear that it may have killed a certain *kind* of romantic movie. But it obviously lit the way to a new look at romance as depicted on film. Romantic movies from then on would be fewer, leaner, a bit meaner, and nearly devoid of sentiment.

The Graduate did not kill romantic movies. But it did change things.

5

WHO'S AFRAID OF VIRGINIA WOOLF?

1966

DIRECTOR: MIKE NICHOLS

STARS: ELIZABETH TAYLOR, RICHARD BURTON, GEORGE SEGAL, SANDY DENNIS

RUNNING TIME: 2 HOURS, 11 MINUTES

Within moments we understand that George is a college professor who has not succeeded and no longer cares, and Martha is a pathologically frustrated wife who loves to compare her husband to her successful father, the president of the college where George is trapped.

The two have invited a new couple, Nick and Honey, to their house for a nightcap.

There ensues a nightmare evening of drinking, attempted seduction, maudlin confessions, and a bizarre episode in which we learn that Martha and George have concocted an imaginary son, whom George proceeds to "murder."

Dawn breaks, Nick and Honey crawl away. George and Martha—spent—go quietly to bed. The audience is left to wonder if their twenty-year marriage survives because of repeated evenings such as the one we just saw.

Note: Cinematographer Haskell Wexler received the last Academy Award for black-and-white photography for *Virginia Woolf.*

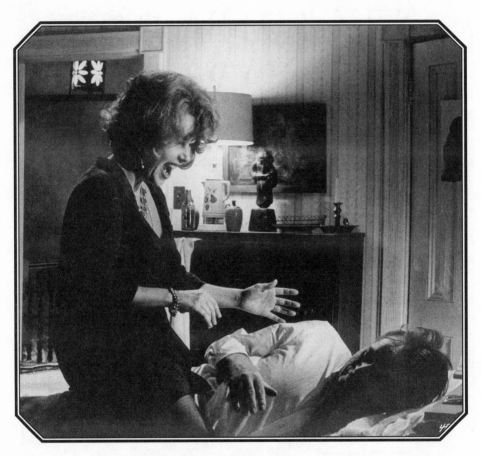

Warner Bros (Courtesy of The Kobal Collection)

J ust this one more time, Old Hollywood gathered the tattered remnants of the vilified Production Code around her and went off to do battle with the forces of vulgarity, profanity, and the seamy side of art.

It was no contest this time around. Vulgarity and profanity won by a knockout, and millions cheered.

In the first days of the Production Code—censorship, really, of the movies in the early 1930s—all the zealotry had been on the side of those who would hold the films uncontaminated by sex, irreligion, or crime that paid.

By the mid-1960s, whatever zealotry remained was on the side of freedom of expression, even if—perhaps *especially* if— that expression might shock or offend large numbers of people.

Who's Afraid of Virginia Woolf? would certainly do that, and more.

Edward Albee's play opened at exactly the moment the United States was closer to nuclear war than ever before or since, the time of the Cuban missile crisis of October 1962. Playgoers who had gone to the theater to forget were instead assaulted by language and situations they had not seen before outside of experimental theater.

The immediate reaction of the audience, eventually voiced by critics, was that Albee had created a play that would be a great success on Broadway, but could never be filmed in anything like its current form.

Neither the critics nor the theater audience understood how much the Hollywood landscape was changing in the 1960s. It was becoming a town and an industry that could no longer live with any meaningful Production Code. *Virginia Woolf* would exorcise the last wisps of the ghost of Will Hays.

The production side of films had, of course, never been comfortable with any part of the "Code." Privately—and, on rare occasions, publicly—stars, directors, and above all writers would poke merciless fun at the twin beds, the "one-foot-on-the-floor" rule, the sanitized kissing, the racial separation, and the scores of other restraints that they felt kept them from telling realistic stories.

In ways large and small, directors and writers would look for methods to convince—or trick—the keepers of the Code. They would find triumphs in a word, a phrase, the careless lift of a skirt, a suggestively raised eyebrow, a sly reaction shot.

On rare occasions, confrontation worked. David O. Selznick simply refused to remove the word "damn" from Rhett Butler's final line in 1939's *Gone With the Wind*. The film was so big, the audience so anticipatory, the buzz so great that the production office simply did not have the power to stand in the way of the juggernaut, so it was the keepers of the Production Code who blinked.

Less clear is why they stepped aside for *The Miracle of Morgan's Creek* in 1944, and a few other groundbreaking films, but, for the most part, censorship held an iron grip on the mainstream film industry well into the 1950s.

The erosion began for the same reason the strict code was adopted in the first place: money.

In the late 1920s, studios were terrified they were losing their audiences because of the "immorality" many in the nation believed they saw on the screen and in the lives of the filmmakers. Powerful groups were organizing and, as we will see in succeeding chapters, they were mounting effective boycotts against movies.

Hollywood fought back with its own production code for what was permissible on screen. They also put an iron grip on the public behavior of their contract players. The restraints were serious and effective.

It worked. Audiences came back to the movies in droves and, essentially, kept coming through the 1930s and 1940s.

Television had been hanging over the heads of movie moguls since the 1930s. Its practical use was given wide currency in the 1939 New York World's Fair when a baseball game between the Brooklyn Dodgers and the Cincinnati Reds was telecast in its entirety. The Second World War set back the advancement of the technology but only by a decade. In the 1950s, television had become a player.

Audiences by the millions began to stay home and watch "Uncle Miltie" and "Gorgeous George," the wrestler. The movies battled back with gimmicks, such as 3-D and CinemaScope.

Still, the erosion continued, and no one was sure where the bottom would be found. There were those who felt the movie business would go the way of its predecessor in mass entertainment, vaudeville.

Others, however, looked at another model and found hope. When the movies really arrived in the 1920s, vaudeville did, indeed, die. But *theater* didn't.

Dramatic and musical theater began to adjust. The stage gave audiences something they couldn't find in movies.

If the movies were sanitized, plays were not. If movies shied from four-letter words, plays did not. On stage, Americans could find adult humor, controversial subject matter, intellectual stimulation, innovative musical plays, and plenty of sex. Theater no longer had a mass audience, so it would not even try appealing to it. They would go after that fragment of the population that wanted something more than they could see in the movies and were willing to pay for it.

The strategy had worked. While movies prospered on a grand scale, theater prospered, too.

Now it was the turn of the movies. They would give audiences something they couldn't get on television. And the Production Code, which had helped stimulate business in the 1930s and 1940s, was now an obstacle to getting the business Hollywood had to have to survive.

A long dance of separation began in the 1950s. The movie industry wanted to dump the substance of restraint without dumping its appearance. There were still powerful parents' groups and others out there who could be troublesome. Complicated—and ultimately meaningless—rating systems were instituted, altered, discarded, reintroduced; a process that continues today.

But *Who's Afraid of Virginia Woolf?* was the ultimate nail in the coffin of Hollywood's forty-year attempt at self-censorship.

A four-character story, black-and-white film, a first-time director, a "talky" script, no action, no "tits and ass," as a later generation would put it. No producer in his right mind, it seemed, would bring this to the big screen.

Enter Ernest Lehman.

Mr. Lehman had been around Hollywood for twenty years as a successful writer who was best known for adapting material from another medium and making screenplays that worked. Major examples included *Executive Suite* (1954), *Sabrina* (1954), *The King and I* (1956), *Somebody Up There Likes Me* (1956), *West Side Story* (1961), and *The Sound of Music* (1965).

But Mr. Lehman was also an original thinker, whose short stories had found their way to the screen as well. In fact, his biting, brutal *Sweet Smell of Success* (1957), written in the 1940s, became a brilliant movie, a screenplay he cowrote with Clifford Odets, starring Burt Lancaster in a role everyone carefully said was *not* based on Walter Winchell. Ernest Lehman was also responsible for the original story and the sophisticated dialogue of *North by Northwest,* which was certainly Alfred Hitchcock's most stylish thriller, if not his best.

Now it was time to bring *Who's Afraid of Virginia Woolf?* to the screen. Ernest Lehman made two key decisions: First, he would *not* change the dialogue, language that had shocked veteran theatergoers in New York only four years earlier. Lehman was going to turn it loose on what was, essentially, still a mass audience. There was serious opposition to his decision, but he prevailed.

Second, he would hire Mike Nichols to direct. Lehman greatly admired Nichols's intellect and his grasp of storytelling. He also knew that Mr. Nichols had a remarkable rapport with actors, a crucial skill in this spare, character-driven movie.

In casting, there was very little thought given to using the two actors who had succeeded in the principal roles on Broadway, Arthur Hill and Uta Hagen. Many film stars lobbied for the parts, notably Bette Davis for the role of Martha, and Henry Fonda for George. Even playwright Edward Albee wanted these two veterans.

Both Lehman and Nichols knew they were in a precarious position. Without proper promotion, this movie would land with a resounding thud, but the subject matter was difficult to promote. Who, after all, was Virginia Woolf? And if she wasn't in the movie, what was she doing in the title? Who was afraid of her and why? And why should a moviegoer want to watch two hours of screaming between a harridan and a wimp?

Hollywood's answer to a difficult story has always been star-power. If you can't sell the screenplay, sell the stars. That is exactly what Lehman and Nichols proceeded to do. They went after the two highest-profile actors in the world at that moment, Elizabeth Taylor and Richard Burton.

The producer approached them with a double-barreled offer.

First, they would be working together in a story with intellectual power and roles that would challenge them both. Miss Taylor seemed particularly vulnerable to that kind of offer at the moment. She had won an Academy Award in 1960 for a role she hated in a film she disliked, *Butterfield 8*. For three years she had been with Richard Burton, whose power and range as an actor were widely acknowledged. Despite her success and her Oscar, her acting skills were still suspect with many critics. Putting on thirty pounds, wearing frumpy clothes, and allowing her hair to become frowsy would at least remove the "glamour" label and allow audiences to see if she could handle the role.

The other inducement was money. Though the Burtons made a lot of money, they spent even more. Mr. Lehman hit them with a high number: one million dollars each. It was a bold move, because his entire budget was just over $5 million and he would have to scrimp in important areas. But it worked. They signed on.

Elizabeth Taylor, it seems to many moviegoers, has been always with us. Her own apparent concerns and those of a number of critics about the extent of her gift as an actress were and are pointless. Miss Taylor is a magnetic presence whose appeal transcends technique and the minutiae of characterization. Since *Lassie Come Home* (1943), she has been part of the world's film life that runs as a corollary to its real life. We watched her grow up on camera. She never seemed to have an awkward age, and audiences would have noticed because she was never off the screen for even one year from 1942, when she was ten, until 1960, when she was twenty-eight.

The indelible moment, the one that etches her in film history, was *A Place in the Sun* (1951) with Montgomery Clift. She was preposterously, impossibly beautiful, and the words from Theodore Dreiser's tragedy came out of her lovely mouth with a poignance that was then and still is utterly believable.

What is *unbelievable*, however, is that Elizabeth Taylor was then not yet eighteen. She would, in fact, marry, the first of eight times, also before she was eighteen. It was startling to note that when she made *Giant* (1956), Miss Taylor, the veteran of fourteen years in film, portrayed a character who was the sexual obsession of the character of newcomer James Dean. Actually, Mr. Dean was eleven months *older* than Miss Taylor at the time.

Welsh actor Richard Burton was seven years Miss Taylor's senior, but two decades behind her star status. Born Richard Walter Jenkins Jr. in South Wales, he would eventually borrow the surname of his favorite teacher, Phillip Burton. After school and stage work as a teenager, he was in the RAF for three years. Resuming his acting career, he soon became one of the most admired and successful of the postwar leading men in Great Britain.

In time, Mr. Burton went back and forth between England and the United States for films for ten years. His reputation and skill were growing and his roles were getting bigger. *The Robe* (1953) had been a breakthrough, but Burton seemed to turn his back on any inflated Hollywood build-up. Few would have called him a major movie star in 1962.

Which was when the Queen of the Nile proved that her magic was no less potent with the passage of a few thousand years. *Cleopatra* was already deeply troubled and famously over budget when the director, Rouben Mamoulian, and two of the stars, Peter Finch and Steven Boyd, were fired. Richard Burton had just finished a small role in *The Longest Day* (1962) and was available, so he and Rex Harrison were brought into the project. And that was that. Taylor and Burton had known one another before, but there had been no spark. Now there was. Both were married. That didn't matter. It was instantaneous attraction.

Their affair burned so brightly it consumed everything around it, including Richard Burton's "great actor/no star quality" reputation. He was now a star, all right, one of the hottest in the industry. Paradoxically, these two actors, now part and parcel of the biggest flop in movie history to that moment, were in demand everywhere, including for *Who's Afraid of Virginia Woolf?*

In a two-hour, four-character play, each actor must carry a large share of the load and there can be no weak link. Again, Lehman and Nichols took chances this time on two relative unknowns and, again, they rolled a seven.

George Segal had made a few movies when he got the call from Mr. Nichols. The director and the actor had a number of things in common. Both were New York based; both had worked the cabaret scene, Mike as a comic actor and George as a jazz musician who also did comic material on occasion. He, in fact, had a gift for comedy that would stand him in good stead for many of the offbeat leading roles he would undertake in years to come.

Still, the character of Nick had undertones and colors no one had yet seen from George Segal. They soon would.

Sandy Dennis turned out to be another inspired choice. Incidentally, like George Segal, Sandy Dennis is her real name. Born in Hastings, Nebraska, Miss Dennis chose acting for her profession early on, working in both amateur and stock productions from the time she was a teenager. Encouraged, she took the plunge and headed for New York, going immediately to the Actors Studio.

Soon she had small parts off-Broadway, with some television as well. At age twenty-four, she appeared in the film *Splendor in the Grass* (1961) directed by Actors Studio founder Elia Kazan. Dennis was neither comfortable nor welcomed in Hollywood. She returned to her first love, theater, where she began to get breakout roles in fine plays including *A Thousand Clowns* and *Any Wednesday*. After two Tonys in a row for those roles, she was a certified star of the theater.

It was that confidence she brought to *Virginia Woolf.* She

had her own connection with jazz lovers George Segal and Mike Nichols. Her companion for many years was the great jazz saxophonist Gerry Mulligan.

And so the filming began. Though stopping short of the still-anathema "fuck," *Virginia Woolf* showered the sound track with multiple "goddamns," "son-of-a-bitches," "up yours," "great nipples," and a memorable "hump the hostess." Mike Nichols called "wrap," the film went to editing, and Warner Bros. waited to see what would come of it all.

There had been warnings: The Catholic Office of Motion Pictures, once the all-powerful Legion of Decency, issued a preliminary report saying that, if what they heard was true, they might have to slap *Virginia Woolf* with the once-dreaded "condemned" rating. Still, they promised to wait until they saw the film. The Motion Picture Association of America followed with an even stronger statement, warning the studio that if they were really thinking of leaving the Broadway play's language intact, they could forget getting a seal. They didn't even promise to wait for a screening.

Warner Bros. executives sat down to look at a rough cut, without music, and a *Life* magazine reporter was there. He printed the following quote from one of the studio chiefs. "My God! We've got a seven million dollar dirty movie on our hands!"

The die was cast. Warner Bros. backed their producer and director. Not a word was cut. In one of the most abject surrenders in film history, the formerly all-powerful Motion Picture Association folded its tent and slunk away. The movie received the Production Seal. Some in Hollywood said if you turned the seal around the other side said "Screw You," a direct quote from the film. Even the Catholic Office refused to "condemn" the film. The Production Code was dead.

All of the publicity about the Burtons, all the controversy about the play, and all those excellent performances turned to gold at the box office.

Who's Afraid of Virginia Woolf? was the number one film of 1966.

The Academy of Motion Picture Arts and Sciences understood that this movie provided a watershed moment in film history, whether establishment Hollywood liked it or not. *Virginia Woolf* received thirteen nominations, including all four actors, the director, the writers, and, of course, a nomination for the film itself.

By the time the big night of the Academy Awards came, however, a new favorite had arrived on the scene. *A Man for All Seasons* and its elegant star, Paul Scofield, had many veteran critics in its thrall, contrasting sharply as it did with the dark view of life represented by other nominated films, including *Virginia Woolf, Alfie,* and *The Sand Pebbles.* Of course, *A Man for All Seasons* could scarcely be said to have a happy ending.

The most obvious feature of the awards ceremony on April 10, 1967, was the absence of many of the nominees. Academy officials were angry and didn't mind telling the press about it. *Who's Afraid of Virginia Woolf?* came in for particular criticism, because three of the four actors nominated, Elizabeth Taylor, Richard Burton, and Sandy Dennis were conspicuous by their absence.

When the evening was over, *Virginia Woolf* had received five statuettes for its thirteen nominations: Elizabeth Taylor for Best Actress, Sandy Dennis for Best Supporting Actress, Haskell Wexler for Best Cinematography, Richard Sylbert and George Hopkins for Best Set Decoration, and Irene Sharaff for Best Costume Design.

However, out of eight nominations, *A Man for All Seasons* scored *six* wins including Best Actor, Best Director, Best Writing, and the big one, Best Picture.

If the Academy was irritated with Miss Taylor for not being on hand for the ceremony, she was furious at them for snubbing her husband. It was, in fact, the fourth time Mr. Burton had been nominated without receiving an Oscar. What neither could know was that there would be two more gala evenings on which Mr. Burton's name would be placed in nomination and, again, he would go home with no "golden doorstop," as Oscar Levant once called the award.

Miss Taylor was so angry she refused to make any comment to reporters about her award and, in fact, would not even accept it until it was presented to her, much later that year, by Lord Mountbatten at the British Academy Awards. As it happened, both she and Richard Burton received the British principal acting awards that night.

For many, all this attention, which began with the opening of Edward Albee's play during one of the most dangerous weeks in history, continued with the almost casual brushing aside of a forty-year film code and ended with matching huffs by the famous Academy and its most famous movie star, begs the question: Who in the world *is* Virginia Woolf?"

It seems simple justice to note that Adeline Virginia Stephen Woolf of Great Britain was one of the most admired of the "modern" novelists. She was also an influential critic. Though never a real best-seller, she influenced writers on both sides of the Atlantic. One of her most unconventional novels, *The Waves* (1931), dealt with six characters whose inner lives are traced by wrenching, subconscious monologues, a radical departure from other narrative devices, including her own.

Personally, Virginia Woolf battled delicate health and serious mental instability all of her life. Though she wrote up to the last of her days, a recurrence of mental problems led her to take her own life in 1941, at age fifty-nine. An ending even darker than that of Albee's couple, whom we leave apparently descending into madness.

Perhaps Albee's Martha and George had reason to be afraid of Virginia Woolf, after all.

But not nearly as much reason to fear as those who had spent the better part of two generations attempting to shackle the creative expression of filmmakers under the banner of "decency." A process which began in 1944, with *The Miracle at Morgan's Creek*, a film we'll visit later in this book, reached its logical—if painfully slow—resolution twenty-two years later in *Who's Afraid of Virginia Woolf?*, a movie that changed things.

6

DR. STRANGELOVE

or: How I Learned to Stop Worrying and Love the Bomb

1964

DIRECTOR: STANLEY KUBRICK

STARS: PETER SELLERS, GEORGE C. SCOTT, STERLING HAYDEN

RUNNING TIME: 1 HOUR, 42 MINUTES

U.S. Air Force Brigadier General Jack D. Ripper goes mad and orders his bombers to attack Russia. He seals off his base, locks down the code, and prevents everyone from contacting the planes, including President Merkin Muffley, who frantically calls in his top advisers, womanizing General "Buck" Turgidson and a demented German scientist, Dr. Strangelove.

Various plots to stop the bombers fail. The Russians are let in on the secret, but remain suspicious. General Ripper, his headquarters invaded, kills himself rather than order his attack to stop. All the bombers are shot down but one, piloted by the crafty Major "King" Kong. When the atom bomb sticks in the bay, Kong personally releases it and rides it to the world's doom.

Note: One of Kubrick's original scripts had the nuclear confrontation ending with a gigantic custard-pie throwing contest among the military, the diplomats, and the politicians.

Hawk Films Prod/Columbia (Courtesy of The Kobal Collection)

Hurry, hurry, hurry, come one, come all, come get your wars! Wars of all shapes and sizes: Great Wars, Banana Wars, Gunboat Wars, World Wars, Great Patriotic Wars, Wars of Liberation, Ethnic Cleansing Wars, Wars on Terrorism, wars for every taste and every occasion!

The twentieth century was a war lover's dream. All those eager little boys who painstakingly set up their ranks and files of lead soldiers in precise formation, then gleefully knocked them helter-skelter had a century to die for.

But, by the century's sixth decade, a surfeit of war was becoming something of a problem. It started to be apparent that too many were dying, which was giving war a bad name. Instead of professional—or at least volunteer—armies slugging it out on isolated battlefields, trained soldiers dying at a rate acceptable to everyone except those who died, the twentieth century produced wars that involved entire populations. No longer was war just a grown-up version of all those six-year-old generals sending phalanxes of metal warriors to their make-believe doom, flags flying and bugles blaring.

Men were getting too good at the destruction trade. Whole towns, then cities, were leveled, the line of demarcation between combatant and noncombatant demolished with the bricks and mortar. So many were dying that too few were left to stand on the sidelines and cheer the heroes. There *were* no sidelines.

Finally, after all the machine guns, the Big Berthas, the tanks, the superfortresses, the blockbusters, the V-2, men found the ultimate weapon, unleashing the very power of nature, splitting the nuclei of uranium 235 and sending fireballs and shockwaves and radioactive fallout in such immense quantities that even the most warlike were given pause.

For once, Hollywood was stumped. They didn't know what to do with the atomic age, an accurate reflection of the bewilderment and anxiety felt by the rest of us. For the brief four years of the American monopoly on the nuclear weapon, major movies made virtually no reference to the revolution that had occurred. If films dealt with war, it was a retrospective on the cataclysm the world had just narrowly survived. Exactly as the Hollywood of the 1930s ignored or made fun of the Depression, Hollywood of 1945-1950 ignored the New Atomic Age.

In 1949, America learned that it no longer had the nuclear secret to itself. The Soviet Union exploded an atomic bomb and they clearly had the delivery system to make it viable.

And so, the most famous and dangerous standoff in history began. It would consume billions of dollars, draining the treasuries of great nations. It would affect, in ways large and small, every living creature on the globe. In a classic irony, it would also prevent what most of those alive on the planet in 1945 thought was inevitable: a Third World War.

The two great antagonists would nibble at the periphery, but neither dared challenge the other directly. Thousands would die, but not millions. In the coin of the Cold War, the rate of exchange was favorable.

We developed phrases for it, eventually. The euphonious "Equilibrium of Terror." The more directly to the point "Mutually Assured Destruction." "M-A-D," indeed.

The 1950s found mainstream Hollywood slow to take on the Cold War, at least directly. Not until the end of the decade did a big-budget film deal with the possibility of the end of life on

earth because of the actions of irresponsible governments;
1959's excellent *On the Beach*, the Nevil Shute novel, directed
by Stanley Kramer.

The 1960s would be different.

Antiwar themes began to appear timidly in films. Writers
who had held their peace for fear of tipping the delicate international balance were silent no longer, and their voices were now
being heard in the central spaces of society; the living rooms.

The Cuban missile crisis raised the temperature to fever
pitch in 1962. The assassination of John F. Kennedy in 1963
unleashed forces of doubt and dissent that would boil, then boil
over, for a decade. Thomas Jefferson once observed "Some will
always prefer the tranquility of tyranny to the boisterous sea of
liberty." America's view of liberty was boisterous enough in the
1960s to shake the foundations of most institutions and
assumptions.

In 1964, in a coincidence of purposes, three remarkable film-
makers released antiwar movies within months of one another.
John Frankenheimer's *Seven Days in May*, Sidney Lumet's *Fail
Safe*, and Stanley Kubrick's *Dr. Strangelove*.

The first presented the possibility of a coup by the American
military, grown powerful and arrogant because of its promi-
nence in the Cold War—and holding the nuclear card as trump.
The second offered the premise that both the United States and
the U.S.S.R. put too much trust in technology to keep nations
from nuclear disaster, by presenting a chilling story of technology gone awry, with the U.S. sending a fleet of bombers bearing
atom bombs to destroy Russia.

Both films, by doomsday standards, had semihappy endings.
In *Seven Days*, the coup is averted. In *Fail Safe*, only two great
cities—Moscow and New York—are annihilated along with
their populations. The rest of the world is presumably saved.

Stanley Kubrick was having none of that. In the darkest
comedy of its age, the closing of *Dr. Strangelove* finds nuclear

blast after nuclear blast going off all over the world, obliterating civilization while that most civilized of singers, Dame Vera Lynn, sings the brave "chin-up" song of World War II, "We'll Meet Again."

It should be no surprise that the casts of those three movies are virtually all male.

Dr. Strangelove or: How I Learned to Stop Worrying and Love the Bomb was the most successful antiwar movie of the nuclear age up to that time. Though it bore no resemblance to 1925's *The Big Parade*, its influence was the same: it opened the gates for antiwar themes in the movies, first a trickle, then a flood in the wind-down of the Vietnam War.

This was Stanley Kubrick's project from the beginning. He was not only the director; he was also the producer and the coscreenwriter.

Mr. Kubrick was born in the Bronx and by the time he was seventeen, in 1945, he was a staff photographer for one of the leading magazines of the day, *Look*. Five years later, he decided to become a filmmaker, quitting his job and putting his energies into documentaries. Within a few years he had borrowed from everyone he knew in order to make a feature film, *Fear and Desire*. Kubrick did everything except the acting. He wrote, produced, directed, loaded film, shot it, then edited it. He was encouraged enough to do another film in exactly the same manner, and then, in 1954, to form a production company, get a bigger budget, hire a professional cast that included Sterling Hayden, and make the crime drama *The Killing*. This is the vehicle that got the attention of critics.

Stanley Kubrick's next film would tell us what he was all about. His work had been seen by Kirk Douglas, who was about to make a major film based on a 1934 novel by Humphrey Cobb, *Paths of Glory*. Mr. Kubrick was one of three writers who would adapt the novel and Mr. Kubrick would direct.

By every measure except one, *Paths of Glory* was a stunning debut. This 1957 film was the most fully realized antiwar film of the decade, even though the war being excoriated was World War I and the military establishment condemned was that of France. The acting, the production values, the directing techniques ranked with the best Hollywood had seen, and the undiluted message was so powerful that the film was banned in France. In fact, it was also banned from many U.S. military bases.

The film's condemnation of the officer corps, the exposing of the heartless and brainless system under which hundreds of thousands had died, was powerful medicine and not many were prepared to take it. The movie was a financial failure.

Kubrick would not make that mistake seven years later. Though *Dr. Strangelove* was every bit as brutal in its renunciation of the military as *Paths of Glory*, it was a comedy. The audience was free to take as much—or as little—from it as they chose.

Some left the theater laughing, quoting one-liners. Others left deeply depressed, wondering if they had seen a fragment of the future. Whatever their motives in going or their reactions after the fact, they made the cash registers ring. Stanley Kubrick, in a film over which he had complete control, had a hit.

The critical community, as it usually is, was divided. *Saturday Review* called it "a true satire with the whole human race as the ultimate target." Many publications noted that satire in the movies was usually box-office poison, but Kubrick's film was breaking new ground in many ways. It was considered newsworthy enough that it was included on the cover of *Time* magazine's year-end issue under the title "The Nuclear Issue." And in the wake of the themes of both *Fail Safe* and *Dr. Strangelove*, the U.S. Air Force released a statement reassuring the world that there were "safeguards" in place, which would preclude the kind of mishaps depicted in the films.

Kubrick's cast choices for *Dr. Strangelove* followed paths as interesting as his plotlines.

Peter Sellers had worked with Mr. Kubrick two years earlier in the offbeat hit *Lolita.* This time the producer-director would require of his star a tour-de-force that would challenge any actor: he would play *three* disparate roles. Sellers took it in stride. He had been on stage since he was a child, traveling with his parents' comedy act. He had been a radio and film star in the U.K. since the late 1940s, often using disguises to play multiple parts in comedy sketches. He would consider it no stretch at all to be President Merkin Muffley, Group Captain Lionel Mandrake, as well as the title character, Dr. Strangelove himself. Perhaps it should be pointed out that after this strenuous role, he plunged into three more American films in 1964, and while filming the last, Billy Wilder's *Kiss Me Stupid,* he suffered a heart attack that set him back for some time. Sellers was replaced in the role by Ray Walston and would undertake a less hectic schedule for most of the sixteen years of life that were left to him.

Second-billed was George C. Scott, a veteran marine who had worked his way through the acting trenches via theater and television. Moviegoers first saw him in 1959 in a fine performance as a prosecutor in *Anatomy of a Murder* and in a low-key Gary Cooper Western, *The Hanging Tree.* His next two projects were equally memorable, *The Hustler* in 1961, in which he was a smooth villain, and in 1963, the star-studded mystery *The List of Adrian Messenger.*

The world did not yet know the intense imperatives that burned in Mr. Scott and would burst into headlines when, six years later, he denounced the Academy Award ceremonies as akin to beauty pageants and said if he were to receive one, he would refuse to accept it. He did receive it for 1970's *Patton* and he did refuse to accept it. A model of consistency, he also received a television Emmy for his work in Arthur Miller's *The Price* and he refused that award as well.

Obviously, Mr. Kubrick knew something about George Campbell Scott that the audience did not. Those complex performances were wrenched from a complex man whose rage we no longer have to guess at.

Mr. Kubrick's next choice was an old colleague from his first days as a filmmaker, Sterling Hayden. Mr. Hayden was another veteran marine but was personally a more adventurous soul than Mr. Kubrick, Mr. Sellers, or Mr. Scott. Twelve years older than Kubrick and nine years older than Scott, Hayden brought a wealth of life experience to any role.

He was born Sterling Relyea Walter in 1916 in Montclair, New Jersey. He dropped out of school at age sixteen to go to sea. He later said he was actually the captain of a schooner by the time he was twenty-one. What is clear is that he never lost his obsession with the sea. He was, in fact, trying to buy his own schooner when an agent suggested he might try modeling for extra cash. Sterling was 6'5" and handsome, and the agent was not the first to suggest he try cashing in on his looks.

The modeling led in short order to a contract with Paramount and a temporary farewell to the sea. A bewildering series of events followed. He made his first film—*Virginia*—in 1941. After Pearl Harbor was bombed, he married one of the screen's true beauties, Madeleine Carroll, quickly made two more films, then just as quickly volunteered for the U.S. Marines.

Even that wasn't quite enough action for him, so when "Wild Bill" Donovan called for volunteers from among the ranks for an organization known as OSS, the Office of Strategic Services, for extremely dangerous duty, he signed on immediately.

His assignment was to coordinate the activities of partisans behind the German lines in Greece and Yugoslavia. It was in the latter country that he established close ties with Yugoslav fighters under a man named Josip Broz, who had since 1935 called himself "Tito." Tito was a Communist, but what impressed Hayden and other Allied agents was that his soldiers killed Nazis as opposed to the other Yugoslav partisans, the Chetniks, who often collaborated with the occupiers and spent as much time fighting Tito as the Germans.

Hayden came to admire the spirit and the camaraderie he saw among Tito's troops, as well as their sense of purpose. For a time, he ascribed it to their politics. When he returned to the U.S.A. after the war and was discharged from service, he joined the Communist Party. Within six months he became disillusioned and left the organization.

By 1947, he was back at Paramount making movies. He surprised everyone by the depth of his performance in John Huston's *The Asphalt Jungle* in 1950.

It was then that he came afoul of the House Un-American Activities Committee. After being summoned several times, he agreed to appear before the panel. Like director Elia Kazan and many others, he admitted he had been a party member, briefly, and went on to name several colleagues in Hollywood who also had been members. Most had already been named, but some had not. Those who knew him best said he never got over his decision to name names. It saved his career, but apparently changed forever his view of himself. His pursuit of parts was thereafter desultory, stopping entirely for large chunks of time when he took to the sea by himself or with family members. His autobiography, *Wanderer*, was ostensibly about his sailboat with that name, but it clearly defined him as well. His General Jack D. Ripper in *Dr. Strangelove*—and the method of his character's death—shows quite as many dimensions and lights and shadows as did Mr. Scott's performance.

In some ways, Mr. Kubrick's most unusual casting choice created the indelible image of the movie.

Slim Pickens had been a rodeo clown, which accounts for his professional name. Born Louis Bert Lindley Jr., he was on the rodeo circuit from the time he was twelve. Headlining as a clown led to movie work when he was thirty years old. For the first fourteen years of his Hollywood career, Mr. Pickens was cast in one forgettable Western after another. For a time, he seemed lost on an endless "trail," with *South Pacific Trail* (1952), *Iron Mountain Trail* (1953), and *Old Overland Trail* (1953). Thirty-one of these horse operas later, he found himself cast in the important role of Major T. J. "King" Kong, pilot of the plane that would send the world to its doom, all the time just "doing his duty."

"Well, boys, I reckon this is it; nuclear combat toe to toe with the Russkies."

That's how we meet Major Kong as he—mistakenly—tells his crew of their mission.

This role lifted Mr. Pickens into a new category. After *Dr. Strangelove*, he would make 40 more movies, many of them big-budget star turns, including *In Harm's Way*, *Major Dundee*, the remake of *Stagecoach*, *Will Penny*, and *Blazing Saddles*.

Slim Pickens used his rodeo training to good advantage when he rode the atomic bomb down to its target, just like the runaway bronco it was. That's the freeze-frame we remember.

Not surprisingly, the praise for *Dr. Strangelove* was not unanimous. The *Washington Post* was of the opinion that "No Communist could dream of a more effective anti-American film than this one." Bosley Crowther of the *New York Times* huffed, "I am troubled by the feeling, which runs all through the film, of discredit and even contempt for our whole military establishment."

Actually, Mr. Crowther was right on the money. Stanley Kubrick *did* have distrust of, and probably contempt for, our military establishment—any military establishment. His deep cynicism and meticulous filmmaking style continued through his last work, *Eyes Wide Shut,* released the year of his death, 1999.

His body of work supports his dark view of life, from *2001: A Space Odyssey, Clockwork Orange,* to *Full Metal Jacket.* Unhappy with Hollywood's filmmaking by committee, Kubrick went to England in 1961, where he felt he could work more independently. He remained there until his death.

In 1964, the Academy of Motion Picture Arts and Science was not quite sure what to make of *Dr. Strangelove.* It was a success at the box office and that always counts in Hollywood.

Still, here was a film making brutal sport of our bulwark against mortal enemies. It was portraying our most cherished leaders as buffoons, not in the usually harmless parodies of Laurel and Hardy or Chaplin, but in sharp, savage satire.

On the other hand, it was obvious that Kubrick had struck a nerve. Millions were weary of being held prisoner in a twilight war that had no winners and for which no end was in sight. Looked at through the upside-down logic of satire, the whole thing was, well, foolish—tragically, comically, fatally foolish.

The clarion call of an antiwar movement had been sounded one year before Vietnam became the issue that would fuel that movement until it burned, for a time, out of control.

There were Oscar nominations for Best Picture; Best Actor— Peter Sellers; Best Director; Best Screenplay for Kubrick, Peter George, and Terry Southern. But in the year of *My Fair Lady,* there would be no statuettes for *Dr. Strangelove.* Kubrick would have to be content with his New York Film Critics Award as Best Director.

And, in the years to come, Kubrick would have to be content with taking responsibility for a film that—for good or ill— altered the public dialogue on the morality of the superpowers' balance of terror.

Dr. Strangelove developed in us an embryonic skepticism for what was beginning to be called the "military establishment," and it fostered a growing skepticism about authority everywhere.

In the years following *Dr. Strangelove,* the lines of national debate were skewed perceptibly. Like *The Dictator* twenty-four years earlier—a film we'll look at in this book—*Dr. Strangelove* used humor to change us.

7

MARTY

1955

DIRECTOR: DELBERT MANN

STARS: ERNEST BORGNINE, BETSY BLAIR

RUNNING TIME: 1 HOUR, 31 MINUTES

Marty is a butcher who lives in a Bronx neighborhood circumscribed by his Italian relatives and friends. He lives with his mother and is the center of her attention. Marty is awkward and unattractive to women. His evenings are aimless excursions with his male friends. His clumsy advances toward women at dances are rejected.

He meets Clara, a plain woman as unattractive to most men as he to most women. They find they can communicate. They like each other. But when he introduces her to his friends, they dismiss her as a "dog," and he allows himself to see her through their eyes. His mother also disapproves.

In the end, Marty finds the courage and wisdom to reject friends and family. He asks Clara to marry him.

Note: Academy Award–winning writer of *Marty*, Paddy Chayevsky, had a small role as an actor in the 1947 Ronald Colman hit *A Double Life*.

United Artists (Courtesy of The Kobal Collection)

It was a form of entertainment that borrowed little from the past and left not much of a legacy. It ruled for just a bit more than ten years, from the late 1940s to the late 1950s, then it was gone.

It was live television drama.

"These live television plays always look like a bad dress rehearsal," drawled Alfred Hitchcock. His contempt had some basis in reality, because too many of the teleplays *were* poorly prepared and indifferently presented. Yet they were more than they seemed, and would preside over the demise of the billion-dollar dream factories, slick production values and all. One of these dramas, specifically, would come to symbolize the end of the forty-year Hollywood stranglehold known as the studio system.

Live television drama is worth more than a casual glance. Those who were not yet on the planet when *Studio One* and a dozen other weekly anthology programs flourished have difficulty understanding what all the fuss is about. A look at grainy kinescopes of some of the "classic" TV dramas leaves many younger viewers scratching their heads. The programs contain little of the careful lighting, expensive sets, quick cuts to energize the pace, and reaction sound tracks to help us know what we are supposed to be feeling.

When the contemporary viewer sees those fifty-year-old

films, he or she is looking at a play with its heart cut out. The entire point of live television was that it was *in its moment*. The very fragility made the experience unique.

In the shorthand of the time, there were those who said the audience was "morbid," "waiting for someone to make a mistake." That was only partially true and then only for a few.

What the majority of the viewers were looking for was to see great artists *risk* making a mistake and to triumph over that added obstacle on the way to success. We wanted to see the special energy that we believed was present only when the players and directors and camera operators were taking a chance on failing in a very public way, as they had done on stage for centuries.

It must be added that these men and women were not risking humiliation because they wanted to, at least not at first. They did so because television technology at the time didn't give them any option. They would perform live or not at all.

Still, in a very short time they came to glory in it, to wear their "liveness" like a badge of honor. They would produce plays like theater, but with only a fraction of the rehearsal time. They would perform for a camera as with movies, but do it all at once in sequence, with no retakes. The result was a hybrid not seen before or since, but one that had surprisingly potent impact on movies.

Live television was headquartered in New York, a fact that galled Hollywood. The actors were, for the most part, theater trained, not tied to any star system, and perfectly willing to be part of what, for a time, was a sort of East Coast repertory company.

While movie executives, directors, talent agents, and, to a certain extent, movie stars themselves poked fun at this upstart medium, the American people turned on their TV sets by the millions every night and, in doing so, created new stars, new directors, new executives, and even new talent agents. Hollywood was scared stiff—and with good reason.

In the midst of detective shows, quiz shows, variety shows, and early talk shows, television drama had an important and highly successful role on the small screen. Just to pick a random week from the fall of 1955, program schedules show eleven prime-time live dramas, each at least an hour in length. Two of them were original plays written by Rod Serling, and the others included *She Stoops to Conquer* with Hermione Gingold and Michael Redgrave, *The Caine Mutiny Court Martial* with Lloyd Nolan and Barry Sullivan, and *The Devil's Disciple* with Maurice Evans, Teresa Wright, and Ralph Bellamy. Among the players listed in the other shows are Tony Randall, Don Murray, Tom Ewell, Elizabeth Montgomery, and Eva Gabor.

In addition to that, the viewer who was housebound during the day had an alternative to soap operas. There was a live one-hour drama *every day* on *Matinee Theater* at 3 P.M.

The *Kraft Television Theater* could serve as a paradigm of the live drama phenomenon. It went on the air in 1947, the first full-hour anthology series. It was a mainstay on TV for nearly twelve years, sometimes producing *two* programs per week. When it shut down operations in 1959, a publicity release told of 650 plays produced and more than four thousand actors employed.

Both the plays and the actors would influence the movie world. But, it must be said, the movie world would influence television much more profoundly and with permanent effect. The film industry had too much to lose to allow upstart television to take away its viewers and revenue. So first they simply overwhelmed it, then they went out and bought it.

The first thing to go was the notion of "live" drama: Too messy, too chancy. All plays became small films, carefully shot and edited so that there was no chance for error. The result was slicker, no doubt about that. The audience came to accept, then to expect, film production values. The brief, yeasty era of live television drama was over.

But after all, what was lost? A unique entertainment experience. That's all.

Still, live television drama had its revenge, first in the actors it developed who would become dominant motion picture stars. Even a partial list is impressive: Paul Newman, Grace Kelly, Robert Redford, James Dean, Eva Marie Saint, George C. Scott, Steve McQueen, Peter Falk, Julie Harris.

The directors who learned their skills in live TV included Sidney Lumet, George Roy Hill, Arthur Penn, Sidney Pollack, John Frankenheimer, and Delbert Mann.

Perhaps hardest of all for Hollywood to swallow was the parade of stories themselves that were lifted directly from live television to become major hits on the big screen. Again, just a short list makes an impressive Academy Award collection: *The Miracle Worker, Judgment at Nuremberg, Days of Wine and Roses, Requiem for a Heavyweight, Patterns, Visit to a Small Planet, Twelve Angry Men.*

And *Marty.*

The lonely butcher from the Bronx was born in the mind of Sidney "Paddy" Chayefsky, who was also born in the Bronx. As a teenager, he tried to be a stand-up comic, but whatever success he might have had was interrupted by World War II, during which he lost an argument with a German land mine and spent months in an English hospital recuperating. That was when he decided to be a writer.

With a few small detours into acting—Paddy had a bit part in 1947's Academy Award–winning *A Double Life*—writing remained his passion. There were short stories and radio dramas and, as early as 1948, television dramas. Chayefsky found he was most at home writing about ordinary people in realistic situations.

In 1953, the *Philco/Goodyear Television Playhouse* presented Chayefsky's masterpiece *Marty*. The director was Delbert Mann, a thirty-three-year-old World War II veteran who had been a bomber pilot. Born in Lawrence, Kansas, Mann had a brief stint as a shoe salesman, but the war changed all that. He gravitated toward the theater and soon found his niche as a director. Television was a foundling at New York's doorstep, and Mann was among the first to take it in and give it respect. By 1950, he was identified as one of the best in the new medium.

The same could be said for the man chosen to play the title role in *Marty*. Rod Steiger had joined the U.S. Navy at age sixteen and served all through World War II and a year or so afterward. It was then that he went to acting school on the GI Bill, eventually making his way to the new Actors Studio, where he became a leading exponent of what came to be called "the Method." By 1953 he was already a familiar face on TV, had even made a film, in 1951, and was just one year away from his movie breakthrough in *On the Waterfront*.

Steiger's costar was also highly respected in television drama. Twenty-five-year-old Nancy Marchand had scored a triumph three years earlier in an acclaimed TV version of *Little Women*. Though she had her greatest success on Broadway, she would become familiar to later television viewers as Ed Asner's boss Margaret Pynchon in the series *Lou Grant*.

If everyone who claims to have seen the original *Marty* in 1953 had actually done so, it would have been the highest-rated drama in TV history. Instead, the ratings were respectable, but not spectacular, and the drama was critically acclaimed, but by no means the most honored of the year.

Still, it got the full attention of two New York natives who were looking for material for their new film production company. They were burdened with none of Hollywood's bias against television because they were mavericks themselves. Actor Burt Lancaster, born and reared in East Harlem, and Harold Hecht, another New Yorker who was Lancaster's agent, had formed Norma Productions in 1947, barely a year after Lancaster gained stardom in *The Killers*. Both served notice they would control every aspect of their future films, from the conception of the idea to the release of the finished product. It was a revolutionary break from the studio system that the Hollywood establishment considered ominous. Their fears would prove to be well founded.

The company metamorphosed into Hecht-Lancaster, then to Hecht-Hill-Lancaster when they were joined by writer-producer James Hill, but the philosophy remained constant.

And successful. From the 1948 film noir with, perhaps, the worst title in movie history, *Kiss the Blood Off My Hands*, to swashbucklers such as *The Flame and the Arrow* and *The Crimson Pirate*, this was an independent company that was making money.

Which leads directly to one of the oddest stories in a town where odd stories abound, Hollywood, California. In 1998, at an event honoring Ernest Borgnine in Jimmy Stewart's hometown, Indiana, Pennsylvania, Mr. Borgnine told me: "We were a tax write-off, Nick. The film was very nearly not completed at all."

Borgnine had been selected for the title role of the film version of *Marty*, and at the time it seemed like very risky casting on the part of director Delbert Mann and producer Harold Hecht.

Borgnine had at least one thing in common with Rod Steiger, who had created the role on TV: He had also been in the U.S. Navy, though in Borgnine's case, his tour had covered a full ten years from 1935 to 1945.

Ermes Effron Borgnino was born in Connecticut, and spent years two to seven in Milan, Italy, before returning to the States and going to school in New Haven. Like Steiger, he took up acting right after his discharge from the service. However, his acting school was in his hometown, Hartford, and his drama workshops were in Virginia. Borgnine had a few roles on live TV and, like Steiger, made his first film in 1951.

But it was as a "heavy" that Ernest Borgnine got the film world's attention. His brilliant, chilling Sargeant Fatso Hudson in *From Here to Eternity* established him as the man filmgoers love to hate, and his Cole Trimble in Spencer Tracy's *Bad Day at Black Rock* reinforced the impression.

How then to turn that tide of hate to love for the nebbish butcher?

"They saw something, I guess," said Borgnine. "I'd really done a lot of different roles by then, but not many that people had seen. On the other hand, both of those films were blockbusters with big stars. Everybody saw me being a badass.

"Besides," continued Mr. Borgnine, "they really weren't expecting anything out of this movie. More than that, they didn't *want* anything out of this movie.

"They told me they had been making too much money and, under the tax laws of the time, they had to lose a certain amount. *Marty* was to be the loser.

"I don't remember the exact amount anymore, but let's say it was $600,000. It was certainly not as much as a million, but it was a specific dollar figure, that much I remember.

"Every day a fellow would be on the set with a calculator and he'd be adding up every penny that was spent for actors, cameramen, grips, catering, transportation, whatever. And one day, when he had reached that magic number, he said, 'Okay, everybody, that's a wrap. We're finished.'

"Swear to God, Nick, we had a third of the movie still to do and they sent us all home! I've never seen or heard of anything like it. Delbert Mann was sick about it and so were the rest of us. We were pretty sure we have a good movie going. Can you imagine how we felt?

"Well, anyway, we went home and my memory is I was at home for a long time. More than a week, I know, because my agent was already lining up other projects.

"Then the phone rang. It was an assistant director, a friend of mine, and he was frantic. He had to get us all back together and finish the picture.

"Guess what had happened? The day after the accountant shut us down, he got a call from one of the company lawyers. 'How's it going?' he asks. 'Fine,' says the accountant, 'We spent the $600,000 we needed to lose, so I closed down the production.' 'You did what?' shouts the lawyer. 'Are you crazy? You got to finish the production, send it out into release, and *then* lose the money! For Chrissake, get 'em back!'

"Can you imagine that? Well, they got us back and we finished the picture, but they still did their best to lose the money. They just released it in a few art houses, but the word got out and pretty soon there were lines around the block, so the company had to change their strategy and back it to the hilt, and then came the whole Cannes thing and the Academy Awards. It just went crazy."

If anything, Ernest Borgnine understated the case. The small, realistic tale of a man who would say to his mother, "One fact I got to face is that whatever it is that women like, I ain't got it" and to his girlfriend, "Dogs like us, we ain't such dogs as we think we are," was a benchmark film.

Playing Borgnine's screen girlfriend, Clara, was Betsy Blair, still another New Yorker who, after stage work, had scored well in two small roles, one in *A Double Life* and the other in *The Snake Pit*. At this point, Blair had been married to dancer-actor-choreographer-producer-director Gene Kelly for thirteen years.

She would share fully in the accolades that were about to pour over *Marty*. The Cannes Film Festival simply could not give *Marty* enough hardware. Blair received the nod as Best Actress, Borgnine as Best Actor, Chayefsky as Best Writer, Mann as Best Director, and the film itself received the Palme d' Or, the first American film to do so. The New York Film Critics gave *Marty* Best Film and Best Actor awards. Clearly, something special had happened.

Even to this day, movie fans, many of whom have never seen

the film, are perfectly familiar with its signature lines: "What do you feel like doin' tonight?" "I don't know, Ange, what do you feel like doing?"

By the time the Academy Awards rolled around, Hecht-Lancaster were fully on board with their low-budget "tax write-off." The trade papers of the day insisted that the movie had been made for less than $400,000, but that the producers had allocated more than $400,000 in promotion. In fact, the *Hollywood Reporter* editor, Billy Wilkerson, asked in print, "Has there ever been a picture where the producer or distributor paid more than the picture's cost in advertising?" It was a question to which he did not have the answer, though the practice in later years would become fairly commonplace.

"Oh, they had us doing all kinds of interviews and personal appearances as the Academy Awards got nearer," recalled Borgnine. "In those days they used to have a TV show announcing the nominees. I don't think they do that anymore, just let the morning news shows do the honors.

"But this one they had all rigged up like *What's My Line?* you know, where the actor would come out and 'Sign in, please.' My memory is that it was a little bit embarrassing because not very many of the nominees showed up. But we were doing that kind of thing all the time."

Hecht-Lancaster was not about to be out-ballyhooed by the big studios they were in the process of challenging. They even sent Borgnine to a Los Angeles area supermarket opening where he was "guest butcher," a moment immortalized when the Meatcutters Union gave him a golden trophy.

Occasion was also found to put young contract actresses in swimsuits—then, as now, a sure camera magnet—holding up placards on Santa Monica Beach declaring "I Love Marty."

Burt Lancaster made himself available to interviewers, and to the inevitable request for an Oscar prediction gave the identical answer, "We're going to take them all!"

"That telecast was fun. We were at the Pantages Theatre and the crowd was revved up." Borgnine smiled at the memory. "It wasn't for me, though, it was for Grace Kelly. She wasn't nominated or anything, but she agreed to make the Best Actor announcement. Just a few weeks before she had told everyone she was engaged to the prince over in Monaco and she was retiring from the screen. This was going to be her last public appearance as Grace Kelly, and believe me, that was a big deal. I've got to tell you, it was great to hear her say my name. Obviously it changed my life."

That's not all it changed. Borgnine and the Hecht-Lancaster company had some rocky days ahead—the actor sued to be released from his agreement—but a sea change had just occurred on that Hollywood stage because of the film they made together.

Many forces were at work to cause cracks in the monolithic structure of the Hollywood studio system, but none made a wider fissure than the first truly independent film to win the movie community's most prestigious honor.

Not only was the film an independent but it was based on material from the despised "live television drama."

The ground was trembling under specific homes in Bel-Air and Beverly Hills that March night in 1956.

The long era of the studio system was over, and it was *Marty* that changed it.

8

ON THE WATERFRONT

1954

DIRECTOR: ELIA KAZAN
STARS: MARLON BRANDO, KARL
MALDEN, LEE J. COBB, ROD
STEIGER, EVA MARIE SAINT
RUNNING TIME: 1 HOUR, 48 MINUTES

The mob rules the New York waterfront through corrupt unions. Terry Malloy is an ex-fighter who does odd jobs for union boss Johnny Friendly. Malloy's brother Charley is the crooked lawyer for Friendly.

Terry Malloy unwittingly participates in the murder of a "troublemaker," one who bucks the mob. At about this time he meets and falls for Edie Doyle. She introduces him to crusading Father Barry, who wants the mob out of the union.

Slowy, Terry Malloy is brought to Father Barry's way of thinking. In a wrenching scene, his older brother Charley attempts to get Terry to go along. Eventually, Charley is killed for his failure to bring his brother back to the fold.

The final scene has Brando, as Terry Malloy, brutally beaten, struggling on the dock to be the first hired for that day's work. All the laborers support him, marking the end for Cobb, Friendly, and his henchmen.

Note: The character Truck in *Waterfront* was played by Tony Galento, known in the 1930s as "Two-Ton Tony Galento," who, on a June night in 1939, fought Joe Louis for the heavyweight championship of the world. He was knocked out in the fourth round.

Columbia (Courtesy of The Kobal Collection)

W ho the hell gives a shit about labor unions?" said Darryl F. Zanuck, speaking for Hollywood, which had always hated making movies about labor unions. The American workers' long struggle to organize into powerful bargaining units was simply too messy, too violent, too difficult a story to tell. Even the heroes were tainted, at least in the eyes of the general public.

And, for that matter, in the eyes of the movie moguls themselves, all of whom were famous capitalists. They resisted the idea of their workers organizing a union just as vigorously as had Henry Ford.

There was more. Significant segments of the American labor movement in the early years of the twentieth century had embraced emerging Socialist doctrines. The eloquent labor leader Eugene V. Debs, jailed during the Pullman strike of 1894, read Karl Marx while in prison and came out of jail a Socialist. Five times he ran for president as a Socialist. Twice, in 1912 and 1920, while the movie industry was struggling through its infancy, nearly a million Americans gave their votes to Eugene V. Debs. It was a sharp, disturbing trumpet call from the far Left.

Its echoes continued even when Debs was gone. After the economic collapse of 1929, a Socialist and a Communist candidate appeared on the 1932 presidential ballot, both men long associated with organized labor.

Hollywood dealt with these compelling movements by ignoring them. Even Warner Bros., famous in the 1930s for gritty urban street stories, largely shied away from realistic portrayals of organized labor, sticking to sanitized accounts of squeaky-clean labor officials and predictably venal managers, always reconciled with one another by fade-out.

One more element must be mentioned: Relations between the studios and their own unions were always fragile. Film barons had fought bitterly against any kind of unions or guilds in their industry. They were successful for a long time, mostly because so many Americans wanted to be in the movies. In no industry did the cliché management threat "I've got ten people waiting to take your job" ring truer than in the movies.

Still, the mood of the country had changed in the 1930s. Government, at least at the federal level, was now an ally of unions rather than their adversary. The public attitude changed, too, as breadwinners saw how vulnerable their jobs were.

Even Glitterland finally got the message. The crafts, the editors, the writers, directors, and finally, the actors got union cards.

Was this, at last, a context within which Hollywood would take a hard look at "Communist" or "mob" or any other insidious influence within America's labor movement?

It was not. The film industry had to work on a daily basis, not only with its own unions, but with unions at location shoots all around the nation. Movies were not about to alienate workers—who could shut them down—by making unflattering films about unions.

It was against this background that Darryl Zanuck shouted his refusal to Elia Kazan when the director came to get backing for *On the Waterfront*.

The New York waterfront was a cesspool of corruption and violence. It had been that way for years, but the rise of crime cells across the country during the 1920s and 1930s made most of the work in ports on the eastern seaboard a crime fiefdom. After World War II, the boss of bosses was Brooklyn-based Albert Anastasia, whose nickname was "Il Terremoto," "The Earthquake." Anastasia came up through the "enforcer" arm of what was already being called the Mafia. His rule was essentially fascist. He was in charge, his goons enforced his rules, "might made right," he brooked no dissent, and union members worked or not at his pleasure.

A tough reporter named Malcolm Johnson was assigned by his editors at the *New York Sun* to investigate what had become a public scandal, the mob-ridden waterfront union. The probing was difficult and mortally dangerous, but Johnson stayed with it. The result was a shocking twenty-four-part series that appeared in 1948, just a week after one of the hiring bosses on the docks was murdered. The stories pulled no punches, describing shakedowns, bribery, beatings, and murder.

The series won a Pulitzer Prize but, more important, it shone a bright light on some of the darkest spaces in New York City.

Writer Budd Schulberg had already taken on organized crime in a novel about boxing, *The Harder They Fall*, which became a film in 1956, and he was sure this story was fertile material for a groundbreaking movie. Elia Kazan agreed and work was begun on a script.

With a nearly completed screenplay in hand, Kazan made the rounds. Then he made them again. Eventually, he had to take "no" for an answer. Not one of the major studios would make this movie. The loud refusal of Darryl F. Zanuck seemed the final nail in the project's coffin. Zanuck, after all, had taken on some interesting topics on the screen since his return from military service, often in conjunction with Kazan. It was Zanuck, the only gentile among all major studio heads, who confronted anti-Semitism in *Gentlemen's Agreement*, with Kazan, another gentile, in the director's chair. They also collaborated on *Pinky*, a story about a light-skinned African American girl "passing" for white. Both films seem relatively tame today, but they generated serious discussion and real controversy in their day.

Apparently, however, neither anti-Semitism nor the color line was as hot to the touch as the subject of corrupt unions in 1954.

Still, Kazan and Schulberg persisted. They believed they had a good story. They didn't know the half of it. As often happens in Hollywood, the subplot rivaled the main theme.

The hero of the screenplay, Terry Malloy, was a failed prizefighter who goes along with the mob's agenda for waterfront workers without protest. If they stole, roughed-up, lied, bribed, it was nothing to him. He was even willing to be used as a tool in the corruption, at least in small ways, so long as he could always go back to his beloved pigeons on the roof of his tenement. In the end, however, his girlfriend and a crusading priest helped him to see that in order to find his own salvation, he would have to inform on the mob. He does so at great personal cost. At the film's conclusion, as Leonard Bernstein's music soars, he stumbles to the front of the worker's line and stands alone, exhausted, bloody, beaten, exonerated, heroic, triumphant.

Now let's examine the parallel some believe is to be found in that image.

Both immigrant Elia Kazan and self-styled "Hollywood Prince" Budd Schulberg had joined the Communist Party in the 1930s. They took entirely different courses to fall under the spell of Marx and, more specifically, Lenin.

Kazan, born in Constantinople, was brought to this country at age four in 1913. The family settled in New York, and his father— real name Elias Kazanjoglou—became a successful rug merchant. So successful, in fact, he could send his son to Williams College, where young Kazan cultivated his interests in drama. It was 1931 and there were many competing forces at work within the intellectual community. When Kazan was attending graduate programs in the drama department at Yale, the stock market crashed and America was plunged into the worst economic depression in its history. By the time he joined New York's Group Theater as an actor and assistant stage manager in 1932, this country's unemployment rate had topped 25 percent. The socialist proposals that had seemed so radical only a few years before began to look pretty good. Old-age pensions, unemployment insurance, savings insurance, health care, limits on stock trading, regulation of banks, graduated tax code, forty-hour work week, farm subsidies, currency regulating, rules to protect workers on the job, lynch laws—all ideas that socialists had been floating for half a century, but had been for the most part hooted down in state and federal legislative halls—were back in play. A few wanted to do even more, nationalizing everything, going so far as to sovietize American life. A pronounced radical streak raced for a time through this country. Before it was spent, thousands of Americans joined the Communist Party. Elia Kazan, known to his friends as "Gadge," was among them.

His flirtation with Communism didn't last long, nor did that of most of the Americans who had been attracted by stories of Russia's "utopian" state. For one thing, the new Roosevelt administration was addressing many of the long-neglected social issues. For another, more realistic reports of life in the U.S.S.R. were emerging, with stories of massive purges and repression evident under the iron hand of Josef Stalin.

When Kazan resigned from his Communist cell, he by no means dropped his support of the politics of the Left. He directed a short documentary about the problems of miners in Tennessee, *The People of the Cumberland*, in 1937. By 1941, he was firmly in the New Deal camp, directing a full-length documentary for the U.S. Department of Agriculture, *It's Up to You*, dealing with the fair allocation of the American food supply.

Budd Schulberg was reared in an America as different from Kazan's as can be imagined. He was born in 1914, the son of a major motion picture executive, B. P. Schulberg. He was a child of privilege in Hollywood, surrounded by moviemakers and movie stars, and went to work in the family business as a publicist when he was seventeen. By age nineteen, he was a screenwriter, but had only moderate success. As noted, it was a time when the nation was having even less success than he, and the younger Schulberg, like Kazan, began to believe the Communists might have some answers that had eluded this nation's undiluted capitalism.

His disillusion wasn't limited to politics and economics. In 1941, he shocked his family and friends with his novel *What Makes Sammy Run?*, a scathing indictment of the film industry. During World War II, he served with John Ford's film documentary unit, producing remarkable records of famous military campaigns. Before and after the war, he continued to support many liberal causes, some of them edging toward the radical.

It was no surprise that when the U.S. House of Representatives took a sharp right turn in the election following the end of the war, long-battered conservatives would attempt to get those farthest to the left of the political spectrum in their crosshairs.

The House Un-American Activities Committee had several incarnations after its inception in the 1930s, but the goal of the panel in 1947 was clear. Now that the Cold War had begun and the U.S.S.R., our wartime ally, was our mortal enemy, political capital could be made by tying liberals to the Communist Party. Hollywood, because of its high profile, had always been a juicy congressional target, and it would be again.

Elia Kazan and Budd Schulberg might not be big-name fish, but they were well-known in Hollywood and had never hidden their left-wing sympathies. Schulberg's novel about Hollywood made him an attractive catch. Kazan had made the Academy Award–winning *A Tree Grows in Brooklyn* in 1945, had directed Broadway's *All My Sons* and *A Streetcar Named Desire* in 1947, and that same year had three Hollywood projects in train, including *Gentleman's Agreement.*

Both men were called before what was by then known as the HUAC. Inquisitors demanded they identify those who had been members of the Communist Party or even attended meetings. Both men gave minimal cooperation and were called "unfriendly witnesses."

The pressure increased and the U.S. Senate now got in on the act. Joseph McCarthy of Wisconsin found an issue that would get him front-page coverage. There was not any aspect of American life that McCarthy could not find riddled with Communists. From the State Department to the Council of Churches to the entertainment business to labor to the U.S. Army, to education, McCarthy promised "evidence" of a massive "Communist conspiracy" to take over America.

Meantime, strengthening the hand of both McCarthy and the HUAC, the Cold War was heating up. There were flare-ups all over the world in the late 1940s, culminating with the invasion of South Korea by the Communist force of North Korea on June 25, 1950. Communism vs. Democracy went from the theoretical to the concrete. Young American men were being killed over this issue.

In 1951, Budd Schulberg changed his mind and decided to testify before the House Committee and name his former associates.

One year later, Elia Kazan did the same thing. Some he named had already been fingered by others. Some had not. Kazan claimed he had come to believe that any former associates who had not come forward to admit their earlier Communist ties might indeed now present a danger to America. On the other hand, critics noted that, immediately after his testimony, Kazan signed a contract assuring him a Hollywood career into the foreseeable future.

There's the alleged parallel: *On the Waterfront* was created by two men who publicly informed on former colleagues. Did they, like Terry Malloy, the character they created and immortalized, believe they did it for a greater good? Did they face public humiliation, metaphorically bludgeoned and bloodied for their decision by former friends? Did they hope one day to stand exonerated, triumphant?

Even at this writing, the subject is too charged for a definitive answer. History will require a little more time. At the 1999 Academy Awards ceremony, reaction to Kazan's being presented with a special honor was decidedly mixed, both in the press and at the event itself.

Whatever the motives of Kazan and Schulberg, the effort to get the film made went forward. An independent producer, Sam Spiegel, undertook to raise the $800,000 it was going to take to get the cameras rolling.

After the funding was in place, Spiegel went to Harry Cohn at Columbia to make a separate deal for distribution.

Once again, *On the Waterfront* faced oblivion because Budd Schulberg refused to work for Cohn. After Schulberg's father had fallen on hard times, he went to work for Cohn who, according to the younger Schulberg, proceeded to humiliate him privately and publicly. Only after delicate negotiations in which Spiegel assured Schulberg that Cohn would have no power to change even one word or one frame of film would Schulberg sign on.

There would be one more major glitch: From the beginning, Kazan wanted Marlon Brando for the lead. Brando was, in some important ways, Kazan's protégé. When Kazan cofounded the Actors Studio in 1947, Brando was his most celebrated student, starring that same year in the Tennessee Williams play *A Streetcar Named Desire*, under Kazan's direction. Kazan had since directed Brando in two films, the movie version of *Streetcar* in 1951 and the highly acclaimed *Viva Zapata* in 1952.

Characteristically, however, Brando balked when Kazan offered him the role of Terry Malloy. He hesitated, said yes, then hesitated again. Kazan, Spiegel, and Schulberg were under the economic gun and could not afford to wait.

That was when the director made contact with Frank Sinatra, who had just scored a triumph in *From Here to Eternity*. The negotiations were serious and the two men were very close to a deal. In fact, Sinatra said later he believed they had already made a deal. That was the moment that Marlon Brandon finally made up his mind and reentered the picture. Kazan promptly broke off the talks with Sinatra and signed Brando. Frank Sinatra later said he believed he had been misled by Elia Kazan.

Coincidentally, filming was done on the waterfront of Hoboken, New Jersey, Sinatra's hometown. When Harry Cohn saw the dailies he predicted the movie would be the year's biggest flop.

Instead, the $800,000 film made $9.5 million in its first release. *Life* magazine wrote, "*On the Waterfront* is the most brutal movie of the year but it also contains the year's tenderest love scenes. Responsible for both is Marlon Brando."

There were twelve Academy Award nominations, including an unprecedented *three* for Best Supporting Actor: Rod Steiger, Karl Malden, and Lee J. Cobb. None of the three won, but the film got eight statuettes, including one each for Best Film, Best Actor, Best Director, Best Story, and Best Supporting Actress for Eva Marie Saint. Cooperating with the HUAC was not yet as generally controversial in 1955 as it would become later, so the awards ceremony went smoothly. Brando was on his best behavior, bantering with host Bob Hope. Budd Schulberg saluted his father, and Eva Marie Saint, expecting a baby any day, declared, "I think I may have the baby right here!"

If, after all these years, there is still ambivalence in the film community about the life roles of Kazan and Schulberg, there is none about the film's excellence.

Nor about its impact on longshoremen and on movies themselves.

The next year, 1955, would prove to be a watershed for the union movement in America. Nearly 25 percent of the total workforce was unionized when the AFL merged with the CIO. Forty years later, despite a small uptick in the 1990s, that percentage slipped to 16 percent.

It would be difficult, in fact, to point to any major difference in the way unionized waterfront work got done as a result of this movie. Albert Anastasia remained the evil genius of the docks right up to the day, three years after the film's release, when he was shot to death in chair number four in the barbershop of the Park Sheraton Hotel on Seventh Avenue in New York City.

What *did* change was Hollywood's unwritten taboo on films about American labor. Prior to this, there had been literally scores of major films about capitalists, depicting them either as heroes or archvillains, but none about the coalescing work forces which were emerging as counterweights to the barons of industry.

Charlie Chaplin's *Modern Times* in 1936 was a sympathetic satire, but showed the worker as a helpless pawn of the system and of technology. John Ford had to go abroad to Wales in 1940 in order to film a hard look at the rape of both land and laborer by unenlightened management in *How Green Was My Valley*. It was a very circumspect treatment. Studio head Darryl F. Zanuck said, "We eliminated the most controversial element in the book, which was the labor-and-capital battle." He very nearly did. He got an Oscar anyway.

On the Waterfront is the direct ancestor of such films as *The Molly Maquires*, in 1970, *Norma Rae*, in 1979, *Silkwood*, in 1983, and *Roger and Me*, in 1989, as well as a dozen or so less distinguished movies dealing with the labor movement. Unions and union leaders, like management before them, are depicted as both heroes and villains these days, but at least now their story is more likely to be addressed than before 1954's *On the Waterfront.*

As to the specifics of the corruption dealt with in the movie, the postscript has elements of both cruelty and poignance.

After all the anger, confrontation, courage, and genuine sacrifice, both the heroes and the villains of the story—and the very real men and women who inspired them—were left irrelevant by technology.

Beginning as a tiny blip on the radar screen in the 1950s, a new development entered the quotient. At the moment labor unions in general and longshoremen's unions in particular were loudly protesting the movie and calling vainly for its boycott, a shadow began to creep over the docks.

A moviegoer can almost see it in terms of a new ending for the film. Marlon Brando, courageous, bruised, nearly dead, stumbles to the gate to be the first worker chosen, triumphant over the forces of evil with which he now stands face-to-face. Lee J. Cobb, the embodiment of the corrupt system, an extortioner, liar, thief, murderer, glares defiant but defeated. The supreme moment of their lives, and of Mr. Kazan's movie, has arrived.

But wait. Both men are suddenly distracted. Instead of looking at one another with visceral hatred, they look toward us in the audience, then off camera right, and up. Their expressions change to puzzlement. They glance back at one another, then at those around them. They are met with shrugs, before all look up again in the direction of the waterfront.

The camera begins a slow pull-out. It's a boom shot and it lifts up, up, fifty feet, then a hundred. We see all the oppressed workers at their moment of victory and all the mob goons at their moment of defeat, but it's beginning to be difficult to tell one from another as they grow smaller.

Coming into frame, from the right, is something we haven't seen before. It is huge and soon dominates the picture, finally squeezing out the actors entirely. It may be a ship, but it is unlike anything seen in any 1954 port. Awkward, odd, the hull appears to sprout huge rectangular boxes.

Containers. The container ship.

Within a decade this new technology would make the life-and-death struggle that went on here seem almost quaint, just as interesting and outmoded as a chapter from Dickens.

Vast technological changes were sparking revolutions in every field of endeavor and at all points of the compass. Labor unions and management would both have to learn to make technology their partner, or disappear.

So would movies.

And labor would have its corner of the American experience depicted on screen, because *On the Waterfront* changed things.

9

THE SNAKE PIT

1948

DIRECTOR: ANATOLE LITVAK

STARS: OLIVIA DE HAVILLAND, MARK STEVENS, LEO GENN

RUNNING TIME: 1 HOUR, 48 MINUTES

Virginia Cunningham seemed perfectly normal to everyone around her, but soon after she had married Robert Cunningham, she began behaving very erratically. Soon, she was too much for her husband to handle, and reluctantly, he has her committed to an institution.

We see immediately the kind of indignity and disrespect that is meted out to many of the patients. We also see the difference one caring doctor can make.

But it isn't enough. Virginia makes small gains, then loses them all in the horror of the open ward. Eventually, with controversial shock treatments and deep psychoanalysis, the problem seems at last to surface and to answer to treatment. Virginia goes home with Robert—and with the hope she'll never have to return.

Note: Costar Mark Stevens, a capable actor and director, had to battle a perception problem later in his career. There was a porno star who spelled his name both Marc and Mark Stevens. No relation.

Dreamworks (Courtesy of The Kobal Collection)

O h, I see, it's a zoo. I like zoos, don't you?"
Olivia de Havilland said that in her role as Virginia
Stuart Cunningham, a woman committed to a state mental
institution. She was walking in a line of patients, all women,
entering the hospital. She looked up and saw another group on
the second floor, staring down at them solemnly, silently. They
were behind iron bars.

Virginia Stuart Cunningham was entering the realm of the
Snake Pit, and Hollywood was at last taking on the long-ignored
abuses in what for generations had been known as "insane asy-
lums."

Mental aberrations of all kinds had been fodder for the
movies from their earliest days, but seldom had the industry
taken a serious look at the core problems of true emotional dis-
connect. The subject was too complicated and hardly entertaining. Not that there wasn't a fascination with diseases of the
mind in Hollywood. There was.

Sigmund Freud was forty years old when movies were born.
At first, neither took much note of the other. An arcade attraction held little interest for a pioneering explorer of the human
mind.

However, before Freud's death in 1939, his ideas had secured
a solid grip on many of the storytellers of Hollywood's dream
factories.

The reason was outlined best by Freud himself in his *Introductory Lectures on Psychoanalysis*. He wrote, "The contribution of psychoanalysis to science consists precisely in having extended *research* to the region of the mind."

Screenwriters believed that implicitly. Mental illness was on the verge of being dissected, categorized, and, in an inexorable leap forward, *cured* by the numbers.

So much had already been accomplished in the physical sciences. Smallpox was virtually eradicated in modern nations. Pasteur had made safe the milk supply, with its promise of so much more. The Curies had opened the possibilities of radiology. Insulin added years of life to diabetics. There were exciting experiments under way with antibiotics, opening an entire world in medicine.

"Cures" were being found every day, real cures for real diseases. No one doubted that mental illness was a real disease. Scarcely one family could be found that hadn't been touched by it to one degree or another.

Now, here was the genius from Vienna and others telling us they could codify that illness by analysis. They could extend "*research* to the region of the mind."

It was a breathtaking promise and the movies fell for it hard. Not long after film found its voice, we began to hear of the significance of dreams to our conscious actions and of the vital role our earliest childhood experiences had on the rest of our lives.

Terms such as "Oedipus complex" became commonplace in our films and, therefore, in our conversations. In fact, it wasn't long before many of us spoke of ourselves or others as having a "complex" of one kind or another.

Hollywood had already accepted the Freud dictum, which stood as such a hallmark of his teachings that it was published by *Time* magazine on the day of his death in 1939. "Neuroses [are] without exception disturbances of the sexual function." Screenwriters needed no convincing on that score.

With characteristic optimism, Hollywood bulldozed its way toward an all-encompassing "cure" for mental illness. Storywriters who didn't know a neurosis from a psychosis nonetheless assumed we were just a few months, or, at worst, a few years away from the key that would unlock a host of subconscious human failings.

Depression, aggression, anger, criminal behavior, all would fall before the precise logic of analysis. Dr. Freud and his adherents were carrying torches into the darkest corners of the human psyche, which was another new word Hollywood liked. The jargon of this emerging faith could be found in films as diverse as *The Big House*, (1930), *Bill of Divorcement*, (1932), and even *The Thin Man*, (1934).

Many of Hollywood's major names, both in front of and behind the cameras, underwent analysis. Most who did became nearly fanatic in their belief in its effectiveness.

But these talented, impressionable men and women baring their souls to psychiatrists under southern California's eternal sun were rich, insulated from the realities outside their silk-lined ghettos.

In the real world, mental illness was treated in an only slightly more enlightened way than in the days of Charles Dickens. The merely eccentric were thrown in among the truly psychotic. There were horrors enough every day to ignite the nightmares of an Edgar Allan Poe or a Stephen King.

Strapped for cash, often inept, sometimes corrupt, local and state institutions did what they could. It was not much. Those who were poor and mentally ill did not have the luxury of hours on a couch-confessional. There would be a brief interview and an instant evaluation. In effect, it was a kind of triage of the mind.

Those deemed hopeless often found themselves warehoused for most of their waking hours in an open ward more horrible than words can describe. "Bedlam" was a term used in Britain for these open wards, derived from the old London hospital for the mentally ill, Saint Mary's of Bethlehem, which slipped to "Bethlem," then "Bedlam."

In America, the words often used were "snake pit."

This 1948 movie holds up surprisingly well as drama, though the treatment of the ill and the jargon used now seem simplistic, even naive. But what cannot be exaggerated is the effect the movie had on its contemporary society. *The Snake Pit* was a thunderclap precisely because it was a successful movie. Forty million Americans saw, bigger than life, a haggard Olivia de Havilland—their own beloved Melanie of *Gone With the Wind*—say to her sympathetic doctor, "I heard a scream and I didn't know if it was me who screamed or not—if it was *I* who screamed."

They saw the horrifying "snake pit," they heard the doctor's—Leo Genn's—rational words exploring, then describing, the causes of her dysfunction. They seemed logical. So did the treatment. The film made it clear that the process would not be quick or easy but, if we were compassionate enough to provide the right resources, those patients could be *cured* and returned to their families.

That was the message of *Snake Pit* and it was received loud and clear.

Of course, the story did not arrive at its moment by accident. A director named Anatole Litvak had seen a novel written by Mary Jane Ward when it was still in galleys before publication in 1946.

Litvak was a ferocious socialite and those who knew him in the Hollywood community thought he cut a "dashing figure." He was certainly in tune with the current movie colony rage for analysis, but he was a step or two ahead of most.

Anatole Litvak had a colorful life. He was born Michael Anatol Litwak in Kiev, Russia, in 1902. At fourteen, he was a stagehand at a theater in St. Petersburg. While he was there,

World War I raged and the Bolshevik Revolution got under way. When he was a philosophy student at age sixteen, the city changed its name to Leningrad. Soon, young Michael Anatol was launching his career. The stage first, then Nordkino Films. He directed his first movie in 1925, *Tatiana*. Its success gave him the momentum to relocate to Western Europe. For the next ten years, most of his work was done in Germany.

Hitler's ascendance changed that. Litvak was a Jew, so he quickly changed his base of operations to London, then Paris. Success was again the catalyst for a move, this time to Hollywood in 1937. His first American film harked back to his days in Mother Russia. *Tovarich* starred Claudette Colbert and Charles Boyer as expatriates from Czarist Russia reduced to working as servants in Paris. The film was a success.

So was his *Confessions of a Nazi Spy* in 1939. Mr. Litvak had married a famous American film star, Miriam Hopkins, shortly after his arrival in this country. With his Continental background and skills as a raconteur, he cut a wide swath in prewar Hollywood. His extramarital affairs fed film colony gossip.

He applied for citizenship as soon as he arrived, and when war came, he joined the U.S. Army. It was Mr. Litvak who teamed with Frank Capra to produce the acclaimed *Why We Fight* documentaries. He produced several other effective documentaries and then was placed in command of all combat photography and motion picture services during the Normandy invasion. For his wartime work he received the Croix de Guerre and the Légion d'Honneur, among other decorations, and was discharged with the rank of colonel.

Some friends thought they saw a different Anatole Litvak return from the war. He seemed more serious. There were definite symptoms of a developing social conscience.

Miss Ward's book fit his new mood perfectly. He saw injustice in the treatment of the mentally ill who were poor. Some were veterans of World War I, and in 1946, he worried that World War II veterans might start falling through the cracks at the Veterans Administration and begin showing up in these abominable "snake pits."

Litvak paid Miss Ward $75,000 for the movie rights to her book, a substantial sum in 1946. He then started pounding the pavement to get major studio backing.

He had some hope for success. The previous year, 1945, director Alfred Hitchcock had a hit with his thriller *Spellbound*, the central theme of which was mental illness and the freeing effects of psychoanalysis. Mr. Hitchcock had himself undergone analysis and was a convinced evangelist of the procedure.

Still, Litvak found *Snake Pit* a hard sell. This story was not a "thriller," not even an "entertainment" as then described in Hollywood. Every major studio with which he had worked before the war turned him down.

But he had an ace in the hole. Darryl F. Zanuck, who had spent much of the war in the military—as had Mr. Litvak— and was proud of it, had come back with something of an increased social conscious himself. He had just released *Gentleman's Agreement* (1947), with Gregory Peck and Dorothy McGuire, taking on anti-Semitism in a way no film had ever done before. He was also toying with an idea that would become *Pinky* (1949), with Jeanne Crain, dealing directly with racial bigotry, using the theme of a young black girl "passing" for white.

But *Snake Pit* was nearly too much for Zanuck. He didn't see what elements in the story would get people to the theater or keep them in their seats once they got there. He found the novelized autobiography unrelentingly grim. He agreed to work with Litvak on a treatment to make the story "filmable." In a few months they believed they had something and turned it over to screenwriters Frank Partos and Millen Brand.

At this point, the writer of the novel, Mary Jane Ward, reentered the picture. She asked that Olivia de Havilland be given the lead role.

Olivia de Havilland was fortunate to have avoided a mental breakdown herself, given the stress of the previous four years. After being "loaned" by Warner Bros. to David O. Selznick for the role of Melanie in *Gone With the Wind*—which earned her an Oscar nomination—de Havilland rebelled at the pedestrian fare *(Princess O'Rourke, Government Girl)* her home studio was giving her. She was put on suspension, sued the studio for release from her contract, and, after three years in courtrooms, won a landmark ruling. In the first year of her new freedom, she received an Academy Award for *To Each His Own.*

Litvak agreed that de Havilland would be perfect. The actress loved the script. Zanuck approved the decision and filming began.

But not before three months of grueling research. Litvak demanded that the entire cast and crew accompany him to various mental institutions and to lectures by leading psychiatrists. He didn't have to convince de Havilland. She threw herself into the research with an intensity that surprised even those who knew her best. She watched carefully each of the procedures then in vogue, including hydrotherapy and electric shock treatments. When permitted, she sat in on long individual therapy sessions. She attended social functions, including dinners and dances with the patients. In fact, when, after the picture's release, columnist Florabel Muir questioned in print whether any mental institution actually "allowed contact dances among violent inmates," she was surprised by a call from de Havilland, who assured her she had attended several such dances herself.

The result is a performance that shines through the decades. Though mental health procedures and jargon definitely appear dated, de Havilland's artistry is timeless.

Mark Stevens, Leo Genn, and Celeste Holm are among the

other players. Betsy Blair, who in 1955 would score heavily in *Marty*, shines in a small role as Hester.

It was also noted by many that Litvak had combined his new skills in making documentaries acquired during the war to his acknowledged commercial storytelling ability in advancing *Snake Pit* to the upper echelon of current Hollywood fare. But this is de Havilland's picture. Her performance indicted an entire segment of public health, and the power of the reaction it caused in America changed things dramatically.

Dr. Milton Rosenbaum has been professor and chairman of the department of psychiatry at the Albert Einstein College of Medicine in New York, and is currently Distinguished Professor of Psychiatry at the University of New Mexico. In February 2000, he received a Distinguished Award from the American College of Psychiatrists for his contributions to the discipline over a period of five decades. At that same time, in an extended conversation with me, he talked about *Snake Pit*. "Certainly, the film had an impact," Dr. Rosenbaum said, "as did a series of hard-hitting articles by journalist Albert Deutsch. They were putting the spotlight on the shame of many public health institutions.

"The superintendents of some of these state hospitals were running them like plantations. They would have big houses on the grounds and patients would be used as house servants and gardeners—they were slaves, really.

"A tour of these hospitals was appalling. Many of the patients would be committed by relatives and just left there. Quite a few were there for life. Often there would be this enormous ward and those unfortunate people would spend their days there, day after day, in beds, on the floor, sitting in corners or pacing endlessly.

"It was a national scandal, but solving it from the inside was nearly impossible. Remember, these state hospitals were major employers, often the biggest business in town. Politicians and merchants and administrators were sometimes in collusion to keep the status quo.

"This movie and those articles and a book or two broke the log jam. There was an immediate outcry. The public was up in arms. It was astonishing how quickly changes came all over the country, and they were radical.

"Conditions improved and so did treatment, almost immediately. The patients, some of them, began to have something that had been stolen from them. Hope."

That point is made poignantly in the film when at a social function one of the patients, apparently a vocalist when she was "outside," begins to sing the tune "Goin' Home." Everyone joins in, each actor's expression making it clear he or she has long since despaired of "goin' home."

The film itself did well. It was a financial success and received six Academy Award nominations, including Best Picture, Best Actress, Best Director, Best Script, and Best Music. It won none of these, getting only a statuette for Best Sound Recording.

However, *Snake Pit* did win the International Prize at the Venice Film Festival in 1949, where it was cited for "a daring inquiry into a clinical case dramatically performed."

The critics were generally kind, with Louella Parsons declaring, "It is the most courageous subject ever attempted on the screen." Walter Winchell wrote, "Its seething quality gets inside of you." On the other hand, Herman D. Weinberg, a noted psychiatrist, was unimpressed: "A film of superficial veracity that requires a bigger man than Litvak; a good film with bad things in it."

Perhaps one measure of the power of the film on 1948 audiences came not from America, but from Great Britain. The British censor required a foreword added to the movie that explained to the audience that everyone in the picture was an actor—and that conditions in British hospitals were *unlike* those portrayed in the film.

In the end, it is clear that none of these comments mattered. Much closer to the heart of it all was Herb Stein of *Daily Variety*, who, shortly after the Academy Award ceremony in 1949, wrote, "Wisconsin is the seventh state to institute reforms in its mental hospitals as a result of *Snake Pit.*"

Publicity releases from 20th Century Fox claimed that twenty-six of the then forty-eight states had enacted reform legislation because of the movie.

That is a very difficult claim to verify because few of the bills introduced or regulations changed or funding increases implemented specifically mentioned *Snake Pit* as a motivating factor.

Still, the studio's speculation is fair. Meaningful changes were made in at least twenty states in the years 1949–51, changes that had been shuffled to the back burner for years, even decades before the movie came out.

But in 1948, movies could be a powerful force. There were 148 million of us in the nation, and that year we went to the movies 3,422,700,000 times. That averages out to twenty-three times a year for every man, woman, and child in the United States. The influence of the big screen was pervasive. What people saw, they could act on if they chose, and after seeing *Snake Pit,* they chose to put the heat on. Public servants had no choice but to respond to an aroused electorate.

Critics might well say that better films have been made on the subject of mental health and they would probably be right. *One Flew Over the Cuckoo's Nest,* for instance, is a better film than *The Snake Pit.*

But it was *The Snake Pit* that changed the nation we live in for the most vulnerable among us.

10

THE BEST YEARS OF OUR LIVES

1946

DIRECTOR: WILLIAM WYLER

STARS: MYRNA LOY, FREDRIC MARCH, DANA ANDREWS, TERESA WRIGHT, HAROLD RUSSELL

RUNNING TIME: 2 HOURS, 52 MINUTES

Three servicemen return home from World War II. One is an infantryman, another a bombardier, and the third a sailor who has lost both hands in a battle at sea.

The infantry sergeant returns to his affluent life to find his children grown, his wife a stranger, and his job at the bank a bore. The air force captain learns the woman he married in haste isn't who he thought she was. For that matter, he isn't who she thought he was, either.

Most poignant of all is the story of the returning sailor, whose well-meaning mother, father, and girlfriend can't accept the new reality of his disability.

Their lives weave in and out of each other's for a time. The captain falls for the sergeant's daughter. His wife runs off with a hood. The sailor spends a wrenching night telling his girlfriend what life with him will be like. The sergeant's wife watches helplessly as he lurches toward alcoholism. Yet all brim with a quixotic hope for the future.

Note: Harold Russell made one more film, 1980's *Inside Moves*. In the early 1990s, he was forced to sell one of his Oscars to meet family expenses, the first recipient ever to do so.

Goldwyn (Courtesy of The Kobal Collection)

They came from Raidersburg, Montana; Racine, Wisconsin; Warsaw, Poland; Collins, Mississippi; St. Louis, Missouri; and Mulhouse in Alsace. They were 23 or 32 or 41 or 58 or 64 years old, these dozens of men and women.

The infinitely complicated trajectories of lives and careers brought them together in a small group of factory-like buildings for one hundred days in 1946. What emerged from their combined efforts was a motion picture that, at long last, deepened the way major studios would portray America to Americans.

It has been said that with *The Best Years of Our Lives* Hollywood ended its long adolescence and came of age. It took a world war to do it.

It also took Sam Goldwyn: illegal immigrant, glove salesman, ambition-ridden filmmaker who had been there at Hollywood's creation. He had tiptoed successfully through the boom-and-bust cycles and the bewildering mergers and break-ups of companies as the new movie industry shook out the deadwood in the cruel calculus of empire-building.

Through it all, the man who began life as Schmuel Gelbfisz in Warsaw, traveled alone at age eleven to London, then to the United States at thirteen where he became Samuel Goldfish, had a deep longing for what Americans have always called "class." He wanted the best to think of him as the best.

When he began making films of his own, he hired the services of some of the best-known authors in the world, then had his picture taken with them. An early advertising campaign for his movies proclaimed "Brains *write* them, Brains *direct* them, Brains are *responsible* for their wonderful perfection." This was the period when Sam Goldfish set up a partnership with Edgar Selwyn. For the company name they took the first syllable of Sam's surname and the last of Edgar's. Sam liked the resulting "Goldwyn" so much, he changed his name legally in 1918, and it was Goldwyn from then on.

Through the years, Goldwyn began or advanced the movie careers of some of the greatest stars of all, including Gary Cooper, Barbara Stanwyck, Ronald Colman, David Niven, Danny Kaye, Merle Oberon, and a dozen others. In the process, he used the writing talents of Sinclair Lewis, MacKinlay Kantor, Lillian Hellman, Ben Hecht . . .

And Robert Emmet Sherwood. Mr. Sherwood would be instrumental in bringing Sam Goldwyn to the moment he had dreamed of all his life.

So would Frances Goldwyn. Sam's second wife had been an actress and was, by all accounts, the only person in whom he confided. He also trusted her judgment. Sometimes.

The "Goldwyn Touch" had brought excellent fare to the screen. Eddie Cantor's *Whoopee!* was among the biggest hits of the 1930s, and Goldwyn's *Dead End, Wuthering Heights, Arrowsmith, Dodsworth, Stella Dallas,* and *The Little Foxes* were well received critically and commercially. He even dabbled in controversy with Lillian Hellman's *We Three,* though he excised the suggestion of lesbianism from the story.

None of his films, however, got the big prize: the Best Picture Oscar from the Academy of Motion Picture Arts and Sciences. Buzz around the town was that Goldwyn produced slick, entertaining pictures but that, in the end, he was purely "commercial."

His choice of films during World War II seemed to reinforce

that perception. While the globe writhed in agony, Goldwyn produced *The Westerner, Ball of Fire, Pride of the Yankees, Up in Arms, The Princess and the Pirate,* and *Wonder Man.* His only obeisance toward the war effort was a fairly routine propaganda effort, *North Star*—filmed at the personal behest of President Franklin Roosevelt—attempting to dramatize for Americans the faraway struggle of the Russian people against the Nazis.

It was at about this time that Frances Goldwyn began a fateful intervention. Their son, Sam Goldwyn Jr., was an eighteen-year-old enlisted man in the army, so Frances was immersed in the war effort and read every scrap of war-related information.

In an August 1944 issue of *Time* magazine, she was drawn to an article in "The Nation" section that dealt with a detachment of marines coming home on a thirty-day furlough after two years in the South Pacific. The reporter followed the bewildered reactions of these young-old men and wrote down their words. Frances was deeply moved and immediately told her husband he should make a movie about servicemen coming home.

Goldwyn's first reaction was negative. He said he would never make such a picture. It was unfilmable. By the time it was made, it would be outdated. He was adamant. However, as a measure of his respect for her opinion, he went to his office that very day and registered two titles, *Home Again* and *The Way Home,* for future use.

By this time, Goldwyn had concluded that the reason he did not get the respect he felt he deserved was because of his image. He was a figure of fun in Hollywood and beyond. It was because of his penchant for twisting his words and spoonerizing clichés. It is unlikely he was responsible for even a fraction of the mangled syntax ascribed to him, but it no longer mattered. His "A verbal agreement isn't worth the paper it's written on," "I can answer that in two words: im possible," and the most famous of all, "Include me out," were legendary. Whether he said it originally or not, Goldwyn eventually accepted authorship. At an Elsa Maxwell party, the hostess asked each guest to write his or her epitaph on a piece of paper. Sam wrote "Include me out."

This curse of twisting the English language came at great personal cost to a man who wanted above all to have "class." He is reported to have said to a close friend, with tears welling in his eyes, "I hate my mouth."

In the fall of 1944, as the end of the war seemed near, Goldwyn became more enthusiastic about Frances's idea.

He first approached MacKinlay Kantor, already a respected novelist whose Civil War story *Long Remember* had cast a long shadow in the 1930s. Kantor would later win a Pulitzer Prize for *Andersonville*. At this moment he was back from an extended stint as a war correspondent during which he flew a number of combat missions with both the U.S. Army Air Force and the RAF. Goldwyn gave the article from *Time* to Kantor and fired up the author with his newfound enthusiasm. "Every family in America is part of this story," he said.

Kantor went off to New York. His announcement that his version would be written in free verse dampened Goldwyn's ardor for the project, but out of Kantor's typewriter came the first outline of a story that would resonate around the world. He called it *Glory for Me*, and the characters were the ones we would recognize in the finished product. Goldwyn paid Kantor $20,000, took possession of the film rights, and went shopping for a screenwriter.

He knew precisely the man he wanted. Robert Sherwood at age fifty was one of America's most distinguished men of letters. He had served in World War I, turned to writing after the war, been the editor of *Life* magazine in its first incarnation, 1924–28, then turned his energies to the stage. His *Petrified Forest* hit Broadway like a hailstorm, then his *Idiot's Delight*, *Abe Lincoln in Illinois*, and *There Shall Be No Light* won three quick Pulitzers in a row. He had spent the war as Director of

Overseas Operations for the Office of War Information and as speechwriter for President Roosevelt.

When Sam Goldwyn contacted him, Sherwood was working on a play about the war. He was interested in the movie project, but immersed in his own stage drama. Goldwyn did what he always did best: He persisted. Sherwood said "no" many times, but he finally relented to the extent of becoming a houseguest of the Goldwyns. For twenty days he struggled with the material, to no avail. Goldwyn found Sherwood and his wife packing for their trip back to New York, defeated.

"Can I talk to you for five minutes?" Sherwood nodded. Goldwyn said, "Your story is beautiful, the words are from heaven. But it's a little bit too political. Just write about the people. If you do, I'll make you a promise. Not one word of your dialogue will be changed." As Sherwood later remembered it, that was a promise that was unprecedented in Hollywood, but Goldwyn kept his word, down to the letter, much to chagrin of the next major player in this drama.

Director William Wyler had been working with Sam Goldwyn for ten years, and the results had been excellent: *Dodsworth, Dead End, The Westerner, Wuthering Heights,* and *The Little Foxes* were all above average films. But the two men wore on one another's nerves professionally. Wyler, a perfectionist, could not stand the constant interference of the studio chief. In exasperation, Wyler would often explode, "What he wants is a Sam Goldwyn picture written by Sam Goldwyn, starring Sam Goldwyn, photographed by Sam Goldwyn, and produced by Sam Goldwyn!"

Wyler was another filmmaker who had found his way to the U.S. from Europe. Born in what then was a part of Germany, Alsace, in 1902, Wyler's early education was in business, but he abandoned dry goods for music, studying violin in Paris. That was where he met a distant relative, Carl Laemmle, head of Universal Pictures, who hired him for his company.

Wyler worked his way up from the bottom, as did so many of the early directors. He was a publicist, prop man, grip, cutter, casting director, and, finally a director at age twenty-four.

During the war, Wyler volunteered his services and was assigned to make combat documentaries. He made one of the best, *Memphis Belle*, following the twenty-fifth mission of a B-17. It was dangerous work, and started the process of a serious hearing loss. For Wyler, that process was complete when he produced *Thunderbolt*, a documentary about an American fighter-bomber, the P-47. An unpressurized flight with his camera in the belly of that aircraft caused permanent hearing loss in one ear and seriously diminished hearing in the other. He was certain he would never be able to go back to his profession.

Already depressed, he was in no mood to accept the bullying and capricious behavior of Sam Goldwyn. Even after a sound engineer showed him that a special earphone would enable him to hear actors' dialogue on a set after all, he resisted Goldwyn's efforts to put him on the *Home Again* project. But, by contract, he owed Goldwyn one more film, and Sam insisted this be the one. Wyler finally agreed, as long as he received 20 percent of the net profits, a relatively new element in contracts in those days. Goldwyn wanted the best, and he was convinced Wyler *was* the best, so he agreed.

In the meantime, Robert Sherwood was fleshing out the men and women who would become screen immortals. For a title, he selected a line he put in the mouth of one of the story's most unattractive characters, the floozy who was unfaithful to her absent soldier husband: "You've wasted the best years of our lives." Sherwood thought the irony was perfect for what he hoped would be the most realistic picture ever made by a major studio. Goldwyn didn't like the title, thought it too long and cumbersome, but let it go for the moment.

He had more important concerns. He and Wyler were working on a cast. Goldwyn got his first choices on a number of the roles easily enough. Many were under contract to him.

Dana Andrews as Fred Derry; Virginia Mayo as his faithless wife Marie Derry; twenty-three-year-old newcomer Cathy O'Donnell as Wilma Cameron, the wounded veteran's girlfriend; and Teresa Wright, three-time Academy Award nominee though she wasn't yet thirty, as Peggy Stephenson who, with Fred Derry, would carry the burden of the movie's central—and unorthodox—love story.

For the wounded veteran, Homer Parrish, Goldwyn chose his rising young star, the Hollywood "heartthrob," Farley Granger. For the mature couple who would anchor the story, the studio chief went after two major names: Olivia de Havilland and Fred MacMurray. Both turned down the roles as too inconsequential. In fact, Fred MacMurray was quoted as calling the character Al Stephenson a "third banana." He would have reason to regret both the decision and the quote.

Myrna Loy, on the other hand, read the script and jumped at the chance to play Milly Stephenson. Myrna Loy had been in the movies since she was a teenager and was still a formidable star. Her earlier sexy and exotic roles had given way to many textures of the "perfect wife" genre. No one did them better. The subject material of *Best Years* was important to Miss Loy. She had given herself over completely to the war effort, taking a leave of absence from films and working full time for the Red Cross. She was given top billing for her return in *Best Years*.

Fredric March was by this point in his career beginning to split his time between Hollywood films and the New York stage. He also understood the importance of the story Sherwood was shaping and enthusiastically accepted the offer to play Al Stephenson. In a way, it was a case of art imitating life: The Stephenson character was a banker who returned, profoundly changed, to his old job. March himself had pursued a banking career, interrupted by service as an artillery lieutenant in World

War I, after which he returned to his apprenticeship at New York's National City Bank. He found the experience most unsatisfactory and within a few years turned to acting. He had a great deal he could—and did—bring to this role.

Great artists and artisans at the peak of their powers were coalesced around *The Best Years of Our Lives.* The famous cinematographer Gregg Toland, whose mastery of "deep focus" gave directors a chance to do things with a camera that would not have seemed possible, joined the team. When it came to scoring the film, Goldwyn wanted his former music director, Alfred Newman, who for five years had been working for another studio. But when Newman recommended the relatively unknown Hugo Friedhofer, Goldwyn accepted the suggestion without question, against Wyler's wishes. It was an inspired decision.

One of the roles that had been set in stone was about to be unset. As it happened, the change would lift this film to a level where few Hollywood movies had been before. It might not be too much of an exaggeration to say *none* had been there before. Realism was about to be given a new definition.

Director William Wyler and writer Robert Sherwood were touring military hospitals, trying to get a feel for the background of one of the protagonists, Homer Parrish. The original Kantor treatment had this character return from combat "spastic," wounded in the central nervous system, unable to control most of his movements. Both men agreed this would be a difficult condition to film and were looking for options when they were shown a training movie, *Diary of a Sergeant.* This was the story of a young man who had lost both hands, and showed his road to rehabilitation. The star was a soldier who had, indeed, lost his hands, and when Wyler and Sherwood saw his natural performance on film, they had an entirely new thought. This young man would be Homer Parrish.

Their enthusiasm swept Goldwyn's objections away. Farley Granger was out. A thirty-two-year-old army veteran named

Harold Russell, with only those few minutes experience before a camera, was in.

Harold Russell was an interesting man by any measure. He had been born in Sydney, Nova Scotia, in 1914. His family soon moved to Boston and that is the city Harold would call home. His background was blue-collar. He was a meat-cutter when the war came. After his time in basic training he asked for transfer to the paratroopers. He was in the last stages of training for combat when, as he put it, "I lost an argument with a block of TNT." The result was the loss of both hands and six inches of both wrists.

What struck everyone who came in contact with Harold Russell was his attitude. He accepted his loss, went immediately into physical therapy, learned to manipulate the hooks and harness so quickly that he was soon teaching others. It was this equanimity and sense of humor that led army filmmakers to use him in *Diary of a Sergeant*.

It was also apparent on the set of *Best Years of Our Lives*. Harold did not seem to be intimidated by his surroundings or the famous faces with whom he found himself working. At one point, he was joking with the legendary Hoagy Carmichael, composer of "Stardust," who portrayed the memorable tavern-owner Butch Engle in the film, and asked Hoagy to teach him to play "chopsticks" with his hooks. The moment was included in an important scene in the movie.

Other personal experiences from all these war veterans made their way into the film. For instance, William Wyler remembered coming home in early 1945. He was over forty years old, he had spent two years overseas, often taking his camera on combat missions. His health had deteriorated and he could no longer hear. He thought his career was finished.

In memory of previous glory days, he asked his wife to meet him at the Plaza Hotel in New York. He saw her at the end of a hotel corridor. She had her back to him, but in a moment of intuition, she turned and saw him. They moved toward one another with an entire panoply of emotion playing over them with each step. Fear, longing, anger, love, puzzlement, all dissolving as they embraced. Wyler incorporated a long hallway into the homecoming of Al Stephenson to his loving Milly in the film.

Myrna Loy later described her motivation: "The two of them just couldn't wait to get into the sack."

Some, including Gregg Toland, thought the war had taught William Wyler a great deal. He had always been a superb studio director, taking advantage of every new "boom-and-dolly" technology brought to his attention.

But in 1946, thought Toland, Wyler had spent a long time in mortal danger using handheld cameras, often doing the shooting himself. It changed his approach. He simplified. The *story* was paramount and technology was used only to serve the story. Like the country, William Wyler had grown up.

When Sam Goldwyn put Harold Russell into acting school, Wyler took him out. When Irene Sharaff showed up with costumes, Wyler and Goldwyn told her to get rid of them. The entire cast was taken to department stores where they bought the kinds of clothes their characters could afford. Then they were told to wear them for a couple of weeks before shooting began.

This was a new world, indeed. One where the "Ruptured Duck" and the "52-20 Club" ruled. Nearly 13 million young Americans had been in uniform at one time or another from 1941 to 1945. The "ruptured duck" was a small gold pin all veterans were authorized to wear. The "52-20 Club" was a fund to help veterans ease back into society. Twenty dollars a week was available to former servicemen for one year or until they found work. This was the background against which *Best Years* was filmed.

Why did it work? William Wyler thought he knew: "Because

it was the truth," he said. At least, it was as close as establishment Hollywood had ever come to telling the truth. What we saw on screen was a mature combat veteran coming back to children who had grown up while he was away and a wife who wasn't sure she knew him anymore. His escape was alcohol and the film left us fairly sure he would descend into alcoholism. Another veteran returned a cuckold, his wife a blowsy blonde whose affection for his uniform and his company disappears with his mustering out pay. His hero's medals make no impression on a town that returned him to his prewar duties as a soda jerk. In desperation he launches an affair with his best friend's daughter, who herself undertakes to break up his marriage.

All of these roles were underplayed, with a brilliance seldom matched in ensemble film acting before or since.

But even these stunning, fully realized roles were overborn by the simple, natural performance of Harold Russell as Homer Parrish. The moviegoer was jolted by what he or she saw unfolding on the screen.

At some level, moviegoers knew that Fredric March and Dana Andrews, Myrna Loy and Teresa Wright, convincing as they were, were actors. They would go on to other roles. Fredric March would be Christopher Columbus. Myrna Loy would help Mr. Blandings build his dream house. Dana Andrews would complicate the life of Daisy Kenyon. Teresa Wright would comfort Marlon Brando in *The Men*.

Harold Russell would do none of that. When his Homer Parrish takes Cathy O'Donnell's Wilma Cameron to his bedroom to show her what life with him would be like—the removal of his harness, his helplessness without his hooks—we all know that the real Harold Russell will be saying the same thing to an all-too-real girl someday. And, when Homer is alone, the tear that rolls down his cheek—the one moment his iron will allows him to be vulnerable—is Harold's tear as well as Homer's.

It is, in fact, impossible to watch the scene even now without a catch in the throat.

On the other hand, if the Breen Office had prevailed, many of the most affecting scenes would not have made it to the screen. Joseph I. Breen was by now the man who presided over "the Code," Hollywood's all-powerful Production Code.

When Mr. Breen and his staff saw the film, they demanded a number of changes. This new "realism" would not get past the gate if they could help it. Specifically, they required that a "passionate" kiss between Milly and Al be eliminated, Al's belch after a Bromo Seltzer be excised, the marriage break-up between Fred and Marie be rewritten so that the tragedy of the divorce be emphasized, Peggy's declaration that she was going to be a "home-wrecker" be taken out.

Following the Production Code was not mandatory but many theaters would not show a film that didn't bear the Production Seal. Moreover, the industry itself fined any producer who ignored the suggestions $25,000. The adverse publicity would bring every advocacy group out, so movie executives routinely caved in.

Not this time. Sam Goldwyn informed the Breen Office that he would not comply with any of their demands. He felt the material reflected America, he said, and would not change one of Mr. Sherwood's words. The Office could do its worst, he was sending *Best Years* out "as is." It was Breen who blinked. The Office withdrew all of its objections. There was no fine. Some Hollywood historians point to *Best Years* as another step in the demise of Hollywood's Production Code, with the true coup de grace arriving with *Who's Afraid of Virginia Woolf?* in 1966.

It will come as no surprise that *Best Years of Our Lives* was not the favorite among Academy Award handicappers on the big night. True, it had received eight nominations, but Sam Goldwyn had never won the big prize, and momentum seemed to be on the side of European invaders, including Laurence

Olivier's *Henry V.* A lot of insiders bet on Darryl Zanuck's *The Razor's Edge* and MGM's *The Yearling,* with Frank Capra's *It's a Wonderful Life* and Wyler's *Best Years of Our Lives* considered dark horses at best.

In one of Oscar's annual injustices, Gregg Toland, who had done some of his best camera work on this film, was not nominated.

On March 13, 1947, all interested parties headed toward the Academy Award's new venue, the cavernous Shrine Auditorium in downtown Los Angeles. There were 6,700 seats, so John Q. Public was invited to the festivities for the first time. Even so, the event was far from a sellout, so the hundreds of uniformed servicemen who were milling around outside in the hope of seeing a pretty movie star were given free tickets.

For what it was worth, *Best Years* rolled into the glittering event on some of the best reviews in recent memory. The *New York Times* wrote, "Sets the highest standards of cinematic quality, then meets them triumphantly." *Time* wrote, "A sure-fire hit with good taste, honesty, wit and even a suggestion of guts." *Newsweek* called it "epic film art." The wonderful creator of World War II's immortal "Willie and Joe," Bill Mauldin, wrote, "The first real, honest-to-God sincere thing I've seen about the war and its aftermath." The lone dissenter, the *New Yorker*, seemed upset that the film didn't go even deeper into the kind of realism postwar Europe was producing, such as Fellini's *Open City.*

Now came Sam Goldwyn's moment of truth. Before the evening was over, *Best Years* had won Best Actor for Fredric March, Best Supporting Actor for Harold Russell, Best Director for William Wyler, Best Screenplay for Robert E. Sherwood, Best Scoring for Hugo Friedhofer, Best Film Editing for Daniel Mandell, Special Oscar to Harold Russell for "bringing hope and courage to his fellow veterans," making Harold the only actor ever to win two Academy Awards for one role, then, the big one,

Best Picture of the year. To top it off, Sam Goldwyn received the Academy's most prestigious honor, the Irving Thalberg Award.

All of Sam Goldwyn's dreams came true in a shower of golden statuettes. But even here, he still had reason to say, "I hate my mouth." Sam had managed a brief acceptance of the Thalberg Award and was doing very well with his "thank you's" for the Best Picture Award, right until the final moment. "Last but not least," he said, "I'd like to thank Hugo Carmichael."

A Goldwynism for the ages.

Frances Goldwyn told biographer A. Scott Berg about the way that night ended: After the parties and the plaudits, she and Sam went home and she went up to bed. Some time later she grew concerned and went down to see why Sam hadn't came upstairs. She saw him sitting on the arm of a couch, holding his Irving Thalberg Award in one hand and his Oscar in the other. He was crying.

Given its moment in our nation's history and, for that matter, in Hollywood history, *The Best Years of Our Lives* is a staggering achievement. For anyone who wants to get a whiff of who we were at the end of the twentieth century's seminal event, it is required viewing.

And for those digging through the fragmented layers of celluloid looking for the beginning of American film's very first serious, big-budget attempt to tell us the truth about ourselves, *The Best Years of Our Lives* is bedrock.

It changed forever the level of excellence that would thereafter be required for our best motion pictures.

11

THE MIRACLE OF MORGAN'S CREEK

1944

DIRECTOR: PRESTON STURGES

STARS: EDDIE BRACKEN, BETTY HUTTON, DIANA LYNN

RUNNING TIME: 1 HOUR, 39 MINUTES

Trudy Kockenlocker lives in the small town of Morgan's Creek with her sister and her father, who is a policeman.

In the slang of the time, Trudy is "boy-crazy," but the one boy she is not crazy about is the one who loves her, the town dork Norval Jones. Trudy uses Norval as a "blind" so she can date the more interesting servicemen stationed nearby. One of them was too interesting entirely. After a party, she *thinks* she might have married the fellow but doesn't know his name or what he looks like. What she soon *does* know is that he left a remembrance. She is pregnant.

Norval does his best to marry Trudy, but mishap builds on misunderstanding and he is run out of town as a philanderer. The only thing that can save the situation is a miracle and they get it. Trudy gives birth to sextuplets, going the Dionne Quints one better. Now the mayor, the governor, and everyone protect the celebrities, giving them a quick wedding and everything they need for a happy life.

Note: Brian Donlevy played the small role of Governor McGinty in *Miracle*, a role he had created in an earlier Preston Sturges triumph, *The Great McGinty*.

Paramount (Courtesy of The Kobal Collection)

How did Sturges get away with it? It's impossible to imagine, even at this distance.

But the fact that he did made inevitable the death of the heretofore invulnerable Motion Picture Production Code, and leads to the inclusion of this frenetic comedy in our list of movies that changed things.

By every standard of the time, *The Miracle of Morgan's Creek* should have been banned from all the theaters in America and its creator, Preston Sturges, hanged from the nearest eucalyptus tree.

But, for a brief shining moment in Hollywood history, Preston Sturges had stardust on his shoulders and could do no wrong. Not even if he impregnated one of his celluloid heroines with sextuplets.

In 1940, the *Hollywood Reporter* said that Mr. Sturges "burst over Hollywood like a comet." Unfortunately, the simile was on target. Sturges was, indeed, a comet. He flared and burned and shone like the brightest star for a moment, then broke apart, cinders barely warm, to scatter over the show business landscape of two continents.

The Miracle of Morgan's Creek may or may not have been Preston Sturges's best film, but it was certainly the one that did the most damage to the film industry's vaunted, feared and hated Code, which reigned from 1930 to 1966.

Reeling under the terrible publicity generated by the excesses of a number of stars, writers, and directors, the studios feared a boycott of their films by middle America. The fear was well founded. Powerful religious groups were, indeed, calling on their flocks to stay away from the product of the "nest of vipers" who had congregated on the left coast.

The frightened moguls looked for the most straight-laced conservative person in the nation for their salvation and found him. Will H. Hays from Sullivan, Indiana, had been a successful lawyer, the chairman of the Republican National Committee, and was the Postmaster General in the early days of the Harding administration.

Fortunately for Hays, he got out of the president's political embrace before the nation found out that the administration of Warren Gamaliel Harding would produce more scandal than Tinseltown had ever dreamed of.

At any rate, Mr. Hays was first hired in 1922 by the newly formed Motion Picture Producers and Directors of America, Incorporated, to clean up Hollywood's image. For eight years he put out localized fires, but it wasn't until 1930 that increased pressures caused the Hays Office to actually impose what was, in effect, censorship of the movies.

The Code remained in development, then was implemented in 1934. Immediately, movies changed. Rules were strictly enforced. What rules?

"Pointed profanity—this includes the words God, Lord, Jesus Christ (unless used reverently). Hell, S.O.B., damn, or other profane or vulgar expressions, however used, is forbidden."

"Sex perversion or any inference to it is forbidden."

"Excessive and lustful kissing, lustful embracing, suggestive postures and gestures, are not to be shown."

And this one which hit Preston Sturges's creativity squarely between the eyes:

"Seduction . . . should never be more than suggested [and is] never the proper subject for comedy."

Comedy was what Preston Sturges was all about, and seduction was often at the very core of his comedies.

Preston Sturges was, by any definition, among a small handful of the most interesting men who ever found themselves in Hollywood.

In his autobiography, published by his widow Sandy after his death, Sturges says that nothing he did in his early days gave any indication of what his life's work would be. It is difficult to argue the point.

True, his mother was a close confidante of the talented, flamboyant dancer Isadora Duncan, so there was a connection with the entertainment world. In fact, in grim family legend, it was Preston's mother, Mary, who gave Isadora the fatal shawl that she threw dramatically around her neck as she stepped into an open car driven by an admirer. The shawl caught around the hub of the rear wheel, breaking her neck and ending her tempestuous life.

In a time now difficult to recapture, Preston Sturges at age fifteen was the manager of his mother's perfume and cosmetics store in New York City. He had spent most of his childhood years in Europe, gone to some famous boarding schools, met many of the Continental glitterati, excelled in boxing and rowing, and learned to drink, a skill he would master, as it turned out, too well.

His life was set. He would be an entrepreneur. And that is undoubtedly how it would have turned out if he had been any good at it at all.

He wasn't. All through his life, businesses he started failed. The huge sums of money he made by his creative genius were squandered on his dreams of business success.

At age eighteen he invented and patented a kiss-proof lipstick. (There is ample evidence he did plenty of research.) In fact, though nothing in his earlier years gave a hint of his success in the movies, his precocious adventures with the opposite sex should have given notice that any Code banning scenes of seduction did not stand a chance against Preston Sturges.

The Hays Office gave him a real battle, however, and won all the early skirmishes.

Let's see if we can follow Mr. Sturges's circuitous path to Lotus Land.

In the midst of his on-again-off-again experience with his and his mother's cosmetics business, Preston at age nineteen joined the Flying Service of the U.S. Army Signal Corps. He got his wings just as World War I ended.

He then reestablished his business, getting it temporarily on a paying basis, only to have his mother come back from Europe and take it away from him. He was by now married to a young woman who had money so he was able to pursue his talent at inventing things. He got a patent for a photo-etching process, designed a vertical-take-off aircraft, the kind that is now in military use, and designed a light automobile with exchangeable power plants for which he did *not* receive a patent.

This was the time he also began to write songs, which led directly to his finding his life's work.

By then his marriage had fallen apart, his songs weren't selling, and he had a near-fatal bout with appendicitis. Then an actress he was dating told him she was only going out with him in order to use him as a character in a play she was writing. He would see himself portrayed, she assured him, as an oaf.

Furious, he responded that he would write a play before she did and that his play would be better than she could ever dream of writing. No matter that he had never written so much as a paragraph of dialogue, at age twenty-nine he sat down and wrote a play. To his astonishment, it was produced. It was not a hit, but he saw his story come to life on a New York stage and he was locked forever to the magnet of theater.

His second play was a smash. *Strictly Dishonorable* was the hit of New York's 1929–30 season and was made into a movie twice, in 1931 and 1951.

Preston Sturges then wrote the dialogue for a few Paramount films—that was in 1930—but he immediately returned to the scene of his triumph, Broadway. It was only after he suffered two flops in a row that he decided to give Hollywood a closer look. That was 1933.

The Hollywood in which Mr. Sturges took up residence was by no means writer-friendly. Oh, the studios paid writers well enough, it was just that they didn't think wordsmiths were really all that important. The writing of every film was a collaborative effort. Since the introduction of sound it was very nearly literally true that *no* film had ever been the work of one writer.

Of course, playwrights and authors, the great names in the field of writing, almost always worked alone. The Hollywood system turned their discipline upside down, in their opinion, and they said so loudly and often.

One writer might write a "treatment," another a "first draft," still another a "rewrite," and a fourth would be brought in to "punch up" the dialogue. The original writer would often not recognize the finished story.

From his first day in California, Sturges began to lobby executives to allow him to direct his own screenplays. It was unheard of and he was turned down month after month. Sturges persisted, because it was clear that in the land of movies, directors got respect and writers did not.

The stature of the true author in the realm of American letters made not one bit of difference. William Faulkner's words were thrown out or rehashed in exactly the same way as those of the greenest writer fresh out of school.

What kept Preston Sturges from being fired for his stubborn insistence on directing his own scripts was that he was turning into a masterful screenwriter and was much in demand. His forte was witty and urbane dialogue, and his contributions improved a dozen pictures from 1933 to 1939.

It was also in that period that Mr. Sturges had his first serious confrontation with the Hays Office, the code enforcement of which was by then the responsibility of Joseph I. Breen.

Universal Studios had bought the rights to Marcel Pagnol's play *Fanny*. It is the story of an older man who marries a teenage girl who has gotten pregnant with her young lover, who deserts her. When the young man returns, the husband is willing to give up his wife, but not the child.

Sturges and several others worked on the script for the better part of a year, but in the mid-1930s they were never able to arrive at a version that would pass Mr. Breen's strict Production Code. (Remember that out-of-wedlock pregnancy theme. It will be important later.)

The Code was only one of the land mines Preston Sturges and other writers had to avoid in the "golden era" of moviemaking. Another was the dictatorial control of films by directors. The seemingly capricious way writing credit was awarded—and withheld—on the finished product was a third, and, of course, the continuing intransigence of studio chiefs on the matter of a writer becoming a director was the crowning obstacle.

Six years is a very long time in Hollywood, then and now, but that's what it took for Mr. Sturges to realize his dream. At the end of 1934, he wrote a story he called "The Biography of a Bum." This, he decided, was his meal ticket. This was the tale he would *not* sell to a studio—any studio—unless he was allowed to direct it.

In 1939, he finally convinced Paramount production chief William LeBaron to let him sit in the director's chair. A major selling point was the price he was willing to accept for the story. Ten dollars. It turned out to be the best investment Sturges ever made. It wasn't a bad deal for Paramount, either.

By now, "Biography of a Bum" had become *The Great*

McGinty, a political satire with a wallop Hollywood had seldom seen. Sturges turned out to be a natural as a director, throwing rules out the window and bringing a fresh look to the big screen.

For the next four years, Preston Sturges bedazzled the film community. Everything he had learned in a rich and checkered life he put on the screen, and, for those four sizzling years, everything clicked.

The Great McGinty won Sturges the Academy Award for Best Screenplay of 1940 and from then on, there was never a question about who would write a Preston Sturges–directed film or who would direct a Preston Sturges–written story.

In quick succession came *Christmas in July*, a charming and very funny film starring Dick Powell and telling the story of a man who went on a major shopping spree under the mistaken impression he had won a big contest. Then, *The Lady Eve*, starring Barbara Stanwyck and Henry Fonda, the title a salute to a very real woman whom Sturges had once dated. Sturges also indulged his passion for pratfalls, giving Fonda five in one scene.

Sullivan's Travels, starring Joel McCrea and Veronica Lake, was a monument to the Sturges credo that comedy was more important than drama, no matter what critics thought. His hero, a film comedy director, feels the lack of respect of the critical community and wants to escape his success and direct instead a heavy-handed drama, to which Sturges gave the title *Oh, Brother, Where Art Thou?* Sixty years later, the Coen Brothers, Joel and Ethan, would borrow that very title for one of their offbeat comedies.

The Palm Beach Story starring Joel McCrea again, this time with Claudette Colbert, featured one of the most outrageous slapstick sequences this side of *Hellzapoppin*, with a group of drunken hunters shooting up the club car of a train. It also marked the comedy debut of crooner Rudy Vallee.

Ending with a flourish, Sturges released two blockbusters in

1944, both starring Eddie Bracken, *Hail the Conquering Hero* and *The Miracle of Morgan's Creek*.

Here's a thumbnail sketch of the plot of *Miracle of Morgan's Creek* that Mr. Sturges actually wrote and shot in 1942.

The heroine, Betty Hutton, is the daughter of a police officer, William Demarest. She's a bit wild and her special delight is to date lonely soldiers from a nearby base. Her father, of course, forbids all such foolishness, so she uses her friend, the hapless and inept Eddie Bracken, as a blind. She goes out with him, leaves him at a movie, goes to the dance with the boys, comes back and picks him up—after a double feature—and goes home. One night things go a bit too far. She finds herself pregnant and has no clue as to who the father is. Loyal Eddie agrees to marry her, but the whole thing is botched and he is run out of town as a philanderer. The day is saved when Hutton gives birth to sextuplets, making the parents, the town and everyone involved, celebrities. Happy ending. Fade out.

There is hardly any statute of the Code that was *not* broken. So how did Preston Sturges get away with it?

"He was just a genius at dealing with the Hays Office," said the star of the film, Eddie Bracken, in a lively conversation in February 2001, recalling clearly the events of 1942. "They would get his script, circle the things that had to go. Then Preston would insert a sentence that seemed to solve everything, looked perfectly innocuous on paper. Only when that piece of business was delivered on screen, it bore no resemblance to the script.

"Let me give you an example. Preston's original script had Betty's character getting drunk and becoming pregnant by someone whose name she couldn't remember. The censors crossed that out. Absolutely unacceptable. So Preston changed it. He had Betty in an exuberant dance hit her head on a chandelier or something and it knocked her silly. That made none of the subsequent events her fault, so the moral misstep could be excused. Of course, when the scene was shot it was clear that everyone was having a merry old time with drinks everywhere, and Betty's exuberance certainly looked to the audience as if she was a little tanked before she hit her head, but the Hays Office bought it.

"It was ridiculous. Not ridiculous that they tried to put some guidelines down for the movies, but the silly lengths they would go to and the iron control they had over the process—Preston was a master at getting around them. None was ever any better."

Describe the atmosphere of a Preston Sturges soundstage.

"If you ever dreamed—ever hoped—that making a movie would be a wonderful experience, your dream would come true on a Preston Sturges soundstage.

"During breaks, it would be like a dinner party with friends. There would be many laughs and great stories. When it came time to shoot, he was all business. He knew exactly what he wanted and didn't waste any time.

"He could be very tough and demanding, but he was also willing to listen to any contribution you wanted to make. For instance, all of that stuttering of my character and the spots he would see before his eyes when he became nervous, that was from a vaudeville act I did. I showed them to Preston. He loved them and kept them in."

You were so young when you made this film.

"Not as young as you think. You've been looking at the biographies and actors' encyclopedias. They all say I was born February 7, 1920. I wasn't. It was February 7, 1915. Now I can tell the truth. I'll only get the old-man parts anyway."

Was there tension between you and costar Betty Hutton?

"To show you how smart I was, I at first said no to doing *Miracle.* I had already done a number of films with Betty." [They had already made *The Fleet's In, Happy Go Lucky,* and

Star Spangled Rhythm.] "I found out the same thing Bing Crosby, Bob Hope, and some others did. If you were in a movie with Betty Hutton in those days, after the shooting was over and you were gone, [Paramount chief] Buddy de Sylva would bring Betty back, have her film two or three more specialty numbers, and put them in the movie. Betty was Buddy's protégé and he was determined to make a star of her. You'd see the movie and realize it wasn't what you thought, a collaborative effort, but a star vehicle for Betty. Of course she was wonderful, so it clicked, but all of us felt as if we had been used a little bit by Buddy.

"So when Preston asked me to do *Miracle,* I said no, because Buddy would put in three extra numbers. Then Preston told me it wasn't a musical, so I said yes right away."

The work with her went smoothly?

"Betty and I were buddies. We worked very well together on screen. We didn't socialize much. I was already a family man and Betty was the queen of the wild Hollywood parties. She would as likely as not take off her clothes and do one of those 'Blonde Bombshell' dances for the partygoers. I can't help but believe that using up all that energy came back to haunt her in the 1950s.

"But the reason I refused to do any more films with her after *Miracle* was that I didn't want to be part of a 'team,' like Abbot and Costello, or Ma and Pa Kettle. I wanted to be an actor, period."

Did you expect a lot of protests when the film was released?

"We didn't know what to expect. By now Preston and I were close friends. I sat in on his writing sessions, watched how his mind worked. We knew—or believed—it was funny, but I'm sure Preston knew he was skating on thin ice.

"In those days, principal actors were not allowed to go to sneak previews. If the film bombed in preview it was thought that would be a blow to our egos. But, Betty and I wanted to go, so we found out where it was showing. Betty, with that blond hair, was recognized immediately and turned away by the studio people. My wife and I sneaked in and found a couple of seats.

"The laughs were so explosive they covered up the gasps. The woman in front of us literally fell off her seat sideways into the aisle. I never heard anything like it. When the movie was over, we were all packed into the aisle squeezing our way out. A man was talking to the woman who had fallen into the aisle, 'Wasn't that the funniest movie you've ever seen?' 'Yeah, except for that jerk kid. Where'd they ever get him?' "

In your opinion, what happened to Preston Sturges after 1944?

"First there were his personal financial troubles. He had the Players' Club, you know, a wonderful nightclub and performance space, everybody in town went there, but Preston had no business sense and it went bust.

"I came back to town and started making the rounds with every one of his friends, asking for money to help bail him out. One visit I was sure would be a forlorn hope. Rudy Vallee had a reputation as a skinflint and he deserved it. I expected to get maybe a hundred bucks out of him. Rudy loved Preston because he had given Rudy a great comedic part in *The Palm Beach Story*. Rudy always thought of himself as a great comedian. He wasn't. He knew every joke ever told but had not a clue as to how to tell them. Anyway, he wrote a check and handed it to me. I took it to Preston, who looked at it, then fell on the floor on his back. I grabbed it and looked. It was for $10,000! What would that be now, half a million? People loved Preston."

Was it the Howard Hughes connection that started his downfall? Sturges signed an exclusive contract in 1945 with Howard Hughes.

"That was certainly part of it, but I believe Preston had a

secret weapon. As I told you, I began to sit in on Preston's writing sessions. He wrote *Hail the Conquering Hero* for me. He worked with what was then called a secretary, Jean Laval. She would be called an executive assistant or creative consultant now. She would rein him in. Preston would sometimes overwrite, or let his enthusiasm carry him away. Jean would say, 'Now, maybe that's funny to you, but it's not funny to me,' or, 'You lost me about a page ago.' He would be mad as hell and stomp out, but he respected her judgment and would listen to her.

"If I'm not mistaken, this was about the time she left him. Jean would probably say she had no role in his greatest work, but my observation is that she did."

With sixty years of perspective, how do you feel about Miracle of Morgan's Creek *now?*

"That and *Hail the Conquering Hero* were clearly the high point of my professional life. I am constantly asked to attend seminars and retrospectives. They worked for me then, they work for me now.

"After those two films my movie career was essentially over. It was not that roles dried up or that I was no longer in demand.

"I went back to what I loved, the place I had started, the stage. In July 2001, in the middle of the run of *Carousel*, I will have made my fifteen thousandth appearance on an American stage. I've been married to my best friend for sixty-one years. I have five great kids, not a clinker among them.

"I even make a movie appearance every now and then.

"And I was part of one of the greatest bursts of creative energy in Hollywood history."

It was all of that, and more. More, perhaps, than Eddie Bracken, Betty Hutton, or the director's brilliant repertory company of comedic actors knew.

In a way, Preston Sturges was more subversive than any of those Hollywood filmmakers who were chased so avidly by ambitious American politicians in the 1930s and again in the late 1940s during the "red scare" eras.

Sturges had in his sights not the politics of right or left but what he and many others in the film community thought of as the Code's hypocritical attitude toward sex, some particulars of which were touched on by Mr. Bracken.

In the temper of the times, sex was an even more controversial subject than left-leaning politics, and more dangerous. While many liberal filmmakers could be found to broach the subject of a more collectivist view of American society, none in mainstream films would venture into the quagmire of sex.

Where those other Hollywood giants feared to tread, Preston Sturges stormed ahead, using his gift for comedy to disguise what he hoped would be a revolution.

His offbeat—to say the least—premise of a young wife accepting the overtures of an old, rich—and also married—man surfaced in *Palm Beach Story*." A young con-woman seducing a rich, but nerdy, young man—twice—in *The Lady Eve* was a bit outside of the current box, as was the obvious sexual liaison between a director separated from his wife and a young, impoverished, vulnerable actress in *Sullivan's Travels*.

But in *Miracle of Morgan's Creek*, Sturges deliberately undertook to use his likeable young costars, Eddie Bracken and Betty Hutton, as bludgeons to hammer the prevailing Code, for which he had such contempt, until it was unrecognizable. As we have seen, he did just that.

The immediate revolution in filmmaking for which he had hoped did not take place. His own star, at its most intense moment of brilliance, inexplicably went out.

But if the toppling of a dam begins with a slight breach, Sturges had supplied it. After *Miracle*, producers and directors raised the film in disputes with Code enforcers over sex in the movies, with limited—but growing—success as time went on.

The Miracle of Morgan's Creek can now be seen as the opening broadside in what would prove to be a glacial—but inevitable—change in the way sex is portrayed in American films.

12

THE GREAT DICTATOR

1940

DIRECTOR: CHARLES CHAPLIN
STARS: CHARLES CHAPLIN, JACK
OAKIE, PAULETTE GODDARD
RUNNING TIME: 2 HOURS, 7 MINUTES

A Jewish barber wakes up from a period of amnesia to find himself in a "Tomanian" ghetto under the tyrannical rule of a dictator, Hynkel—who looks just like him. The barber is beaten by brownshirts, but escapes.

He is then mistaken for Hynkel, and then meets his fellow dictator, Napaloni, of "Bacteria," played with Academy Award–nominated verve by Jack Oakie. Neither will let the other's head be higher, so each raises his barber-like chair.

Hynkel is surrounded by Garbitsch, chief of propaganda, and party chief Herring.

Eventually, the Jewish barber without a name escapes with a Jewish laundress named Hannah, leaving Tomania to the mercies of Hynkel and his henchmen.

Note: This was the last Charlie Chaplin film in which he wore the "little tramp" mustache.

United Artists (Courtesy of The Kobal Collection)

How did America handle the run-up to the seminal event of the twentieth century, World War II? What role did movies play in that? The answer to either question is not unanimous.

Memorial Day 1999: An anonymous caller to a radio talk show in New York addressed the day's subject, which was newsman Tom Brokaw's book *The Greatest Generation.*

"Look, I don't want to be a fly in the soup here, but what makes these thirties and forties people so great? They worked their way out of a couple of messes, but it was messes they got themselves into. All right, maybe they had some help with the Depression, what with Wall Street and bankers and then the government sitting on their hands till Roosevelt. But if this 'greatest generation' didn't want something for nothing, the Crash wouldn't have happened in the first place.

"And look at World War II. Everybody knew about the Nazis, they weren't hiding under a bench. They'd been raising hell since the 1920s, and Hitler wrote a book saying what he was going to do if he ever got power, for God's sake. Then he's the big cheese and he starts doing it all, one-two-three, the laws about Jews and then beating them up on the street; then gobbling up little pieces of property along the border, and breaking treaties and building up the military.

"Roosevelt and some insiders knew what was going on, but

any time they tried to do something, 'the greatest generation' would scream bloody murder." The caller's voice got thin, an imitation of a whine. "Hey, hands off. We're antiwar. Forget the rest of the world. No army. No navy. No air force. If they'd started to get ready ten years earlier, even five, you think Hitler would have had a walkover like he did in those first years?

"Sure, those Americans back then got the job done when it was nearly too late. But if they'd taken care of business *before* all these Jews and gypsies and others got exterminated, then they *would* have been the 'greatest generation.' "

The caller identified himself as a thirty-six-year-old student, changing careers from construction worker to accountant. His comment set off a storm of calls for the remainder of the program. World War II era listeners angry at a lot he said, and a surprising number of younger callers were sympathetic to his point of view.

Generation gaps are nothing new, but these all seemed extraordinarily important and troubling as they played themselves out on the radio for the next hour.

The exchanges proved again how difficult it is to slip into someone else's skin. Those who were not yet alive can't be expected to understand the deep fear and anger generated by a threat that could literally destroy the economic system upon which one's homeland was based—and a total war one could actually lose.

By the same token, the Depression and World War II veterans couldn't understand their children's and grandchildren's puzzlement at their fierce pride of survival and their death-grip on the verities that sustained them.

The baby boomers grew up in an atmosphere precisely upside-down from their parents. They lived in an era of unbroken prosperity, but during which those verities progressively weakened. Only twice in the long twilight of the Cold War did Americans born after the Second World War get a glimpse of the mortal national peril that was the daily portion of the generation that preceded them: first when the Cuban Missile confrontation took us to the edge of the abyss for a few days in October of 1962, and then when inflation was dangerously out of control for a few months in the late 1970s.

The limited wars of post-1945 didn't forge a bond between old soldiers and young. It did the opposite. These were wars in which the U.S. could lose a great deal, but never its nationhood. The stakes didn't approach those of World War II, but the young man who risked everything in Korea and Vietnam was just as dead as the one on Omaha Beach when his number came up. That fact alone bred cynicism among the post-World War II generations. During the "police action" or the "limited war," life back home went on pretty much as usual. Unlike the early 1940s when every aspect of national activity was dedicated and subordinated to the war effort, these "presidential" conflicts seemed to be supported by the general population precisely because they caused so little disruption in the nation's pursuit of commerce and pleasure.

So old and young soldiered on, using the same words but meaning different things. The rift deepened and widened. Which brings us to the charge that Depression-era Americans were blind and deaf to the onset of the Second World War.

It's true.

The drumbeat of 1920s and 1930s antiwar sentiment in the popular culture conditioned Americans to react with a reflexive negativity to even the mention of the possibility of armed intervention elsewhere in the world.

That is not to say that the antiwar theme was by any means the dominant theme of movies or pop music or radio broadcasts of the 1930s. It just wasn't that important. The top spot went to escapism, pure and simple. Singing, dancing, comedy, romance, historical dramas. Anything to take us away from the dreary present for a few hours. The Depression itself, the central fact of daily life in the 1930s, was largely ignored, too.

Six-year-old Shirley Temple assured us "We're Out of the Red" in 1934, but Bing Crosby's 1932 hit "Brother, Can You Spare a Dime" was considerably closer to reality. Both were rare mainstream pop culture connections with the economic disaster gripping the nation.

If movies could largely ignore the ever-present Depression, we shouldn't be surprised that the looming world conflagration didn't even make Hollywood's radar screen.

Still, not everyone in Tinseltown was deaf to what Winston Churchill was to call "The Gathering Storm."

The brooding, self-absorbed giant of cinema, Charlie Chaplin, was restless. January 1937 found him back on center stage. Five years after *City Lights*—stubborn rebuttal to the need of the spoken word in film—Charlie had triumphed again. His masterful *Modern Times* was one of the major hits of 1936 and, again, Chaplin had disdained sound, leaving his immortal Little Tramp as speechless as he had been twenty years earlier.

Only an artist of Chaplin's towering reputation could have pulled it off. A decade had passed since *The Jazz Singer*, when Al Jolson's spoken aside "You ain't heard nothin' yet" changed movies forever—all movies, apparently, except those of Charlie Chaplin.

That January morning, Chaplin had received a telephone call from Flint, Michigan. The General Motors Fisher Body Plant Number One in Flint had been the focus of the nation's news since December 30. That was when workers would begin what was to be called a "sit-down strike."

It was in many ways the most important confrontation between labor and management in the twentieth century. Others were more violent, but none had the long-lasting impact of Flint.

Even in the middle of the Depression, auto-making was the nation's number one industry, and General Motors owned 43 percent of the American passenger car market. In 1936, GM sales were $1.5 billion, on which they reported pretax profits of nearly $300 million. These astounding numbers were ascribed to the management skills of GM president Alfred P. Sloan Jr., who was not about to slice off any of those profits to benefit an upstart union called the UAW.

Long negotiations ended during Christmas week of 1936. Anticipating a strike, Sloan ordered stamping equipment out of the factory to be sent to other plants which had no union. UAW organizers looked at the crowd of workers in front of Fisher One and said, "Well, what do you want to do?"

A man shouted, "Shut her down! Shut the goddamn plant!" Others picked it up and it became a chant.

So they walked back in the factory door and shut her down. It was to remain closed for forty-four days, and in the end the UAW would win a titanic struggle. None of that was clear in these early January days, however. Lower courts issued injunctions and levied fines against the union. They were ignored. Even the Supreme Court of the United States, in one of its less remembered and least memorable decisions, ruled that sit-down strikes were unconstitutional. None of that mattered. Court ruling and management intransigence would be swept away by events.

The caller told Charlie Chaplin that on the previous evening, a friend had brought a projector and showed *Modern Times* to the strikers inside the plant. They had laughed and cheered, stamping their feet and whistling. The Little Tramp, coming to grips with increasingly faceless technology, was their hero.

Charlie was gratified, but already preoccupied with something else. Despite his long flirtation with socialism, Charlie Chaplin was one of the most conspicuous capitalists of his generation. And despite the love lavished by millions on his Little Tramp character, Chaplin himself chose near isolation rather than personal interaction with his fans.

Even those counted as close friends were never sure which was the real Charlie: the underdog flickering on the screen, feeling every blow, sharing every indignity of the common experience and fighting back with unconquerable optimism; or the cool, cultured, silver-haired plutocrat in the gated estate under the endless sun?

Perhaps the answer was always in his work. Charlie Chaplin clearly mistrusted authority and power. He knew what the misuse of both had done to his own early life.

So it was no surprise that his unfailing instinct led his gaze to fall upon Adolph Hitler. As early as 1931 he had wondered aloud to friends if Hitler did not know that his Little Tramp character had made Hitler's signature mustache ridiculous? Didn't Hitler ever go to the movies, Chaplin asked?

If Hitler did, he apparently had no sense of the absurd, nor, for that matter, a sense of humor. Slowly, Chaplin began to understand that the mustache would be the tool of his counterattack. It appeared there was never any question that Chaplin would take Hitler on. From the moment the Austrian ascended to Germany's ultimate halls of power, Charlie Chaplin recognized mortal danger to everything be believed. A man who could call himself the Führer with a straight face—and get people to listen to him—was a threat.

It is a curious fact of Charlie Chaplin's career that in his final fifty productive years he made only fifteen movies. Much of this glacial pace, to be sure, can be traced to self-indulgence. His ego was legendary and he demanded that he dictate every aspect of every frame of his films.

Dictate: Odd, that word. Perhaps Chaplin understood Hitler better than we knew.

In 1937, however, the amount of time required to get *The*

Great Dictator on film cannot be laid at Chaplin's door alone. In the mid 1930s, Germany, Austria, and Italy were still among the most lucrative markets in the world for Hollywood films. It was not just reluctance to get caught in the crossfire of competing ideologies that kept studio moguls out of the democracy vs. fascism debate. It was commerce.

And it was more than that. For example, Warner Bros. executives—alone among the big studios—could clearly see the direction that world affairs were taking and, by fits and starts, began producing films with a "preparedness" theme. Often the results were little more than flag-waving "B" pictures extolling the U.S. military—a military, incidentally, that was largely illusory. But in a memorable effort, the studio decided to take sides on the main issue of the day.

It was late in the game, to be sure. The humiliation of the Allies by Hitler at Munich was, it appears, the final straw for Warner Bros. They undertook to make a film out of a series of articles, "Storm over America," profiling the activities of Nazi spies who were actually tried and convicted of espionage in the U.S. in 1937, and their clear association with many Bund groups, still powerful in some regions of America.

Confessions of a Nazi Spy, released in 1939 and starring Edward G. Robinson, George Sanders, and Paul Lukas, got a storm of protests from the groups Warner Bros. expected, and one they did not. It is reported that the U.S. State Department informally requested that some aspects of the film and its promotion be cooled down because its tone might hinder "sensitive negotiations."

There was more. Germany, of course, banned the film, but so did seventeen other foreign counties, all afraid to offend Hitler. That cut materially into the film's revenue, and *Confessions* was only a moderate success. A few distributors on the East Coast had been told that Bundists and other Nazi sympathizers might start riots in first-run cities, so squads of detectives were hired to patrol the theaters, just in case. But there were no reported major incidents.

In the meantime, Charles Chaplin was working furiously on his screenplay. In the earliest stages, he decided two things: His Little Tramp would speak for the first time and be seen for the last time.

There was no lack of friends and associates to tell him he was making a serious mistake and should abandon the project. A small but influential minority of Americans in public life believed that Hitler's Nazi Party was the wave of Europe's future and was, in any case, unstoppable. Charles Lindbergh and Joseph Kennedy, among others, believed accommodation would be more difficult if the arts community was hostile to the new order. Charlie Chaplin forged ahead.

After the fall of France in June 1940, Chaplin was asked by a Scripps-Howard reporter if he would now drop the project. "Of course not," said Charlie. "In fact, I would like very much to offer my film for an audience of one. Herr Hitler."

He knew what others did not. Anyone he could make ridiculous, he could make vulnerable. Hitler had given Chaplin the priceless gift of the mustache. No one on earth knew better how to use it.

Many believe the funniest scene in the film is a sort of ballet in which Hynkel the dictator dances with a globe, which he obviously covets.

To make sure no one misses any part of the Nazi menace, Chaplin plays a double role. In addition to Hynkel, he is a nameless Jewish barber.

At the end of the film, Chaplin's character does an extended monologue extolling peace and world brotherhood. In spite of misgivings by some in the audience at hearing the Little Tramp speak—nothing could compete with their own imaginings of what the little fellow sounded like—the film and its closing sermon were well received at the time.

In the years since, critics have not been kind to those closing remarks, many saying it ruins the impact of the film. Perhaps they are right, but in fairness, most of the critics were not around at that culminating moment with Europe prostrate, Hitler triumphant, and England standing alone.

Franklin Roosevelt contacted Chaplin and asked him to recite the closing speech at his birthday party in the White House in January of 1941. It was Charlie's first visit to the nation's capital since a Liberty Bond rally in 1917.

Of course, *The Great Dictator* was banned in all the predictable countries, but it did excellent business in the U.S.A. The music was particularly praised even though, for once, it was not the work of Mr. Chaplin. Meredith Willson, already a music director of major radio programs and something of a comic character himself, wrote the score. It would be nearly twenty years before his masterpiece, *The Music Man*, would enchant audiences around the world.

The year 1940 saw several more movies dealing forthrightly with the situation in Europe, all reflecting, of course, the events of 1939: Hitler's shocking nonaggression pact with Stalin and the U.S.S.R., which led many in this country who had believed the Soviet Union to be an altruistic state to rethink their assumptions; the almost immediate invasion of Poland, in which Russia participated from the East; the declarations of war by the Allies; the obliteration of Poland; the long "phony war" in the West while Hitler redeployed his armies. All were hammer blows to our complacency.

And all were background to *The Great Dictator; The Mortal Storm*, with Frank Morgan, dealing with persecution of the Jews; and *Foreign Correspondent* with Joel McCrea, directed by Alfred Hitchcock, in which the McCrea character ends the film by saying "The lights are going out in Europe. Ring yourselves with steel!" *Arise My Love*, with Claudette Colbert and Ray Milland, begins in the closing moments of the Spanish Civil

War and ends with the sinking of the *Athenia* by U-boats in the Atlantic. All of them were hard-hitting, heart-stirring films.

The Academy Awards presentation for 1940 films took place on February 27, 1941. The United States was at peace and would remain so for another nine months; Britain had surprised everyone by surviving the Blitz; Hitler had failed to mount an invasion of the British Isles; Japan was growing more bellicose in the Pacific. An international sea change was under way.

President Roosevelt had been invited to attend the Oscar ceremonies at the Biltmore Hotel in Los Angeles. He told organizers that the international situation required him to remain in Washington, but he agreed to make a live radio address to the assembled celebrities. It was carried coast-to-coast.

Roosevelt praised Hollywood for promoting "the American way of life." He also asked the public for support for his Lend-Lease plan to help Great Britain. Prominent Hollywood Republicans, including most of the studio chiefs, were not pleased to be giving Roosevelt the free air time, but the third-term argument was over. Voters had decided FDR would go where no president had gone before, so the entrenched wealthy of Los Angeles shrugged and swallowed their comments.

Films that had what can only be called anti-Nazi themes did well with Academy voters, accumulating a total of twenty-six nominations.

The Great Dictator received four of them, including Charlie Chaplin as Best Actor. The smart money, however, said the "New York incident" would keep him from getting the award. A scandal had erupted after Charlie and Katharine Hepburn won the New York Film Critics' Award as Best Actor and Actress. A critic for the *Daily Mirror*, Lee Mortimer, who would later dog the life and career of Frank Sinatra, charged that the voting was rigged.

According to Mortimer, *New York Times* critic Bosley Crowther had personally petitioned other writers to vote for

Chaplin because he would be a top attraction for their own awards radio show. Even before the brouhaha was resolved, Chaplin had refused to accept the award, but most insiders assumed the damage was done. For whatever reason, *The Great Dictator* was shut out.

The most dramatic moment of that long ago February evening came when the award was announced for Best Original Story. It went to Benjamin Glazer and John S. Toldy for *Arise, My Love.* Mr. Glazer walked to the podium and electrified the audience by telling them there was *"no* John S. Toldy." It was, he said, a pseudonym for a writer still living in Germany. If his identity was known, said Glazer, Toldy would end his days in a concentration camp.

The maker of *The Great Dictator* may have left the Academy Awards empty-handed, but he could be content in the knowledge that his was the most successful of the 1940 war-related films.

And, I submit, the most important. Like the other films, it focused the attention of the only nation that could, in time, defeat Hitler. The vastness of Russia might stop him, but it would take the resources, the manpower, the know-how, and the cocky optimism of America to put the Nazis out of business.

Chaplin had the key. The mustache.

He made Hitler a figure of derision. After Chaplin, others did the same thing in movies and in pop music, notably Ernst Lubitsch with the brilliant Jack Benny and Carol Lombard film *To Be or Not To Be,* and Spike Jones with his novelty tune "Der Führer's Face."

Now, looking back on the unbridgeable chasm filled with the Holocaust dead, these films and songs seem feather-light, insubstantial, almost silly.

But they weren't.

Their purpose and result were deadly serious. Leni Riefenstahl's film *Triumph of the Will* had made Hitler seem invulnerable, inevitable. *The Great Dictator* made him seem a laughing stock, a ridiculous figure on the world stage.

Hitler understood the difference very well. According to one postwar report, the Führer had prepared a list of enemies to be eliminated immediately upon his ultimate victory over the Allies. Following the release of *The Great Dictator*, Charlie Chaplin's name was placed in the top ten.

The young caller to the radio station was right. Americans *were* slow to recognize the true threat to humanity that Hitler represented.

However, I would argue that they were encountering a force that was beyond any rational expectation or previous experience. There is, thank God, only one Hitler every thousand years.

But for every Hitler, there is also a Charlie Chaplin.

And that changes everything.

13

STAGECOACH

1939

DIRECTOR: JOHN FORD
STARS: CLAIRE TREVOR, JOHN WAYNE,
THOMAS MITCHELL
RUNNING TIME: 1 HOUR, 37 MINUTES

Seven people board the stage to Lordsburg, and we get to know them all: the good-hearted prostitute, the gambler with the Confederate past, the whiskey salesman with a soft heart, the alcoholic doctor, the elegant, distant, very pregnant cavalry officer's wife, and the banker with a guilty secret.

They cannot know it, but because of an Indian uprising, they are riding into the most dangerous hundred square miles on the continent. Their first encounter is with an escaped convict, the Ringo Kid, who joins them.

In the ensuing running battle, the Ringo Kid and Dallas, the prostitute, fall in love, Lucy has her baby, Hatfield, the gambler, is killed, Mr. Peacock, the whiskey drummer, is wounded, Dr. Boone is redeemed, and banker Gatewood is apprehended.

In Lordsburg, the Kid has his revenge on those who killed his family, and the sheriff helps him and Dallas to escape to a new life.

Note: The original negatives of *Stagecoach* were either lost or destroyed. John Wayne had one positive print that had never been through a projector gate. In 1970, he permitted it to be used to produce a new negative, and that is the film seen today at film festivals.

United Artists (Courtesy of The Kobal Collection)

Here's a piece of information that will win you a bar bet even among film buffs. Who directed Shirley Temple in her 1937 feature *Wee Willie Winkie?*

John Ford, that's who.

Yep, the same irascible, profane John Ford who was either the reigning genius of American film, or the most overrated moviemaker of the twentieth century, depending on which critic you read.

What cannot be denied is that Ford sat in the director's chair for at least a dozen of this country's most memorable motion pictures, including one that would change forever America's own original storytelling form: the Western.

Stagecoach is the 1939 movie that invented the clichés which, for forty years, would be copied, refined, parodied, reviled, and worshiped by many filmmakers, including Ford himself. It was clearly the most dynamic leap forward in the genre since the introduction of sound a dozen years earlier. Its impact is felt even yet on the rare occasions the Western métier is used to tell stories these days.

Yet everything about the making of *Stagecoach* was improbable, especially the director, Sean Aloysius O'Fearna. The youngest of thirteen children, he was born in 1895 in Cape Elizabeth, Maine, the son of Irish immigrants. He spent most of his childhood in Portland, Maine, where his father ran a saloon.

It is no stretch of the truth to say that Sean got into the movies because of his trail-blazing brother Francis, who had taken the stage name Ford and had become a successful actor/writer/director in early Hollywood films. After high school, Sean O'Fearna, who became Sean O'Feeney in school, went to join his brother in California and again changed his name to Jack Ford, to match his brother's new surname. He did a bit of everything in those days. He was even one of the hooded riders of the Klan in D. W. Griffith's *The Birth of a Nation.*

These early Hollywood careers are difficult to sort out with any hope of accuracy, but it appears that Ford began directing as early as 1917. Most of the first silents for which he was responsible were Westerns, many with cowboy star Harry Carey.

In 1923, after he had moved from Universal to Fox Studio, he changed his name again to the more dignified *John* Ford. He also made one of the best films of the 1920s, the epic Western *The Iron Horse* in 1924.

After this, however, the veteran of the Hollywood Westerns widened his horizons. Over the next fifteen years, both in silents and soundies, he would explore antiwar themes, comedy, drama, biography, and social stories virtually to the exclusion of Westerns. By 1939, in fact, most filmgoers had forgotten his early emphasis on "horse operas," as they were derisively called, because his success for more than a decade had relied on stories such as his dark view of the internal Irish agony *The Informer,* for which he received an Academy Award in 1935. His credits in the 1930s included *Arrowsmith, The Lost Patrol, Steamboat 'Round the Bend, Mary of Scotland, The Hurricane, Young Mr. Lincoln, The Plough and the Stars*—and *Wee Willie Winkie.* Not a Western among them.

Then, in 1937, he read a short story by Ernest Haycox that appeared in *Collier's* magazine. It was called "The Stage to Lordsburg," and John Ford thought he saw a major movie. He called Haycox and bought the movie rights for $4,000. If he was to return to Westerns, this was the stage he would ride.

In truth, the tiniest seed of an idea began to germinate in John Ford's mind as he read the story. It was an idea that raised many eyebrows in Hollywood when he announced it.

His star would be John Wayne. John Wayne?

John Wayne had been out of the major movie mainstream since the spectacular failure of *The Big Trail* in 1930. In a way, Ford had been an important part of that film, too. He had talked to its director, Raoul Walsh, about a young property man, not long out of college. "Why don't you take a look at that kid," said Ford, "the one with the funny walk, like he owned the world."

Walsh took Ford's advice, then launched a project that would put both his and Wayne's careers in eclipse for the better part of a decade.

The Big Trail was a huge project, the first major outdoor spectacle of the age of sound, and it had a stupendous budget of more than $2 million. There were hundreds of extras, a full cast of principal players, and wide vistas of the Southwest, still largely unpopulated.

To take advantage of the breathtaking scenery, a new process was developed, utilizing innovative cameras and lenses, plus a revolutionary 70mm film. The system was called Grandeur. When audiences saw it many stood and cheered. Unfortunately, only a handful of theaters could actually show it to advantage on large screens. For most, the extra effort was wasted.

Fifth billing went to Tyrone Power Sr., father of the future superstar who was still in high school in Cincinnati, Ohio, at that time. It would be the elder Power's last performance. He died as the production was completed.

The star of this major film was to be the neophyte actor, twenty-three-year old John Wayne, who had appeared only in bits, often billed as "Duke Morrison." Walsh rolled the dice in a breathtaking gamble on an unknown.

It was too much. The young man could not fill the frame in competition with the great West, even at 6'4". His dialogue was, of course, stilted and amateurish, and there was too much of it. The "walk" was everything Ford had said, but it was not enough.

The Big Trail flopped and the young actor, top billed, was swept away in the failure. For many years, *The Big Trail* was spoken of in the movie community the way a later generation would speak of 1980's *Heaven's Gate.*

"Duke" Wayne was relegated to the offerings of the studios on "Poverty Row." Wayne later estimated he did as many as eighty Western features and serials from 1931 to 1939. That was in addition to such fare as *Men Are Like That, Control Airport,* and *The Deceiver,* in which his role was that of a *dead body!* There was even an attempt to make him a singing cowboy, another failure. In other words, John Wayne was mired deep in the "B" world, the permanent second-class citizenship of 1930s and 1940s Hollywood.

Even in the year of his breakout in the benchmark *Stagecoach,* 1939, his other roles were in *Three Texas Steers, The Night Riders, Wyoming Outlaw,* and *Frontier Horizon.*

But all that was about to change. John Ford had kept in touch with Wayne during Duke's long period in limbo. The story as it was later told goes like this: Ford had his friend, the top screenwriter Dudley Nichols, write a screenplay of "The Stage to Lordsburg." Then he invited John Wayne out to his yacht to read the script. He asked Wayne, "Who do you think should play the outlaw?" John Wayne started to list some of the major stars of the day. Ford stopped him. "Goddamnit, Duke, I bought this thing for you. Can't *you* play it?"

So buried in the bottom layer of the Hollywood pecking order was John Wayne that his own name near the top of the cast list in an "A" picture never occurred to him.

It didn't occur to Hollywood executives, either. It was true that Westerns coined money for the studios, but no one took them seriously. They were strictly matinee fare, not "prestige" films.

In fact, since the Academy of Motion Picture Arts and Sciences had begun making awards for Best Picture, ninety-two features had been nominated through 1938. Only *four* of those had what could be called Western themes, and of those just *one*, *Cimarron* in 1930–31, received the top honor. Some would balk at calling Edna Ferber's sprawling story a traditional Western, but it certainly qualified under a general category of "films that take place in the West."

Still, it is clear that the movie establishment had limited respect for the ten-gallon hat no matter how revered the director bringing them the project. Studio after studio turned Ford down flat. His insistence on John Wayne in a key role did nothing to help his case.

Eventually, he showed up at the door of Walter Wanger, who, at this stage of his career, was an independent producer. A very interesting, three-dimensional character, Wanger had served as an army intelligence officer in World War I and was on President Wilson's staff at the Paris peace talks. After leaving the service, he became a producer for Paramount and other studios, before setting up shop on his own.

Wanger was a great admirer of Ford, but had the same reservations about "A" Westerns and, even more, about John Wayne, as the other producers. He said he wouldn't risk his money unless Ford replaced Wayne with Gary Cooper.

Ford refused to budge. It would be Wayne or no one. However, they did reach a compromise of sorts. Wanger would put up $250,000, just a bit more than half of what Ford was asking, and Ford would give top billing to Claire Trevor, a far better-known name than John Wayne in 1939.

John Ford would make two more decisions that would prove to be crucial to the film's final result.

First, as pointed out earlier, he turned screenwriting chores over to Dudley Nichols. That was not surprising, because the two had already collaborated on ten films by then, including *The Informer*, which had earned both men Academy Awards.

Still, Nichols had never undertaken a Western. Dudley Nichols was probably the best-known native of Wapakoneta, Ohio, before a space-traveler named Neil Armstrong took "one small step for a man, one giant leap for mankind" in July of 1969. Nichols had been a very successful reporter, notably for the *New York World*, before permanently relocating to California in 1929 and casting his lot with the new "sound" movies. It was a good decision.

The critics who associate Mr. Nichols's work only with John Ford, however, don't do the writer justice. It was he who provided the screenplay for Howard Hawks's famous romp with Katharine Hepburn and Cary Grant in 1938, *Bringing Up Baby*. He incurred the wrath of Ernest Hemingway by daring to paraphrase the master in *For Whom the Bell Tolls* in 1943. He collaborated with some of the best directors of his era, including Jean Renoir, Leo McCarey, Fritz Lang, Réné Clair, Delmer Daves, Anthony Mann, and George Cukor. It was his screenplay with which young director Elia Kazan made a timid, but earnest, foray into the topic of race relations with *Pinky* in 1949.

Nichols had also directed three films, all of which were well thought of by most of his contemporaries: *Government Girl*, a social comedy made during World War II; and two vehicles for Rosalind Russell, the biopic *Sister Kenny*, about a controversial Australian nurse and her early treatment for polio, and Eugene O'Neill's *Mourning Becomes Electra*.

Not a bale of hay or a six-gun among them, but Nichols was a superb writer and "The Stage to Lordsburg" was a story of nine disparate individuals, no matter what the locale. The danger imposed on them by the rigors of the Old West was only the catalyst for character studies. Nichols seemed immediately at ease.

The second important decision Ford made was the location itself. Monument Valley became an unbilled costar in *Stagecoach*. Ford would go back again and again after 1939, but this was the first time a full feature film had been made there.

Hugging the Utah-Arizona border, Monument Valley was— and is—one of the most isolated, desolate, and spectacularly beautiful pieces of real estate on the planet.

Situated, for the most part, in the Navajo Nation, Monument Valley is not really close to anything. A town called Mexican Hat clings to cliffs over the San Juan River and a few crossroads settlements are scattered here and there. You can drive past a Monument Valley High School and shop in a Monument Valley Tourist Center. Guides can drive you to one astounding vista after another, many of them familiar because of John Ford's films. But all intrusions by man seem less depredations than irritants, temporary blemishes that will disappear in a wink of time, leaving everything as it was.

The Navajo guide will tell you that Native Americans have long held that ground to be sacred. Moviegoers will not be surprised. *Stagecoach*, *Fort Apache*, *She Wore a Yellow Ribbon*, *The Searchers*, and a handful of other films have long told them that John Ford thought so, too.

Monument Valley is high desert, about a mile up. A traveler does not happen upon it by chance. One must search it out. The formations that give the valley its name are beyond description, which, it must be supposed, is the reason Ford never referred to them verbally in his films. The eloquence was in the visual image. In no way symbolic of the West—they are unique to this relatively small, circumscribed place—they have come to evoke the Western myth created, in substantial measure, by John Ford himself.

Ford packed up his crew, nearly ninety strong, and headed for Monument Valley to make his movie. He liked location shooting, far from studio interference. He was master of his company and took full advantage of his power.

The cast Ford assembled, while short on stars, included some of the best character actors to be found anywhere. John Carradine as a dangerous but aristocratic Southern renegade gambler. Thomas Mitchell as an alcoholic doctor. Andy Devine as the comic driver. Stage actress Louise Platt as the pregnant, arrogant wife of a cavalry officer. Donald Meek, the most fortuitously named actor in Hollywood, as the mild-mannered whiskey drummer. George Bancroft as the implacable lawman. Berton Churchill as the venal, hypocritical banker.

And, at the top of the heap, Claire Trevor as the prostitute who desperately wanted to have a normal family life, and John Wayne, a good man turned bad by his passion for vengeance.

From the beginning, Ford believed he was creating something special. What he was seeing through cinematographer Bert Glennon's lens is exactly what he imagined on his personal trips to the location. One of the establishing shots was actually filmed from nearly forty miles away. No one had seen anything quite like it before. The tight character studies contrasted with the broad visual strokes and Ford's unerring instinct for action sequences brought the form to life in a way that was new.

In 1957, on the set of a film called *Handle with Care*, I had a series of conversations with Thomas Mitchell, the principal supporting actor of that movie, which starred Dean Jones and Joanie O'Brien. The subject of the extended conversations over a ten-day period was Mitchell's most productive year, in terms of quality of roles and performances: 1939. In addition to his Academy Award–winning role in *Stagecoach*, Mitchell portrayed Scarlett O'Hara's father in *Gone With the Wind*, was a major supporting actor in *Mr. Smith Goes to Washington*, had an important role in *The Hunchback of Notre Dame*, and, arguably, had the key role in Howard Hawks's interesting *Only Angels Have Wings*. That, obviously, would be an entire career for some successful actors. For Thomas Mitchell, it was one year.

The conversation turned to *Stagecoach:* "I was out there the whole time," Mitchell said, "three months, I think. The place was so beautiful it was terrifying, especially at night. We were staying in awful accommodations. No cooling during the day, no heating at night. My cabin, sort of a tourist court, didn't have indoor plumbing.

"The assistant director put up a shower with a few stalls. That was about it.

"Ford was a son of a bitch on location. He chewed up actors and spit them out. Duke Wayne would take anything from him because, you know, Ford invented him.

"Things would start off pleasantly enough with a few drinks, a few laughs, then Ford would zero in on someone for the cruelest kinds of jokes and hazing. That's when you really found out how he thought you were doing in the film. As he got drunker, he got meaner toward one actor or another.

"Usually he just ignored the women. I don't ever remember seeing him give Claire [Trevor] a direction. Or the slim girl [Louise Platt] or the Mexican [Elvira Rios]. Perhaps I missed it.

"He came after me in the barroom scene at the end of the film. I wasn't strong enough, he said. Who would believe a limp-wristed Irishman would stand up to Luke [Tom Tyler]? he said. He got pretty abusive and the evening was fairly unpleasant.

"Some have said that was a technique he used to get the performance he wanted out of an actor, that he didn't know how to communicate verbally what he wanted. So he did it emotionally. I don't know if I believe that or not. He was articulate enough when he wanted to be, damned articulate as a matter of fact. I just think he was a mean drunk.

"Anyway, the result was that I gave a performance with a bit more backbone, and, when I saw the finished product at the preview, he was right in the context of the total film.

"I wish the bastard had another way of communicating with his actors. But that was one of the three or four best pieces of work I was ever associated with, so I suppose I would crawl over those goddamned rocks again to work with him."

Louise Platt, the "slim girl," nearly forty years later confirmed many of Mr. Mitchell's observations and conclusions. It was late summer 1995. The voice on the phone was still genteel, each sentence complete, each memory clear. She was now Louise Platt Gould, living on Long Island.

"I was under contract to Walter Wanger and it was he who assigned me to *Stagecoach*. I'm afraid I got off on the wrong foot with Mr. Ford. He and the others constantly played practical jokes on the set. I guess I took them too seriously and was about to leave the company when someone explained that it was all a joke.

"I was twenty-four. My mother had been something of a Southern belle and my father was in the military, so when I learned my character was from Virginia and was taking the stagecoach to meet her husband who was in the cavalry, I had a great deal to draw from.

"It was my experience that Southern women were very strong, but never hard. I wove that into my characterization and worked on a very light Southern accent.

"In my first scene I could see Mr. Ford was not pleased. He took me aside and told me my character had to be 'hard.' 'Hard as a rock,' he told me. 'She wants only one thing: to get through. To get to her husband.' That was the only direction he gave me throughout the entire filming.

"Mr. Ford understood the medium. Remember the scene just after my baby was born? He spent a long time—a very long time—getting the light to glint in Claire's eyes for her close-up. She only said three words, 'It's a girl.' From those three words and that close-up, you knew everything about Claire's character. Whatever life had done to her, she would be a wonderful mother.

"It was brilliant acting and brilliant direction.

"Ford understood the theme of a story on film. He knew what each individual actor needed to do to develop that theme.

"When the film was completed, we all went to a preview. I saw that my character's role in the story was unresolved.

"I went home and called Mr. Ford. 'You told me all Lucy wanted was to get through to her husband,' I said, 'But in the film you never see her get through.'

" 'Who do you think you are?' he said and hung up.

"Five minutes later his assistant called and said, 'I understand we're shooting a new ending for you tomorrow. Who do you want to be in it?' I said, 'Claire Trevor should be there because of her association with the baby.' We shot it the next day and that's the scene you see in the movie.

"Was *Stagecoach* the best piece of work I was ever associated with? Probably. But I'm much prouder of my daughters, Abigail and Lucy."

Not a surprising conclusion from a woman who, at twenty-four, could take on the formidable John Ford—and win. Then go on to name her youngest daughter Lucy, Louise's character name in *Stagecoach*.

The New York critics were impressed. They named John Ford the Best Director for *Stagecoach* and, individually, gave the film uniformly glowing reviews.

Establishment Hollywood was cautious. Still, even they knew something was in the air. In the film capital's most productive year, this Western received seven nominations. In the face of the hurricane called *Gone With the Wind, Stagecoach* could not repeat its New York triumph. Two Oscars were all it could manage, one for Thomas Mitchell for Best Supporting Actor and one for the musical score that incorporated more than a dozen folk tunes and was the corporate work of Richard Hageman, W. Franke Harling, Louis Gruenberg, Leo Shuken, and John Leipold. If this film put Westerns into a new category, it did that and more for John Ford. There came to be a cult of believers and they included some famous names, indeed.

When the boy genius Orson Welles stormed into Hollywood two years later to make *Citizen Kane*, he was asked how he would prepare for his first venture into movies. "By studying the masters," he replied. "By which I mean, of course, John Ford, John Ford, and John Ford."

On the other hand, perhaps his most vocal detractor is British critic David Thomson. What others call "visual poetry" he refers to as "claptrap." He says of Ford, "No one has done so much to invalidate the Western as a form." Mr. Thomson's opinion is so isolated and so virulent it might qualify as prejudice.

Moreover, it doesn't matter. John Ford is firmly ensconced in the pantheon of great film directors, and *Stagecoach* is the vehicle that took him there.

Many will say that Ford's later Westerns and those of Howard Hawks, Anthony Mann, and others were better, more mature, darker, truer visions of the West. Certainly Hawks's *Red River* and Ford's own *The Searchers* would qualify. Any number of anti-Westerns, such as Clint Eastwood's *Unforgiven*, draw the contrapuntal inference from Ford's earlier, towering, mythical vision of a time that never was, except in John Ford's unparalleled gift for storytelling and moviemaking.

If the child is father to the man, John Ford's celluloid child, born in 1939, is father to all the serious Westerns that followed, and follow still.

Stagecoach lifted the movie Western of the sound era from the Saturday matinee "oatburner" to an essential and original form of American expression. Along the way, it invented a view of western history that prevailed for a generation and changed moviemaking for even longer.

14

BOYS TOWN

1938

DIRECTOR: NORMAN TAUROG
STARS: SPENCER TRACY, MICKEY
ROONEY, HENRY HULL
RUNNING TIME: 1 HOUR, 36 MINUTES

Father Flanagan believes there is no such thing as a bad boy and spends his life attempting to prove it. He battles indifference, the legal system, and often the boys themselves, to build a sanctuary outside Omaha, which he calls Boys Town.

The boys have their own government, make their own rules, dish out their own punishment. One boy, Whitey Marsh, is as much as anyone can handle. His brother is in prison for murder and Whitey himself is a poolroom shark and sometime hoodlum. Father Flanagan takes him to Boys Town. Three times he runs away, the third time because he hears his brother has escaped. He joins him, but Father Flanagan rescues Whitey and helps capture the gang in the act of robbery.

Whitey and Father Flanagan go home to Boys Town.

Note: MGM Studio head Louis B. Mayer, known privately for his deep reservations regarding the Catholic Church, later called this his favorite film of his tenure at MGM.

The story deals with a real man and a real place.

The events are largely fictional.

MGM (Courtesy of The Kobal Collection)

I n the year 2002, American Catholics—and particularly the Catholic clergy—found themselves in a place they had not been for half a century and more. They were under the hot light of controversy and scandal. Admitted incidents of sexual abuse of children by priests and long-term cover-ups by Catholic hierarchy rocked parishes from coast to coast.

It was a painful time, particularly for the oldest Catholics, who recalled an even more difficult time. They remembered all too well when Catholics—laity as well as clergy—were charged, indicted, and convicted in the hearts of many fellow Americans, not for real breaches of the law, but for imagined offenses born in the heated cauldron of prejudice.

From the beginning, Catholicism had been a hard sell in mainstream America. In a land that revered the God-fearing individual, Catholics stressed God-fearing religious conformity. In a country proud of its uniqueness and convinced of its superiority, Catholics bonded with coreligionists around the world. In a nation where family-building was synonymous with nation-building, Catholics required celibacy of their clergy. In a land settled by plain-dressed believers who prayed in spartan places of worship, Catholic priests dressed in silk and raised golden chalices in soaring cathedrals. In a nation needing respect for disparate creeds, Catholics claimed infallibility in matters of faith. The differences gave birth to often-scurrilous myths that had the half-life of atomic waste.

As a result, well into the twentieth century, Catholics were among the most conspicuous victims of bigotry in all the land.

This story will deal with how all that ended, and what role the movies had in it.

Before we get to screenplays, we'll begin with a real man in a real place and time.

The year after the movies found their voice, Alfred E. Smith of New York was buried in a humiliating defeat in his bid to be president of the United States.

Governor Smith would not have won the election, even under normal circumstances. He was a Democrat and it was not a year for Democrats. The nation's economy appeared to be booming and successive Republican administrations were getting the credit for it. But in 1928, the element that turned defeat into a rout was a dark streak that had run through the American experience from the earliest days of the European settlement of the continent.

Al Smith was a Roman Catholic.

For many early colonists, "Rome" smacked of many things they had come to these shores to escape. Even when Catholics became a substantial part of the population of the New World, the fear—and the prejudices spawned by the fear—did not diminish. Rome was an issue in political campaigns through the nineteenth century. Men and women of good will addressed the problem, with some success, as the twentieth century dawned.

Movies were, in their silent days, largely circumspect on the subject of Roman Catholics. Priests were, for the most part, portrayed sympathetically, when they were portrayed at all. They were by no means central figures in any major film projects.

The Smith candidacy threw down the gauntlet once and for all. Did Catholics belong at the highest levels of American life, or not? When the dust settled in the fall of 1928, the nation had its answer.

Absolutely not.

It had been brutal.

"Every rumor and innuendo that had been bandied about for a hundred years was dredged up again," said Dr. John Kenneth White, professor of politics at Catholic University, who wrote among other books *The Fractured Electorate,* dealing with the 1928 election: "The Ku Klux Klan, very powerful at the time, even spread the word that if Smith were elected, the pope would so control this country that a secret tunnel was already planned between Rome and Washington. In some quarters, they were believed," Dr. White told me in an extensive interview.

"Catholic churches and convents were physically attacked, even in the northern states. There were terrible speeches, filled with fantastic charges.

"Of course, Republican candidate Herbert Hoover made a very civilized statement, saying, 'We will not make religion an issue in this election.' Smith himself wrote a major article explaining his position on separation of church and state, making many of the same points John F. Kennedy would make thirty years later, often in the same words. Prohibition remained a major issue and what few remember today is that prohibition was less concerned with the consumption of alcohol than with immigrants. Many prohibition supporters thought of immigrants as dirty, lazy drinkers of wine, beer, and hard liquor, with loose morals and criminal tendencies. 'Prohibition' was often used as an euphemism for 'anti-immigrant' and because so many immigrants were Catholic, anti-Catholicism.

"When the issue was 'wet' or 'dry,' voters knew exactly what was meant when Al Smith was called 'wringing wet.'

"Of course, so did first-generation Americans. Though Smith was a pariah in the South and Midwest, his appearance in Boston drew a crowd larger than even the pope's much later visit of 1978. When he appeared in big Eastern cities his audiences were larger than Charles Lindbergh's, the hero of the previous year's epic flight across the Atlantic," said Dr. White.

Nothing made any difference. It was no contest. The Solid South, which had voted unanimously Democrat since the days of Reconstruction, was shattered. Seven states—Virginia, North Carolina, Tennessee, Kentucky, Florida, Oklahoma, and Texas— voted for Herbert Hoover.

Hollywood stood firmly on the sidelines through all of this. Politics, though very important off-screen, as movie titans culti- vated whichever elected officials were in power, was an on- screen no-no. The seismic struggle against superstition and prej- udice represented by the 1928 election might have happened on the dark side of the moon as far as the film industry was con- cerned. No films even hinted at that melancholy period in American life. That didn't mean, however, that the industry took no notice. Quite the opposite. Hollywood knew the impor- tance of tolerance better than most.

The men who ran America's dream factories were well- suited to the job specifically because they were for the most part Eastern European Jews. In their homelands, dreams had been thwarted by intolerance, a bigotry often sponsored and codified by governments. They knew firsthand that tolerance was no mere exercise in limp-wristed liberalism. It was life and sinew and blood to any free society that claimed to offer opportunity for everyone.

In subtle ways, the evil of prejudice began to be hinted at, nibbled upon in the hundreds of stories that poured out of the studios. Nothing groundbreaking. Tiny steps. The prejudice of the big-city dweller against the country bumpkin, for instance. That had importance, because 1928 had been the first election in which more Americans lived in big cities than in towns and farms.

The prejudice against expanding roles for women was approached in a less obvious—but possibly more effective—way. Women were simply cast in a dizzying array of film roles as the 1930s progressed.

The color line was less amenable to solution and, unfortunately, was poorly served by movies for decades. In fact, films hurt more than they helped by burning stereotypes into the national consciousness. What *The Birth of a Nation* had begun, *Gone With the Wind* could continue, albeit with more benign images. Among successful films in wide release, perhaps only 1934's sentimental *Imitation of Life* gave black actors a three-dimensional role in the broader culture. Interestingly, when remade in 1959, five years after, *Brown vs. the Board of Education* had found segregation in public schools to be unconstitutional, the subject matter was still relevant, still controversial, and still handled with a soap opera sentimentality. Progress by African Americans, measured in Hollywood terms, had been very slow, indeed.

Roman Catholics were another matter. For one thing, most were white, easily assimilable in the majority population. They were also growing more numerous by the year, the largest minority in the nation by 1928. Finally, most of them lived in big cities, where movies were a primary form of entertainment. To Hollywood, they were customers.

Here was a prejudice Hollywood could take on with some real hope of making a difference. Perhaps Catholics could be demystified, brought into the mainstream.

Not that Hollywood moguls were pro-Catholic. That would have been asking too much. Jews had suffered for centuries in nations that were predominately Catholic. The Hollywood attitude would become not so much pro-Catholic as anti-bigotry. As years passed, they went to work. What was needed were good stories and they were not lacking.

In 1936, the blockbuster *San Francisco* had as its principal sympathetic character a clergyman, standing up for morality in corrupt San Francisco just before the earthquake of 1906, and played by Spencer Tracy. The clergyman could have been any denomination. He was a Catholic priest.

When Jimmy Cagney's big-city character in 1938's *Angels with Dirty Faces* went wrong, his lifelong pal tried to set him straight. Again, a cleric, the Pat O'Brien role, could have been Methodist or Episcopalian. He was a Catholic priest.

Then, most important of all, came a hugely successful movie in which the central character was a Catholic priest and the central activity was a Catholic project. *Boys Town*, in 1938, was a breakthrough. Americans saw a tough priest slapping the cigarette out of a delinquent Mickey Rooney's mouth, yet a man who could say, "There is no such thing as a bad boy." Moviegoers saw a stern keeper of moral standards who would also rush to help a kid—struggling under his human burden— who was saying the immortal "He ain't heavy, Father, he's my brother."

The writers of the true, original story of Father Flanagan were Eleanor Griffin and Dore Schary, who shared an Academy Award for their effort.

Mr. Schary, who had worked on stage as an actor and, in fact, had supported Spencer Tracy on Broadway in *The Last Mile* in 1930, had a lifelong interest in what he felt to be important civil rights causes. Anti-Catholicism in the 1930s would certainly qualify as one of them. He was eventually a playwright and studio head of MGM, where he produced as many "message" pictures as "entertainment" vehicles, and he served as national chairman of the Anti-Defamation League. He also strongly opposed the Hollywood blacklist during the McCarthy era.

Director Norman Taurog, himself a former child actor, again proved he was superlative working with children. He had received an Oscar for directing his nephew, Jackie Cooper, in *Skippy* in 1931, and would get a nomination for *Boys Town*.

Spencer Tracy went personally to Boys Town, near Omaha, to get a feel for the place and the man he was to portray.

When he received his Oscar for the role in February 1939, Tracy responded graciously by spending all of his acceptance speech talking about Flanagan. "If you have seen him through me, then I thank you."

All was not moonlight and roses, however. An overzealous publicity man announced that Tracy was donating his Oscar to Father Flanagan. Problem was he had forgotten to ask Tracy. "I earned the damned thing," Tracy said. "I want it." The Academy hastily struck another inscription, Tracy kept his statuette, and Boys Town got one too. It read, "To Father Flanagan, whose great humanity, kindly simplicity, and inspiring courage were strong enough to shine through my humble effort. Spencer Tracy."

The next entry into what might be called the reinvention of American Catholics at the movie box office came in 1940. No Oscar nominations this time, but *Knute Rockne, All-American* was a runaway hit at the box office and has been quoted in the intervening years as often as any film of its moment.

This time, sports is leavened into the mix, with remarkable effect. Notre Dame, the little Catholic college in Indiana, was put on the map by football. And we see a new element. The hero, Knute Rockne, the famous football coach, is a non-Catholic. The message is clear. Non-Catholics and Catholics can work together, without intruding on one another's beliefs, and produce an All-American success.

As Professor White notes, "This message was so important, President Franklin Roosevelt called the studio to congratulate all the filmmakers involved, and to permit his approval to be made public."

Under the relatively benign hand of the studio heads, a band of filmmakers had come together whom later historians would call "The Irish Mafia." There was never a formal organization and the numbers changed from time to time. They were actors, writers, and directors, most at least nominally Catholic, nearly all male. The names included Jimmy Cagney, Spencer Tracy, Pat O'Brien, George Brent, Leo McCarey, Frank McHugh, Bing Crosby, and a dozen or so others.

None rose to the rank of studio head, but together they comprised a powerful pod of influence in the film business. Leo McCarey, one of Hollywood's funniest men, was also one of its most gifted directors. He was what some future critics would call an "auteur," a person who stamped a picture with his vision and had his hand in virtually every aspect of the process. McCarey was a writer, producer, and director. Some experts eventually found his approach to be overly sentimental and his later work handicapped by politics, but no one challenged his talent, then or now.

Mr. McCarey's work was by no means burdened with any religious sensibilities in the beginning. He wrote most of Laurel and Hardy's silent shorts, was the director for, perhaps, the Marx Brothers' best film, *Duck Soup*; he directed major hits for W. C. Fields, Harold Lloyd, and Mae West; directed and produced the brilliant *Ruggles of Red Gap*, then received the Academy Award as Best Director for the sex comedy *The Awful Truth*, starring Irene Dunne and Cary Grant, in 1937. It was McCarey who gave us *Love Affair* in 1939, which became *An Affair to Remember* in 1957. His own favorite was an overlooked gem, an indictment of pre-Social Security family life, brilliantly made—with no stars—and called, in gentle irony, *Make Way for Tomorrow*.

It was Leo McCarey who, with the inspired casting of Bing Crosby and Barry Fitzgerald, would bring the Hollywood effort to mainstream American Catholics to its peak with 1944's *Going My Way* and the sequel in 1945, Father O'Malley's second adventure, *The Bells of St. Mary's*. Both of these were among the biggest pictures of the year and both in Academy Award contention. *Going My Way* garnered Mr. McCarey two Oscars, one as director and one as screenwriter. Both Bing Crosby and Barry Fitzgerald also walked away with statuettes for that film. Crosby, McCarey, and Ingrid Bergman were nominated for *Bells* too, though none was a winner.

All through the years of World War II, Hollywood films

struck the theme of religious tolerance. Every combat movie had the requisite Protestant, Catholic, and Jew. Only atheists, Hindus, Buddhists, and Muslims got short shrift.

Once again, Catholics were in the forefront with the harrowing true story of the five Sullivan brothers of Waterloo, Iowa, all of whom were killed when the cruiser *Juneau* was sunk in the waters off Guadalcanal. *The Fighting Sullivans* was briefly withdrawn from release because some in the military thought it would be a blow to morale on the homefront, but cooler heads prevailed and it was allowed to run its course.

The message, again, was clear. If an Irish Catholic family could make the greatest sacrifice of any during the entire war, it would take a mean-spirited bigot indeed to hold their religion against them. After the war, Roman Catholics continued to be portrayed in a positive light by Hollywood. Even the all-American icon John Wayne got into the act with *Trouble Along the Way* (1953), in which his character is a tainted football coach who comes to the rescue of a small Catholic college, and then the splendid *Quiet Man,* the entirety of which is played out in conspicuously Catholic Ireland.

It should be said that in every one of the films noted here, Catholic priests are rarely shown—whether by coincidence or design—in their chasubles on the altar, holding the chalice, consecrating the host, or murmuring Latin. Instead, we see them in their black suits, or in sweatshirts with baseball caps. If there were Americans still put off by "papist" rituals and mysteries, Hollywood would not rub their noses in it.

Actually, Professor White believes that World War II and the Cold War that followed had the greatest impact moving Catholics into the center of American life:

"After World War II, when the time of the Iron Curtain and the Cold War began, American Catholics were positioned to be seen as more patriotic than most. The Catholic hierarchy had, after all, been staunchly anti-Communist for years and that now dovetailed with our national purpose. Entreaties to heaven against 'godless Communism' had a good sound to Americans whose sons were being shot at in Korea," he told me.

"There was a poll in 1950 asking which groups in this country were more inclined to be soft on Communism. Topping the list were actors, reflecting the headlines generated by the House Un-American Activities Committee. Second were Puerto Ricans and that was because of the recent attempt on the life of President Truman. Next in order were New Yorkers and union members. But at the very bottom of the list, in a virtual tie, were Catholics and Protestants.

"Most amazing of all, popes began to appear on the lists of 'most admired persons' in this country, something that would have been unthinkable in the days of Al Smith. The stage was being set for John F. Kennedy."

Yes, it was. Being set by demographics, by World War II, by the Cold War . . . and, I submit, by the movies beginning with the blockbuster tale of Father Flanagan..

None knew it better than the young Democrat from Massachusetts himself. The day after his narrow and historic victory in November 1960, there was a private dinner for his closest associates, perhaps a dozen or so. Among them was his key aide, Kenneth O'Donnell. In 1968, five years after President Kennedy's assassination, Mr. O'Donnell told me during an interview, "As I recall, the first toast was to the American people. The next one, also offered by the president-elect, with a chuckle went something like this: Here's to the good Father Chuck O'Malley, wherever he is. We owe him a lot."

They all laughed. But they also drank the toast.

The real Father Flanagan of Boys Town had begun a process that, by the time the fictional Father O'Malley arrived, was little less than a revolution.

They had changed prejudice into acceptance.

15

TRIUMPH OF THE WILL

1935

DIRECTOR: LENI RIEFENSTAHL
STAR: ADOLF HITLER
RUNNING TIME: 1 HOUR, 50 MINUTES

This documentary has no real story line, nor was one intended.

The director opens by taking us through the clouds, an endless time, it seems. Just when the anticipation is about to turn to irritation, we see the aircraft circling, landing.

Hitler emerges, a man of the new technology. He has energy and command. He is stern. Everyone runs to do his bidding. He is whisked from the stage to be saved for a climactic moment.

Speaker after speaker, rank after rank, battalion after battalion pours into Nuremberg. It is a tide, an irresistible tide of youth full of ardor for their Führer. At night the gathering becomes mystical, torch lit. At last, Hitler speaks. Tens of thousands respond hysterically. No one is responding to other leaders that way in 1935, the film tells us. None can stand before him, is the message.

Note: In 1952, Leni Riefenstahl was cleared by a West German denazification court of Nazi collaboration, though she admitted witnessing Polish civilians massacred while she was accompanying the German army in 1940.

(Courtesy of The Kobal Collection)

There are some who insist that one film, *Triumph of the Will*, facilitated a world war with immeasurable consequences that will be felt for the next thousand years. Are they right?

The filmmaker was a woman of genius. Her name is Leni Riefenstahl. Did she know she was the drum major of a parade that was leading the world back and down into a barbarism more profound than any epoch of the Middle Ages? That remains open to question.

Forty years after *Triumph of the Will* a brand-new film festival in the Colorado Rockies decided to pay tribute to her body of work, including a number of "Mountain Films." As it turned out, forty years was not nearly long enough. Wounds were too deep, too raw.

"We tried to isolate her from the protests, no question about it." Jim Bedford paused for a moment. "We understood how sensitive it all was. There were only a few protesters, maybe a dozen, maybe less, but some were holocaust survivors. Naturally, they were going to get national press.

"Still, we had invited Miss Riefenstahl to Telluride to present a tribute to her artistry as a filmmaker. We knew it would be controversial. We did what we could to protect her." Mr. Bedford is now operations manager of the Telluride Film Festival in Colorado. In 1974, when Leni Riefenstahl arrived for her tribute, he managed a theater in town.

"Have you seen *The Blue Light?* We had a wonderful 35mm print of it. Beautiful. And then, all those mountain films produced by Arnold Fanck in which she acted. We are a very small mountain community, Mr. Clooney. Used to be a mining town. We could relate to all that. And *Olympia* is surely one of the great documentaries ever made. Of course, it has propaganda overtones, it would have to have them because of the time and place where it was done. But have you seen it? The 1936 [Berlin] Olympics are celebrated, frame after frame as athletes competing only against their own limitations, an Olympic ideal.

"As for that other film, everyone knows about that. We showed it only at a minor venue. Should an artist be judged only on one project out of a body of work, even if that piece has profound negative political implications?"

Mr. Bedford's question may be logical in the abstract, but the answer does not matter. Despite what anyone says or does, Leni Riefenstahl will be judged by one film and one only for all time: *Triumph of the Will.*

There is little argument that this was the best propaganda film ever made, and the most effective. Some even claim its air of inevitability contributed materially to concessions made by Hitler's neighbors, including France and England, in the years leading to the humiliation of Munich in 1938, and in another year, to world war.

Even now if you watch the film alone in a darkened room it has the power to clutch at your heart and make the roof of your mouth dry.

Imagine, then, what it must have been like on the evening of March 28, 1935, at the glittering UFA Theatre on the Kurfürstendamm in Berlin. The locals called it Gloria Palast, the city's major cinema palace.

Hitler walked across the lobby and was met by Leni Riefenstahl. He took her hand in both of his, smiled, and walked with her to their seats. The theater was, of course, packed.

What they saw on the big screen was more than *Triumph of the Will*. It was a triumph of filmmaking and it justified Hitler's uncharacteristic decision to give a young woman an important, meaningful task within the Nazi party.

Leni Riefenstahl was just thirty-two when the man Germans called the Führer told her to film the 1934 party rally in Nuremberg. That was it. No detailed instructions. More important, no limitations.

What Ms. Riefenstahl proceeded to do was to break many old filmmaking rules and invent several new ones.

Where did this burst of creativity come from? True, there was talent from the beginning, but it was a talent in the performing arts, and contemporary critics found it decidedly limited.

She was a dancer who wavered from style to style. She was also the daughter of a successful businessman who wanted no part of a daughter who was a professional dancer, so he suggested she leave home. Helene Bertha Amelie Riefenstahl was glad to do so, because she was just as mortified to be living under the roof of a man who sold toilets as he was to have a daughter on stage.

Leni was attractive and athletic, so she soon gravitated toward the film industry, especially outdoor film. Gossip columnists in Berlin, particularly Bella Fromm, kept close tabs on her affairs. One could read hints that Leni lived with a film star, a dance instructor, a tennis star, a painter, and two ski champions in a row.

But it was her association with producer Arnold Fanck that led her eventually to her life's work. Fanck made what were called "Mountain Pictures" and Leni appeared in six of them. Mr. Fanck and Miss Riefenstahl also reportedly entertained at a comfortable duplex, welcoming guests such as boxer Max Schmeling and famous director Ernst Lubitsch.

By now, it was the process of filmmaking that was beginning

to intrigue Riefenstahl. There was a deepening sense that she had a knack for it. Her questions became more technical and more penetrating.

When she was thirty years old, she took a screenplay by Béla Balázs, rewrote it, produced it, directed it, edited it, starred in it, and distributed it with her own company. The name was *The Blue Light*, and it was a salute to mountain mysticism. It was that film and that quality that caught the attention of Telluride's Film Festival organizers forty years later.

The film also caught the attention of an important contemporary audience in 1932. Adolf Hitler had admired Ms. Riefenstahl's work as an actress in the earlier "Mountain Pictures" and was now reported to be very impressed by her skill in making *The Blue Light*. They met for dinner on a number of occasions. Details of these meetings are in dispute, but the result is not. Leni Riefenstahl got the commission to film the Nuremberg Party Rally in 1934.

There is no evidence that Miss Riefenstahl ever joined the Nazi party. But there is every evidence that she was drawn to the sheer power, the emerging new mythology, the pageantry with its subtext of violence. She was clearly convinced she had caught the wave of the future.

And she had the talent to convince others of the same thing.

No part of the process would be easy. The Nazi regulars were notoriously antifeminist and Leni Riefenstahl was the only woman with a position of power in the entire Party establishment. Albert Speer, Hitler's architect and eventual munitions chief, remembered it clearly: "[Nazis] could hardly brook this self-assured woman, the more so since she knew how to bend this man's word to her purposes. Intrigues were launched and slanderous stories carried to [Rudolph] Hess in order to have her ousted. But after the first Party Rally Film *Triumph of the Will*, which convinced even doubters of her skill as a director, these attacks ceased."

No one had ever seen anything quite like it before in film-making. Riefenstahl was tireless in staging each element so it would work as a piece of cinema.

American journalist William L. Shirer was there and told of the rally in his *Berlin Diary.* "I'm beginning to comprehend, I think, some of the reasons for Hitler's astounding success. Borrowing a chapter from the Roman Church he is restoring pageantry and color and mysticism to the drab lives of twentieth-century Germans . . . [At the opening meeting] the band stopped playing. The was a hush over the 30,000 people packed in the hall. Then the band struck up the 'Badenweiler March,' a very catchy tune . . . Hitler appeared in the back of the hall and, followed by his aides, Göring, Goebbels, Hess, Himmler, and the others, he strode slowly down the long center aisle while 30,000 hands were raised in salute."

For seven days the show went on. Hitler introduced his Arbeitsdienst, the Labor Service Corps, which turned out to be 50,000 paramilitary young men, the first 1,000 of them shirtless, all carrying shining spades or other tools. When the first of them reached the massive crowd in the city, they broke into a perfect goose step, driving the onlookers into a frenzy of excitement.

Leni Riefenstahl was everywhere. She and her chief photographer, Sepp Allgeier, had as many as thirty film cameras rolling at one time, using a dozen different lenses. There wasn't an angle she missed and nothing was left to chance.

Speer had designed an ingenious light technique for the after-dark rallies. While 200,000 of the faithful gathered, he enclosed the perimeter with columns of light, klieg lamps at regular intervals, pointing straight up, piercing the night.

There was much more. Some 300,000 watched and cheered a sham battle staged by the Reichswehr. At night another 15,000 snaked through the narrow winding streets of the old town, holding torches.

Hitler himself told correspondents what the purpose of these huge party rallies was and why they were so carefully staged.

"The half-million men who attended all week," he said, "will go back to their towns and villages and preach the new gospel with new fanaticism."

Leni Riefenstahl's mission, on the other hand, was vastly more important. If she could catch that mood, that unanimity of purpose, that religious fervor, and that mystical bond between the people and the Austrian who told them what they wanted—needed—to hear, her audience would not be confined to the borders of Germany.

It would pour like liquid fire over every great capital that Hitler coveted. Vienna, Paris, Warsaw, Moscow, Rome, London. Yes, and New York and Washington, too.

Leni Riefenstahl worked like a woman possessed. During the shooting she was everywhere. Then, for six months she was buried in the editing process.

Many in Berlin believed Riefenstahl was merely a facade, a "beautiful advertisement for the Nazi Party." Social columnist Bella Fromm wrote in a diary published only after she escaped Germany in 1938, "The Nuremberg Rally official film will carry her name. Many say the real work will be done by competent collaborators."

Apparently Miss Fromm had not seen *The Blue Light*, which Miss Riefenstahl made with almost no collaborators at all.

The furious pace of reducing hundreds of thousands of feet of film to a two-hour documentary wore on Riefenstahl. Already slim, she became painfully thin. Music director Herbert Windt later said he was driven hard, often eighteen hours a day, particularly in the final weeks.

The party rally had ended on September 10, 1934. The finished film premiered March 28, 1935, at Gloria Palast.

If Hitler had overruled the advice of those closest to him in choosing a young woman for one of the most important tasks of his new regime, he could now point to the decision as one more proof of his invincibility. The film was more than he expected, more than anyone could have imagined.

Historian Robert Payne wrote, "To see the film made by Leni Riefenstahl at Nuremberg is to be aware of the intensity of emotions aroused by Hitler's presence, the ferocity of the acclamation, the blindness of the obedience. Her cameras celebrated the strange magician who could reduce hundreds of thousands of people to mindless robots."

And mindless robots could wreak a lot of havoc if turned loose on a peaceful Europe. That message was sent as a stalking horse through countries large and small by Leni Riefenstahl's *Triumph of the Will*. Those who shared Hitler's worldview were encouraged. Those who remembered too well the blood bath only twenty years earlier were frightened. Those who believed Hitler would be mollified if he were given back the bits and pieces that had been taken from Germany at Versailles carried the banner of appeasement to the bargaining table.

And those who had thought Hitler was a domestic German phenomenon were awakened to looming mortal danger.

All in all, *Triumph of the Will* was a cold shower for Europe's body politic, ruthlessly chilling each nation's deepest fears and vulnerabilities. Those in public life who would face down Hitler looked around for support and found only former friends shivering on the periphery.

Miss Riefenstahl's Blitzfilm foreshadowed Hitler's Blitzkrieg by half a decade.

How did it all seem to the filmmaker after the last cannon was fired, the last bomb burst, the last atrocity committed? In the mid 1960s, thirty years after her grim masterpiece and twenty years after the end of the war, Leni Riefenstahl responded to an interviewer:

"A commission was proposed to me, I accepted. I agreed to make a film others could have made. It is for making this film that I spent years in camps and prisons.

"Have you seen the film? It contains no reconstructed scenes. It's all true. There is no editorial commentary. It is history, it is cinema verité. It is a documentary, not propaganda."

Her protests are understandable, but disingenuous. Of course, there are reconstructed scenes. The camera tracks past individual party members, each shouting a word or phrase as he gets in frame. The move must have taken hours to set up. Moreover, many scenes did not require reconstruction; they had been constructed in the first place with a view to the film she was making. Everything was subordinated to her requirements. The 1934 party rally was, in fact, a made-for-film event.

Miss Riefenstahl had no compunction about reconstruction, at any rate. Albert Speer again: "I recall that the footage taken during one of the solemn sessions of the 1935 party congress was spoiled. At Leni Riefenstahl's suggestion, Hitler gave orders for the shots to be re-filmed in the studio. I was called in to do a backdrop simulating a section of the congress hall, as well as a realistic model of the platform and lectern. I had spotlights aimed at it . . . [Rudolph] Hess arrived and was asked to pose for the first shot. Exactly as he had done it before an audience of 30,000 . . . he solemnly raised his hand. With his special brand of ardor, he turned precisely to the spot Hitler would have been sitting, snapped to attention and cried, 'My Leader, I welcome you in the name of the Party Congress . . . The Führer speaks!'

"He did it all so convincingly that from that point on I was no longer sure of the genuiness of his feelings . . . I was rather disturbed; Frau [sic] Riefenstahl, on the other hand, thought the acted scenes better than the original."

Leni Riefenstahl was at the heart and center of the Nazi juggernaut in the 1930s. She gave it the face it would present to the world, even after war was declared. None have done it better. It is pointless for her to disavow her central role.

Or the stamp it leaves permanently on her work.

Bill Pence is a founder and director of the Telluride Film

Festival. "It was our first festival, you know. We're locked in this box canyon up in the Rockies, and Leni Riefenstahl's work—her *other* work—matched our situation. It seemed a natural fit.

"Yes, we realized there might be controversy, but we didn't have any idea how big it would be. The press coverage was international. Suddenly everybody knew how to pronounce and spell Telluride.

"Because of her past associations, she had not received much recognition for her artistry over the years, so she was truly thrilled and very gracious. I should make the point that the protestors were gracious, too. They had picket signs, but they never attempted to stop people from attending the events.

"Our other two tributes that year went to Francis Ford Coppola and Gloria Swanson. They did not question Miss Riefenstahl's appearance. In fact, Mr. Coppola seemed to spend a great deal of time with her talking about film techniques.

"I must say, I did have the impression that Miss Swanson was a bit miffed at all the attention Miss Riefenstahl was getting.

"We would have preferred not to get the type of attention that was being shown us, but, I suppose it did give us a kind of jump-start. From our first festival, everyone knew who we were."

Miss Riefenstahl has published books of photography. In 1993, there was a documentary about her life. She has written an autobiography.

All interesting, but, like her other films, many of which are brilliant, all are side shows.

Her masterwork, *Triumph of the Will*, has Leni Riefenstahl marching in lockstep with Adolf Hitler down the halls of history, for as long as anyone remembers the twentieth century—a tragic fraction of which was changed forever with the help of *Triumph of the Will*.

16

LOVE ME TONIGHT

1932

DIRECTOR: ROUBEN MAMOULIAN
STARS: MAURICE CHEVALIER,
JEANETTE MACDONALD
RUNNING TIME: 1 HOUR, 44 MINUTES

A Parisian tailor is charmed by a titled but impoverished playboy into extending him credit. When the tailor learns the man in his best suit is a notorious deadbeat, he decides to confront him at his château.

On the way he meets beautiful Princess Jeanette, a widow, and there is instant attraction. The tailor learns that the château belongs to the princess; the playboy is a poor relation with no money. The deadbeat begs the tailor to keep his indebtedness a secret, then introduces him to the household as a baron. Many adventures ensue and the tailor/baron and the princess fall in love.

At last his identity is revealed in a hilarious sequence. He leaves on a train, but is pursued by the princess on her horse. Clinch. Fadeout. Happy ending.

Note: Watch for the grocer played by George Hayes, not yet known as "Gabby," the toothless sidekick of Roy Rogers and Hopalong Cassidy.

Paramount (Courtesy of The Kobal Collection)

The greatest movie musical ever made received no Academy Award nomination, is on no list of "100 Best of the Century," and made little money then or since. Moreover, it is highly probable you have never seen it. Nor are you likely to. It is not available on video.

The movie is *Love Me Tonight*, made in 1932.

Why is it the most sparkling, witty, vibrant, and innovative musical ever made? Because of its director, Rouben Mamoulian. Why is it now completely forgotten? Because of its director, Rouben Mamoulian.

Before we get deeper into this story, let me ask *you* what musical you think is the greatest ever made? Many will say *Singin' in the Rain*. The man who produced *Singin' in the Rain*—and even wrote the lyrics for the song in 1929—is quoted as saying *Love Me Tonight* was the greatest influence on his career in musicals. His name was Arthur Freed and he was responsible for many of the great MGM songfests of the 1940s and 1950s, from *For Me and My Gal* to *Cabin in the Sky, On the Town, Annie Get Your Gun, An American in Paris*, and *Gigi*.

If a little more evidence is in order, note that Vincente Minnelli, director of *Meet Me in St. Louis* and *The Band Wagon*, and Charles Walters, director of *Easter Parade* and *High Society*, said exactly the same thing.

How can a film that had such a powerful influence that it

actually *changed* the way musicals were made for decades to come now be so obscure to all except film buffs and historians?

Rouben Mamoulian was an upstart. Some called him a dilettante in film. He had a rage for details. Studio executives always found him a stiff, unbending pain in the neck. His name is now nearly as forgotten as his masterpiece. On the other hand, even casual film fans have heard the name Ernst Lubitsch. Even if they have not seen many—or any—of his films, the "Lubitsch touch" is famous . . . and justifiably so. One of the early European pioneers, Lubitsch stormed through the silent era, and by 1919 had already established himself as both artistically and commercially successful.

From 1924 on, Lubitsch moved effortlessly from Europe to the United States and back again, directing blockbusters, moving in the highest reaches of international society.

The arrival of sound, terrifying to many, was welcomed by Lubitsch. His films continued to have a unity, a style, a "Lubitsch touch." Moreover, they coined money, which made Lubitsch dear to the hearts of Hollywood executives. The films were also always good. In fact, they were assumed to be the best. Assumptions die hard, both among contemporaries and among historians. For a moment in 1932, the careers of Lubitsch and Mamoulian would intersect in a way that would have fateful consequences for both of them.

Lubitsch is important to the Mamoulian story: Among his great successes in the years 1929 through 1931 were the musicals *The Love Parade*, the debut of Jeanette MacDonald and the first time she and Maurice Chevalier appeared together; *Monte Carlo*, with Miss MacDonald teamed with Jack Buchanan; and *The Smiling Lieutenant*, with Maurice Chevalier this time in pursuit of Claudette Colbert. All the films were innovative, taking the Hollywood musical out of its "backstage" rut and beginning to integrate the songs into the story. Each was a classic Lubitsch "Ruritanian" operetta, taking us to a fictional country where the principals march through a light farce, winking at us along the way. Each was great fun.

But 1932 dawned on a fundamentally different world. To put numbers to it, the gross national product of the United States was down 23 percent from the year before. Inflation was actually *deflation* at an annual rate of minus 4.7 percent. Automobile sales were down a shocking 80 percent from 1929. Unemployment closed at a paralyzing 23.6 percent. Ominously for Hollywood, one of the few areas to prosper was the sale of radio sets, with 2.5 million additional receivers in 1932. Americans were staying home in droves, listening to new heroes premiering that year, including Jack Benny and Fred Allen.

Musicals, which had been a staple of successful movies from 1927, began to go out of fashion in 1931 and were all but dead in 1932. Ernst Lubitsch knew this and decided to cast his lot with a straight comedy and a downbeat antiwar drama that year. He was scheduled for another musical with Jeanette MacDonald and Maurice Chevalier, but all he could see was another Ruritanian operetta, so he passed.

Enter Rouben Mamoulian. We'd better take a closer look at him, because he was then and has remained something of an enigma to the Hollywood community.

Six years younger than Lubitsch, Mamoulian was an Armenian born in Russia of affluent parents. He studied criminology, lived in Paris, gravitated toward theater, studied under a student of Stanislavsky in Russia, toured England with a Russian Stanislavsky repertory company, and stayed there to study drama at the University of London.

Here is where we begin to get a hint of what Rouben Mamoulian was all about. Though by all accounts he was an able student and teacher of the naturalistic Stanislavsky style of acting that came to be known as "the Method," he totally rejected it in his mid-twenties. He later said, "What survives best is myth, poetry. Realism dies." He then set out to prove his point.

While Lubitsch was the toast of two continents, Mamoulian was working his way to the United States. For three years, 1923 to 1926, he directed operas and operettas at the Eastman Theater in Rochester, New York. His great success there led him to a teaching and directing position—at age twenty-eight—for the prestigious New York City Theater Guild. It was here that he first came to national attention with his innovative directing of the major theater success *Porgy*. This and other hits, plus a growing reputation for inventiveness, prompted a call from Hollywood. He was offered an opportunity to direct a 1929 film called *Applause,* a vehicle for torch singer Helen Morgan.

Until then, Mamoulian had had no serious connection with film. That's important to remember. Most of the giants of the medium, D. W. Griffith, Cecil B. DeMille, Josef von Sternberg, John Ford, Fritz Lang—and Ernst Lubitsch—had virtually cut their teeth on celluloid. They were the inner circle.

Mamoulian was a stage director. He would, in fact, later be associated with some of the most successful plays in American theater history. At least two of them, *Porgy and Bess* and *Oklahoma,* were clearly revolutionary.

It has been difficult—even to this day—for Hollywood to accept the possibility that an interloper from Broadway who directed no more than sixteen films could, in fact, be just as revolutionary on nitrate as he was before footlights, and deserve to stand with the titans of moviemaking, but the hard evidence leaves no doubt. If there is a small double handful of great filmmakers of the twentieth century, Rouben Mamoulian is among them.

From the moment he walked onto a soundstage, Mamoulian saw this visual medium with new eyes and heard it with new ears. Miss Morgan would not be glamorized in *Applause,* music would serve the scene, cameras would move as he wanted them to, even if ways had to be invented to do it.

His next two films, both in 1931, showed equal grasp of the

métier and caused heads to turn in Hollywood. In *City Streets*, with Gary Cooper and Sylvia Sidney, he took a routine underworld melodrama and, by unique vision and obsessive attention to detail, lifted it to the level of a superb film. But that wasn't a patch on what he did with Robert Louis Stevenson's *Dr. Jekyll and Mr. Hyde* the same year. Many critics still feel that this version, starring Fredric March and Miriam Hopkins, is the best of them all. Mamoulian's eerie atmospherics set a style that holds up even now, and March's performance won an Academy Award.

And that was it. The sum and total of Rouben Mamoulian's film experience when he was asked to direct the musical that would be *Love Me Tonight*. It was a form—the musical—that was decidedly out of favor, and it was ground that had already been ploughed successfully by the master, Lubitsch, and with the same two stars! An impossible position for a virtual neophyte director.

So Mamoulian proceeded to make the greatest movie musical of them all.

He had plenty of help. Richard Rodgers and Larry Hart wrote an original score that is as good as any ever done, including "Isn't It Romantic," "Lover," and Chevalier's signature "Mimi."

But it was the way Mamoulian wove it together that lifted this musical to the sublime. From the beginning metronome-like sounds of a wakening Paris, to the exhilarating way the theme "Isn't It Romantic" carries us from a tailor shop to a castle, to the off-screen sound effects that make a dropped flowerpot sound like an explosion in order to emphasize how shocked a lady-in-waiting was to learn a count was a tailor, everything is fresh and new and sexy and witty.

For those who have only seen Jeanette MacDonald in her stylized duets with Nelson Eddy, this saucy confection in see-through negligee will be a serendipity. And if you think of Myrna Loy only as the perfect wife, wait until you see her as the oversexed cousin of the princess. And if you think of Chevalier as only the caricature of an aging boulevardier, wait until you see his genuinely witty characterization as the tailor-cum-Count.

Mamoulian was putting his money where his mouth was: "What survives best is myth, poetry." He even introduces rhyming dialogue, but it is so well done it never seems forced.

In fact, *Love Me Tonight* is seamless. A phrase becomes a poem, the poem becomes a song, a step becomes a stroll that moves to a skip, then a dance. Just when the fantasy seems to be losing control, Charles Ruggles or Charles Butterworth comes in with a deadpan one-liner that centers us again.

It is nothing less than a stunning achievement. When it was screened in Los Angeles in 1932 Lubitsch was there. Afterward he generously told reporters that he "envied" Mamoulian's gift for moving the story and his light touch on the sexy scenes.

Lubitsch did more than that. Like all great talents, he learned from what he saw. His *Merry Widow*, two years later with the same Jeanette MacDonald, had noticeably easier flow than his earlier work.

If Mamoulian had done nothing but *Love Me Tonight*, he would be an interesting Hollywood footnote. However, in spite of heavy Broadway commitment, Mamoulian was in the director's chair for two films in 1933, guiding a pair of Hollywood's grand dames to successful roles. He was the first man besides Josef von Sternberg to direct Marlene Dietrich in an American film. The movie was *Song of Songs*, and Dietrich remained a fervent admirer of Mamoulian's talent for the rest of her life. That same year he directed Greta Garbo in *Queen Christina*, which most critics call her best film.

His body of work is worth exploring, and we will, but nearly as interesting is the list of films from which he withdrew or was dismissed. One was the excellent film noir *Laura*, which found Mamoulian at odds with studio executives from the first day. Though he did not know it, he was also squarely in the path of the bulldozing ambition of a man named Otto Preminger. The voracious talent of Preminger had focused on *Laura* even before Mamoulian was brought into the picture. The autocratic Preminger helped Darryl Zanuck decide that Mamoulian's early scenes showed him to be uncomfortable with the suspense formula. He was dismissed, Preminger brought in, and nearly every scene was reshot, with the result that a classic movie emerged in Preminger's image, with no vestige of Mamoulian remaining.

Ten years later, Paramount had in mind a small film they hoped would be a "sleeper." They had signed popular singer Rosemary Clooney, who had tested very well in her initial film work. The plan was to make *Red Garters* a star vehicle for her.

It was a completely offbeat musical spoof of the Western genre that then dominated Hollywood offerings, and the task of pulling it off was given to Rouben Mamoulian.

"His idea was that this movie would be experimental, very avant-garde," recalled Miss Clooney years later. "He had been working on the project for some time before I was brought in. My costar was to be Don Taylor, a young romantic lead of whom the studio thought highly. Singer Guy Mitchell was cast, with Pat Crowley as his love interest.

"Mr. Mamoulian was of medium height, he had good eyes behind thick glasses, his hair was dark and combed straight back in the European fashion. We worked together for more than six weeks. I liked him right away.

"It was clear from the beginning he was intense about details. Our set was not a set at all, but the suggestion of a set. There were no walls, only frames for windows, stairs leading nowhere, unsupported doors, chandeliers hanging in space. The entire thing was shot on a soundstage, with sand painted bright yellow for day shots and an enormous matching yellow cyclorama all around the walls. For night, the sand was dark blue and so were the walls. It was remarkable.

"I recall only one disagreement with him: He was checking everyone's makeup, wardrobe, and hair. He had a specific notion for the way he wanted my hair. It didn't fit me at all, little curls all over the forehead, and I suddenly realized that it was a copy of Marlene's hair in *Destry Rides Again*, the earlier Western spoof with Jimmy Stewart.

"Mr. Mamoulian wanted the story line straightforward and the comedy to flow from the situation. We were given to understand that there was some dissatisfaction in the front office with the early results, but we had no idea how serious it was.

"One morning Mr. Mamoulian came to my house. He told me that he had been dismissed from the project and he didn't want me to hear about it from someone else. He also told me Don Taylor would no longer be in the film. His demeanor was always courteous and correct.

"There was some irony in Paramount's choice to replace him. George Marshall had been the director of *Destry Rides Again.* The entire attitude of the film changed. Jack Carson was brought in to work opposite me, so it was clear comedy would be emphasized. More jokes were added.

"As it turned out, *Red Garters* was a disappointment to all of us. There had been some anticipation in the critical community and several major magazine pieces, most emphasizing the offbeat set and stark colors.

"Perhaps the clash of two visions made it impossible to produce a more coherent film, I don't know. But, the point should be made that Rouben Mamoulian only took on interesting, chancy projects. And if they weren't interesting before he took charge, they certainly were afterward."

Six years later, in 1960, there were few projects thought to be more interesting than the remake of *Cleopatra*. A talented and volatile international cast, a location far from the front office, an enormous budget, and a presold story. All of that before the love story within the love story drove everything else off the front pages of the tabloids. The man chosen to stir this heady stew was Rouben Mamoulian.

Shooting began in September 1960. The stars were Elizabeth Taylor, Peter Finch, and Steven Boyd. Five weeks and $5 million later, Miss Taylor became ill and production was shut down. When *Cleopatra* began again on New Year's Day 1961, Miss Taylor wanted the scenes with Mr. Finch rewritten. Writers, director, producer, far-away studio chief, and star were at an impasse. With what eventually proved to be only ten minutes of useable film in the can, Mamoulian (a) resigned, if you believe the producer, or (b) was fired, if you believe the star.

He wasn't alone. Finch and Boyd went with him, to be replaced by Rex Harrison and Richard Burton. The new director was Joe Mankiewicz, the brilliant writer who had directed *All About Eve* and *Letter to Three Wives* a decade earlier. And *Cleopatra* clanked on to its doom. Its staggering $40 million cost was not recouped until most of its principals had disappeared from the scene. Those ten expensive minutes would be the last the screen would see of Rouben Mamoulian.

What was his legacy? *Love Me Tonight,* the wholly unlikely masterpiece, of course. But there was more.

He was also the man invited by MGM to direct Hollywood's first full-length, three-color Technicolor film, *Becky Sharp,* in 1935. Even now, a moviegoer's jaw drops to see the subtle yet pervasive use of color that never allows the new technology to intrude on the story or the players. In its way, *Becky Sharp* is a Hollywood milestone.

Mamoulian's most beautiful use of color is 1941's *Blood and Sand,* but some find the washes almost too beautiful, distracting the viewer from the film's baseline. Nonetheless, frames of this film could be mounted on an art gallery's wall and rival Goya and El Greco.

To prove his versatility, Mamoulian was also at the helm of the witty swashbuckler *The Mark of Zorro,* starring Tyrone Power in 1940.

After some in Hollywood labeled him as "too artsy," "too

prickly," or, as one famous mogul said, "a pain in the ass," Mamoulian directed only two more films, *Summer Holiday* in 1948, and nine years later, Fred Astaire's last MGM dance turn, *Silk Stockings*. Both were received with decided reserve by critics at the time, but both now have been found admirable by most film historians. The first was a charming variation of *Ah, Wilderness* and the other a musical remake of *Ninotchka*.

Mamoulian was responsible for only sixteen movies over a period of twenty-eight years. Among them were the best film version of a horror classic, Hollywood's best musical, the first three-color Technicolor movie, Garbo's best film, a breakout movie for Marlene Dietrich, William Holden's debut, Tyrone Power's signature role, and Fred Astaire's last great musical.

At the same time, he was directing on Broadway *Porgy*, *A Farewell to Arms*, the unique American opera *Porgy and Bess*, the revolutionary American musical *Oklahoma*, and, perhaps, the darkest, most three-dimensional musical up to its time, *Carousel*.

Against this must be weighed his willingness to abandon projects when he didn't get his way and his unwillingness to hear other points of view. He could occasionally be cruel in comments about colleagues. He certainly did not fit easily into the show-business social scene on either coast. He was devoid of even the most rudimentary skills in self-promotion. But his influence burns through his films and his genius has proved, to borrow from Hemingway, to be a "moveable feast" across the decades.

History will—or will not—reassess his contributions. As for the rest of us . . .

We'll always have *Love Me Tonight*.

Watch it sometime if it shows up at a film festival or on a classic movie channel. It changed movie musicals for the next quarter century.

17

MOROCCO

1930

DIRECTOR: JOSEF VON STERNBERG
STARS: MARLENE DIETRICH, GARY COOPER, ADOLPHE MENJOU
RUNNING TIME: 1 HOUR, 30 MINUTES

A beautiful nightclub singer, Amy Jolly, arrives by ship in Morocco, already pursued by a rich, smooth villain, Le Bessier. She rejects him, and is instead attracted to an enlisted man in the Foreign Legion, Tom Brown.

Their relationship is stormy and at one point she agrees to the advances of Le Bessier because she is furious with Brown. At the engagement party she hears marching feet and runs to them, only to learn Brown is probably dead in a recent battle.

He survives and, after a few more plot twists, rejoins his unit to march off on another expedition. Jolly sees women trailing in their wake, asks about them, and is told they are camp-followers, staying as close as they can to their men. She takes off her high-heels and joins the women, determined to be with Brown.

Note: The shooting script showed the title *Amy Jolly, Woman of Marrakesh*. It was reportedly changed at the behest of Gary Cooper's agent.

Paramount (Courtesy of The Kobal Collection)

The woman seemed neither young nor old. She was striking rather than beautiful in a tuxedo, walking though the smoky saloon. She was singing about selling fruit, but the audience was pretty sure she was selling something else.

The men in the nightclub had grown quiet when she began singing. She rewarded them by giving them languorous, lingering looks as she passed them.

One of the men, who obviously knew her and was also obviously wealthy, gestured for her to come to his table. She hesitated for a moment, then deliberately strolled to another table where two couples sat. She glanced at them all, then her gaze fell on only one. A young woman. The singer touched the woman's hair lightly. It was a caress. She smiled. A shy smile. Then she leaned over slowly and kissed her on the lips.

The year was 1930 and that tux and that kiss on the big silver screen portrayed a great deal more than sexual ambivalence. It was the opening salvo in a decade of film during which actresses would have more choices, be more successful, and wield more power than at any time before and, arguably, since.

The movie was *Morocco* and the star was Marlene Dietrich. It was the first time we had seen her. The international hit *Blue Angel*, made first, was actually premiered in New York on the same day that her first "American-made" film hit the theaters.

Josef von Sternberg, the mercurial and brilliant director, had been sent by his studio to Germany the previous year to direct a fading star, Emil Jannings, in the story of a teacher doomed by obsessive sex.

It was there that von Sternberg saw Marlene Dietrich perform in a revue and obsession had its turn with him. He saw something other directors—very good directors such as Fritz Lang and William Dieterle—had not seen in the seven years Miss Dietrich had played small roles in German films. He gave her the part in *Blue Angel* and told her she should go to Hollywood with him.

Marlene promptly left her husband and five-year-old daughter in Germany and sailed with von Sternberg for the New World.

They were an odd couple in many ways, but they were embarking on what would be the five defining professional years of their lives. In spite of his name, von Sternberg was more American than Austrian. True, he was born in Vienna, but he was brought at age six to New York, where he entered elementary school in Jamaica, Queens. Relatives took him back to Vienna as a teen, but he returned as soon as he could. In fact, when America went to war, in 1917, he joined the U.S. Army. His name was then Josef Sternberg, which he sometimes shortened to "Stern." It was only after he landed in Hollywood in 1924 that a zealous publicity man added the "von" to his last name.

His reputation was growing. It was clear that he was a magician with a camera and understood dramatic lighting as few have done before or since.

He would bring every ounce of his skill to bear on what he planned to make his ultimate creation: Marlene Dietrich.

The roundness of her face disappeared, transformed by diet to slimmer lines and prominent cheekbones. Her eyebrows were shaved. One reason she wore pants in that famous nightclub scene was to disguise the bandages he had wrapped tightly around her already famous legs. He detected pockets of fat on her ankles and thighs and he intended to squeeze them out before filming later sequences where Marlene's legs would be exposed.

If Miss Dietrich doted on him—and she did—many did not. Both Emil Jannings and William Powell nearly came to blows with him. According to director Peter Bogdanovich, von Sternberg later told a student audience that Mr. Powell had it put in his contract that he never would have to work with von Sternberg again. On the *Morocco* set, he and Gary Cooper had a verbal battle that shut down shooting for a day.

Recently, the actress Janet Leigh, who was directed by him in one of his last films, *Jet Pilot*, made in 1951, said to me, "That was not a good experience. I never resorted to public profanity until I encountered Mr. von Sternberg. He ordered and drilled and screamed until I finally screamed back. I always thought he would have been happier if Duke [John Wayne] and I goose-stepped around the soundstage."

Still, in 1930, von Sternberg had fired both barrels at the film industry and hit the bull's-eye twice. *The Blue Angel* and *Morocco* were both hits. In addition, *Morocco* was nominated for five Academy Awards, including Miss Dietrich for Best Actress and Mr. von Sternberg for Best Director. It won only for Best Sound Recording and at that had to share the award with other Paramount productions. Still, studio chief Adolph Zukor was heard to say that the box-office returns earned by Dietrich "saved Paramount."

He wasn't exaggerating. Nothing occurs in a vacuum, not even the products of a dream factory, and Hollywood was in trouble, along with the rest of the nation.

The previous September 5, an economist by the name of Roger W. Babson had said "There is a crash coming quite soon and it may be a big one, 60 to 80 points on the Dow-Jones barometer." Since the Dow at that moment stood at its highest level ever, 381.17, an 80 point drop would represent 20 percent of Wall Street's wealth wiped off the big board in a single swoop, an unthinkable disaster.

Barron's weekly, a conservative economic bible, called Mr. Babson a "scaremonger" and a number of other uncomplimentary things. Less than two months later, October 28, when the market had free-fallen exactly 80 points, *Barron's* shifted ground, blaming Babson for the crash, saying his prediction had caused panic.

It is just as well that *Barron's* and the rest of the business community, including movie studios, didn't know what was coming. By mid-1932 the Dow would drop from that 1929 high of 381.17 to a stunning low of 41.22. The entire market was virtually wiped out, retaining only a little more than 10 percent of its value.

President Hoover's Secretary of the Treasury didn't see anything wrong with that. As Hoover later conceded, Andrew Mellon wanted to "liquidate labor, liquidate stocks, liquidate the farmer, liquidate real estate. Let it all go right to the bottom, then begin again. It will build character." Hoover by no means agreed with Secretary Mellon, but his view of government wouldn't allow him to do much. He sincerely believed that "nature will cure all while government intervention might ruin all."

In November 1929, the president said, "Any lack of confidence in the basic strength of business is foolish." As stocks continued to plummet and businesses close, he said in January 1930 "Business and industry have turned the corner." As stocks neared the 200 level in May, Hoover said, "We have now passed the worst."

We hadn't—neither the country, the movies, nor Mr. Hoover. Prices for wheat, corn, cotton, wool, and tobacco had dropped 40 percent in one year. Consumer spending went down a like amount. Unemployment rose by leaps and bounds, heading toward a heart-stopping 25 percent in 1932.

This was an unprecedented crisis, because the politics of the 1920s had been based on business and nothing else. President Calvin Coolidge made two famous statements that tell us all we need to know about the times. First, " The business of America is business." Those who said they found no justification for that statement in either the Declaration of Independence or the Constitution were shrugged off. Later, when Mr. Coolidge was asked by World War I allies for a moratorium on war debt payments so that England and France could, in turn, ease ruinous reparations payments from Germany, which was in financial chaos, he replied to his Secretary of State, "They hired the money, didn't they?"

If business was America's prime reason for being, and business failed, what then?

These were questions many were asking in those early chilling days of the Depression, and they were getting no answers from Washington.

In 1931, when the Academy Awards for 1930's films were announced at the Biltmore, the special guest was Hoover's vice-president, Charles Curtis. Curtis, whose mother was a Kaw Native American, had the lifelong nickname "Indian." However, he displayed no stereotypical surefootedness. On his way to the podium, he tripped over a chair and dropped half his speech. Unaware of what had happened, he continued on his way. He must have lost the part of his talk dealing with the economic crisis, because he made no reference to it at all except a rambling salute to the industry's "glorious opportunity to render a great and *steadying* influence to your fellow Americans."

The movie business needed more than platitudes. Ticket sales had plummeted. But the industry was slowly, by fits and starts, beginning to recognize a virtually untapped resource.

Women.

The Depression was a crisis of family. Just to survive, just to stave off the dreaded "breaking up housekeeping," required the full energy, talent, and ingenuity of everyone in the family. Women took on tasks that would not have been considered appropriate in the previous decade. Sometimes unofficially, often unpaid, women took their place beside men. Their voices were heard with increasing authority in the family circle. As men went far away for employment, women became heads of the family, at least pro tem.

Their entertainment of choice was the movies. Films were relatively inexpensive and gave a blessed few hours once a week to escape the grim reality outside the theater door.

Hollywood took note. It was a quiet revolution, but a real one nonetheless. Women on the screen became partners, full partners, with their male counterparts. No longer would they just be long-suffering victims or ingenues or sex kittens.

Look at the decade *Morocco* unlocked. Of the eighty-eight top ten box-office stars named by the film industry, an unprecedented forty-two of them were women. Even more significantly, the very top money-makers in eight of those ten years were female.

These women were by no means stereotyped. Leading the list two years in a row was sixty-two-year-old Marie Dressler. The "sweetheart" Janet Gaynor was in there. So was the dramatic Greta Garbo, the perfect smart-aleck partner Myrna Loy, feisty Joan Crawford, everybody's favorite little girl Shirley Temple and her nemesis Jane Withers, the diva Jeanette MacDonald, the emerging teen culture icons, Deanna Durbin and Judy Garland, the professional woman Rosalind Russell, the bombshells Jean Harlow and Mae West, the ideal wives Kay Francis and Ann Harding, the cute, sexy girl next door Paulette Goddard.

Of the great names that resonate even today whenever memorable women of film are named, virtually all rose in the 1930s. Can any other decade come close to Katharine Hepburn, Claudette Colbert, Bette Davis, Ginger Rogers, Loretta Young, Irene Dunne, Carole Lombard, Olivia de Havilland and her sister

Joan Fontaine, Jean Arthur, Madeleine Carroll, Alice Faye, Barbara Stanwyck, Hedy Lamarr, Greer Garson, Vivien Leigh, Joan Blondell, Joan Bennett, *all* the box-office winners I've already named—and Marlene Dietrich!

It is true that we could produce an equally impressive hit of male stars, but their roles on films would be familiar. Cowboys, soldiers, doctors, pilots, lawyers, gangsters.

For these women stars, the barriers dropped for the first time, and we saw them in roles rarely—if ever—available to them before. Pilots—Katharine Hepburn in slacks and Rosalind Russell ditto. Doctors, lawyers, reporters, business moguls, cold-blooded killers, writers, explorers, politicians, spies, labor activists, cab drivers, preachers.

All of this in addition to the traditional long-suffering wives, temptresses, teachers, ingenues, singers, dancers, actresses, nuns, and dumb blondes.

It was a stunning avalanche of diversity, but it did not last. The middle years of this century piled one major crisis on top of another, and the two crises were not the same.

If the Depression was a crisis of family, requiring everyone— men, women, and children—to strain every nerve to work together in order to save what they had, there loomed a World War, which was a crisis of violence and separation. In the early 1940s, nearly 13 million young men would for a time be separated from the millions of women who loved them and feared for them.

The separation bred something different. The men began to idealize the absent women. In a less attractive sense, they began to objectify them. The women became pictures, two-dimensional; in a way, untouchable.

The movies, as they always eventually do, took note of the sea changes. The female star of 1941–45 was more conventionally beautiful, but less real. The surrogates for the girl back home—our movie stars—were airbrushed pinups.

The woman who had worked shoulder to shoulder with her husband, her father, her brother, her male friends in the 1930s was set at a distance, up on a sort of pedestal. Her legs were near perfect, and her breasts and her teeth and her hair, too.

The "girl back home" may not quite be Betty Grable or Rita Hayworth or Linda Darnell or Veronica Lake or Dorothy Lamour, but that was now the goal. The diverse movie women of the 1930s would be just a fading memory.

It is not clear that we have ever fully recovered from the results of that crisis of separation, at least as far as films are concerned. With honorable exceptions, women in films, particularly young women, are still treated as set decoration. They are even yet unlikely to be cast as doctors, pilots, truck drivers, or preachers.

If young actresses today are in any way aware of the films of the 1930s, my guess is they might be curious at first and then, finally, frustrated to see and hear the great roles afforded those women who were contemporaries of their grandmothers—make that great-grandmothers. If, indeed, they wish to begin a voyage of retro discovery, they could do worse than to start with 1930's *Morocco*.

This was the film that signaled to the world that, at least for the forseeable future, Hollywood was going to take another look at the evolving society around it. Dietrich's tuxedo was a uniform for a new army that would occupy the cinema capital for a decade and change it dramatically.

An army of women.

18

THE JAZZ SINGER

1927

DIRECTOR: ALAN CROSLAND
STARS: AL JOLSON, MAY MACAVOY
RUNNING TIME: 1 HOUR, 29 MINUTES

New Yorker Jakie Rabinowitz longs to be a performer on stage, an ambition thwarted by his father, Cantor Rabinowitz, who insists Jakie follow his footsteps in the higher calling.

Embittered, and despite the efforts by his mother, Sara, to mediate, Jakie leaves home, changes his name to Jack Robin, and sings jazz in public.

On the night of his Broadway debut, he learns his father is dying. He leaves the theater to be with his family, sings for his father, then returns to the stage where they have been holding the curtain for him.

He performs to an ovation, joined in by his mother, whom we see in the audience.

Note: Six months after this "part-talkie," Warner Bros. released the first "all-talkie," *The Lights of New York*. It was a crime drama, opening an era of "gangs, gats, and gams" that would dominate the coming decade.

Warner Bros (Courtesy of The Kobal Collection)

WAIT A MINUTE! WAIT A MINUTE! YOU AIN'T HEARD NOTHIN' YET! WAIT A MINUTE, I TELL YOU, YOU AIN'T HEARD *NOTHIN'* YET!"

What a way to begin the sound era in the movies.

It was the sixth of October, 1927. There had not been this kind of buzz about a motion picture since *The Birth of a Nation* twelve years earlier.

This would either be a revolution or the biggest bust in the thirty-one-year history of the movies.

Sound. Talking pictures. There had been rumors about them for years. Futuristic ramblings, most thought, like trips to the moon.

Hadn't Thomas Edison, the great Edison himself, dabbled in sound-on-film before setting it aside as impractical? Hadn't Lee de Forrest, whom most called the "Father of Radio," actually produced some shorts with sound four years earlier, an experiment that most found decidedly unsatisfactory?

For the four Warner brothers, all their chips were in the pot. This great leap forward would work or they would be bankrupt. *The Jazz Singer* was about to premiere. Chances were that the Warners would have their answer before the evening was over.

Or at least three of them would. Sam, the second youngest, the man who, more than anyone else in the family, had pushed for this great gamble, would not see how it turned out.

Sam had not accompanied Albert, Harry, and Jack on the trip east. He had a sinus infection again and it was giving him trouble. Sam had broken his nose as a younger man and nothing had been right since then. He had actually undergone five surgical procedures to repair the damage. The last time, an infection set in and the doctor decided to perform surgery one more time to see if they could get to the core of the problem.

It was too late. The infection ran rampant through his body as his physicians looked on helplessly. On October 5, while his brothers were making preparations for the biggest professional day of their lives in New York, Sam Warner died in Los Angeles at the age of forty-one.

Albert, Harry, and Jack, devastated, immediately boarded a train for California. Their employees and their star, Al Jolson, would have to handle the premiere at the Warner Theater in Manhattan the next night.

The brothers could be forgiven if, in their grief, they saw this death as the worst possible of omens. It was impossible to exaggerate how instrumental Sam had been to this project. When enthusiasm flagged or naysayers seemed to be getting the upper hand, it was Sam who bucked everyone up. "This is the future. We're starting a brand-new business."

If they could pull it off, that is exactly what the Warner brothers were doing. It would be just as important a tidal wave of change as *Birth of a Nation* had been in 1915, but this time without the adverse social implications.

Perhaps on the three-day train ride west, the three brothers did what many families do at a time of crisis. Perhaps they discussed what had brought them to this moment.

The Warner family had arrived in Baltimore from Poland in 1883. For the next fifteen years, the Warners moved about the northeastern United States and Canada. Finally they settled in Youngstown, Ohio, where the head of the family opened, first, a cobbler's shop, then a butcher shop, then a bicycle shop. All of the Warner children—there were twelve of them—took part in the family businesses.

A turning point occurred in 1903. Father, mother, and children invested every dollar they had been able to save in a nickelodeon in Newcastle, Pennsylvania. As a practical matter, the four brothers, Harry, Albert, Sam, and Jack, took over the operation of the new business. They saw its potential and soon were involved in the emerging field of distribution of film shorts. In a few years, they also began dabbling in production.

Very soon it was more than dabbling. They had a major success in 1917 in California with a film called *My Four Years in Germany*. It staked the brothers to a growing role in the movie business.

When Warner Bros. was established, Harry was president, Sam the chief executive officer, Albert the treasurer, and Jack the production chief. They began in 1925 the difficult process of acquiring motion picture theaters. This was crucial. Without a string of theaters the production studio was a cut flower in a vase. It could bloom for a while, but without the guaranteed income stream the movie houses provided for its product, the studio was doomed.

The Warner brothers understood the rules. They were turning out successful films, many of them spearheaded by the young writer who would soon be their production chief, Darryl F. Zanuck from Wahoo, Nebraska. There was the series of Rin-Tin-Tin films and serials, based on the exploits of a German shepherd who had been found in a trench near the end of World War I by Captain Lee Duncan, who, after the Armistice, brought him straight to Los Angeles with the specific purpose of training him for the movies.

The success of Rin-Tin-Tin, and of a few stylish Ernst Lubitsch comedies, kept Warner Bros. afloat while they searched for a way to lift them to the next level of distribution, where the major studios ruled.

But by the mid-1920s, the rule of the giant studios was uneasy. Despite the boom times, motion picture attendance was dropping. Major productions such as *The Big Parade* or *Ben-Hur* could still draw record crowds, but the everyday drama and comedies had lost their luster. In some cases, the revenue loss was alarming. Theater operators began to bolster their movies with live entertainment, sometimes full light operas or musical comedies. A few old show-business troopers gloated in trade papers that movies, as they always said, were a flash in the pan and that "vaudeville is back."

The new film industry was not about to roll over and play dead, however. They searched desperately for something that would lure the regular customers back. There were sporadic flings with animation, color, and sound, but all were dismissed by the money men as expensive "gimmicks," much as 3-D would prove to be thirty years later.

The Warner brothers were not so sure. Besides, what had they to lose? The way things were going, their studio was on a slow boat to nowhere, destined to sink. The business graphs were undeniable.

Of all the options, sound seemed the most feasible. Bell Telephone had been floating a system they had developed called Vitaphone. It was creaky and primitive by any later standards, synchronizing a record with the film image.

Every studio, after getting a look and a listen to the Bell demonstration, dismissed Vitaphone as unworkable. The sound was scratchy and the synch seemed unreliable, but even if the technology was fixed, the costs of refitting thousands of theaters coast-to-coast put the idea out of the question.

On the other hand, Warner Bros. did not have the comfort level of their rich competitors. They decided to give Vitaphone a try. To be sure, their first steps were tentative. They commissioned several shorts using the technique.

It is likely that the first voice ever heard on film in public performance belonged to Will H. Hays, the former chairman of the Republican National Committee and postmaster general under President Warren Harding. Hays had been hired by the studios to head up the new organization called the Motion Picture Producers and Distributors of America. His job was to clean up the image of Hollywood after a string of scandals caused outrage in many parts of the country, bringing threats of boycotts, as we have seen previously.

On August 6, 1926, a small audience at the Manhattan Theater in New York saw—and more importantly *heard*—Will Hays as he stood before a microphone and said, among other things, "Sound will usher in a new era of pictures and music."

Note the emphasis on "pictures and music." Vitaphone believed the future of sound lay in synchronizing music with film. The possibilities of dialogue for an entire drama had not yet occurred to anyone. To make the point, another of the shorts shown that night featured the nation's most famous entertainer, Al Jolson, singing one of his trademark songs.

Then came what Warner Bros. hoped would be the deal-closer. The audience saw a full-length feature, *Don Juan*, starring John Barrymore. There was no dialogue, but the sound-on-disc Vitaphone system provided the first full musical sound track accompanying the action on the big screen.

Unsure how to market the new technology, Jack Warner told assembled theater operators that by installing Vitaphone, they would no longer have to hire orchestras to provide appropriate music.

It was no sale. The operators didn't believe the new technology was cost effective. Besides, where was the product? They would have to have fifty Vitaphone features in train before they could commit to such a major makeover in their movie houses.

The Warners had to settle for outfitting a few theaters for Vitaphone, providing them with prints of the shorts and *Don Juan*, then going back to the drawing board in Los Angeles.

They were ready to give up on sound and look in some other direction for their salvation. They were almost out of money. Maybe they should cut their losses and get into another business, some in the family suggested.

The holdout was Sam. He believed that sound was the future of the industry, and within a few months he had at least some tangible evidence on his side.

Those few theaters that Warner Bros. had rigged for sound began to send in some interesting reports. While other movie houses were pulling out all the stops in late 1926 and early 1927 to get customers through the door and failing, the Warner Bros. "sound" movie, along with the shorts, were attracting a steady—and increasing—number of moviegoers.

Sam implored the rest of the family to go back to their money sources and to put in their own savings as well on the biggest gamble of their lives.

At this distance, no one can point to the precise moment they all said yes. It is likely that it was less a dramatic meeting with all shaking hands in an instant of solidarity than an incremental "two steps forward, one back," until they were all up to their necks with Lady Luck the only life preserver.

In 1926, one of the biggest hits on Broadway was a sentimental songfest called *The Jazz Singer*, starring Georgie Jessel doing his best Al Jolson impression. This was chosen as the vehicle that Warner Bros. would ride to the revolution. The road would be bumpy.

George Jessel was signed to star, then he learned that something new would be added. Moviegoers would *hear* him as well as see him. He doubled his asking price. The brothers turned him down flat and went to another New York star, Ziegfeld headliner Eddie Cantor. Talks went on for a few weeks before Eddie's friends convinced him it was too risky. The movie was likely to flop and Eddie's film career would be over before it started.

This time it was Jack who came up with the idea. Since they

were fully committed anyway, why not go for the biggest star in the world, the one everyone was imitating? Why not approach Al Jolson himself? Jolson had already put his toe in the water by agreeing to do the short last year. Why not ask him to jump in with both feet?

Their timing was good. Jolson's show had just closed and, as usual, he needed money.

By common consent in show business, Al Jolson was the greatest entertainer in America and, perhaps, the world. Even as severe a critic as Charlie Chaplin called him "riveting" in performance. Russian-born Asa Yoelsen was the son of a cantor. The family came to America when Asa was a child. By the time he was a teenager, he was entertaining in nightclubs and restaurants, using the popular technique left over from minstrel shows, black face.

Jolson rose above the burnt cork and the mawkish material to mesmerize audiences coast-to-coast. He dominated the new recording industry, and his appearances in shows and concerts were routinely sold out. He became something of a one-man industry. The public loved him. That was by no means true of those who knew him best. He could be rude and domineering. Many, including songwriter Sammy Cahn, called Jolson the biggest "cut-in" in history. A "cut-in," according to Cahn, was an artist who would perform or record a composer's song only if his name appeared as cowriter. This way, not only did artist get half the credit, he got half the royalties.

This did not bode well for the upcoming negotiations, but the Warner brothers were determined to hitch their project to this star, and they did.

Interestingly, there are two versions of what happened next: A news story in the early 1930s, using some quotes from Jolson, indicates that Jolson was offered $50,000 plus a hefty percentage of the net, but instead opted for $75,000 cash up front, much to his later regret.

But other accounts, including biographies, tell a more convincing story, including specific numbers. Jolson did, indeed ask for $75,000, one-third of it on the signing of the contract and the rest at $6,250 per week. But a substantial part of the weekly salary, said to be one-third, was to be withheld and invested in the production. That investment of $16,000, according to a Jolson radio interview, eventually returned more than $2 million.

All of that was well into the future when Jolson showed up for work. When he saw the Vitaphone camera and heard his instructions from director Alan Crosland, his spirits fell. He was sure he was about to be associated with the biggest disaster of the century. When his friends Charlie Chaplin, Douglas Fairbanks, and others threw a big party welcoming him to California, that's exactly what Jolson told them. Most agreed with him.

On the set, the technical difficulties were formidable. The Vitaphone camera was noisy, so it had to be enclosed in a padded, boxlike soundproof booth. There was no air conditioning, so the camera operator could only stay in there a few minutes at a time. Even so, he emerged drenched and dehydrated.

The microphone was a stern master. There could be none of the camera movement directors had come to rely on as silent films matured. Actors had to cluster around the mike and an ingenious way had to be found to hide it.

For the first feature-length "talkie" there would be precious little talking. In fact, most of the "dialogue" was ad-libbed by the veteran Jolson around his songs. The following year, it would be a schoolyard exercise to count how many words Jolson actually spoke, but no one could agree because of Al's partial words and sentence fragments. Most pegged it at about 250.

Director Alan Crosland was in no way intimidated by his principal actor, though Jolson was clearly what later generations would call a "superstar." Crosland ordered Jolson around as if he were the rawest prop boy on the payroll, demanding take after take.

One of the sentimental tunes brought Jolson to tears. Crosland asked for another take, then another, each time with Jolson dissolving in sobs. After five versions, Crosland strode onto the stage and, according to bystanders, said, "Look here, Jolson, let's try it again and this time put some *feeling* into it!"

While the filming went on and the Warner brothers watched their bank balance diminish, America was in one of its yeastiest times.

As 1927 dawned, Lizzie Borden died in Fall River, Massachusetts, never again to hear schoolchildren chant, "Lizzie Borden took an ax / And gave her father forty whacks / And when she saw what she had done / She gave her mother forty-one."

Al Capone, irritated by some inconsequential raids on a few of his enterprises, told the newspapers, "I am going to St. Petersburg, Florida, tomorrow. Let the worthy citizens of Chicago get their liquor the best way they can. I'm sick of the job—it's a thankless one and full of grief. I've been spending the best years of my life as a public benefactor."

The presiding judge at the controversial Sacco-Vanzetti trial, Webster Thayer, says from the bench, "This man [Bartolomeo Vanzetti], although *he may not have actually committed the crime* . . . is the enemy of our existing institutions . . . The defendant's ideals are cognate with crime." Both were found guilty, appeals were denied, and they were executed.

In Paris, a young man landed his monoplane at Le Bourget airport, stepped out, and said to the huge crowd on hand the most superfluous sentence of the decade: "I am Charles A. Lindbergh."

As the summer wore on, Babe Ruth wore out opposing pitchers, finally slugging sixty home runs, breaking his own record of fifty-nine.

The cameras continued to roll at Warner Bros. Jolson's best friend in the cast was character actor William Demarest. Years later, when Jolson's life story was made into a movie, he insisted Demarest be given a major role. On the soundstage, all male eyes were on a dark-haired, dark-eyed beauty playing a chorine, whose name was Myrna Loy. Portraying Jolson's cantor father was Warner Oland, whom later moviegoers would know as Charlie Chan.

At last, filming was done, the cantor's voices were dubbed, editing was complete. Cans of film and delicate sound equipment were shipped east.

The finished product was pure schmaltz from first frame to last, but the director made an excellent decision by taking his camera on location to New York. We get a glimpse of the Jewish sections of the Lower East Side and of the Great White Way, Broadway itself in 1927.

Then came the moment. The Warner brothers were on their way back to California, but Jolson was there, hiding his apprehension and skepticism with the star's mask, waving and smiling at his fans.

The film and disc started simultaneously. Many in the audience were aware that the play, and the film, were considered to be Jolson's biography. First they heard Bobby Gordon, as Jolson at thirteen, utter a few words. There was a nervous rustle through the crowd. After a montage, they saw Jolson, much bigger than life, singing to the audience from the screen. The murmur in the theater whipped from aisle to aisle like wildfire.

But it was at the end of the song when Jolson—the great star Al Jolson—actually *talked*, that the dam burst. "Wait a minute!" they heard him say. "Wait a minute! You ain't heard *nothin'* yet!" Jolson was right. They couldn't hear even the rest of the sentence because they were standing and cheering. They were still cheering through most of Jolson's next song, "Toot-

Toot-Tootsie." When the one hour and 29-minute film was over, they stood and cheered again.

It was a triumph. No one had seen anything like it since *The Birth of a Nation*. Word went immediately to the Warner brothers on their train. It also went that very night to the top executives of every motion picture company in the world.

The gamble had paid off. It was an entirely new ball game, although some hoped they could hold back the dawn. A few, including D. W. Griffith, suggested a conspiracy among the major studios and their thousands of theaters to keep sound out, at least until it was perfected.

But the genie was out of the bottle and that was that. Sound was in, silents were out. Stars, writers, and directors who couldn't make the transition were out, too. In an astonishingly short time, the entire landscape of Hollywood changed.

Very quickly, technology went to work to improve sound. Vitaphone gave way to Movietone, which was itself soon eclipsed. Warner Bros., better positioned than other studios, prepared their next "talker." Meantime, $3.5 million poured into their coffers within six months. In those theaters not equipped with sound, *The Jazz Singer* ran as a silent and *still* did record business. Warner Bros. bought more theaters.

Studios with large inventories of expensive silent films scrambled to attach some element of sound to them. Overnight, silent films, the sole product of a thirty-year-old industry worth billions even back then, were dead.

Warner Bros. studio, on the other hand, was now a player.

Two years passed and a brand-new organization called the Academy of Motion Picture Arts and Sciences surfaced. The avowed purpose was to honor outstanding achievements in the movie business. The celebration began modestly enough, a dinner for 270 in the Blossom Room of the Hollywood Roosevelt Hotel. Janet Gaynor later called it "More like a private party." A statuette—not yet called "Oscar"—was designed for the awards.

At that first event, May 16, 1929, it was decided to salute the pictures of 1927 and 1928. It was also decided that it was unfair for "talkies" to compete with "silents," so *The Jazz Singer* was ruled ineligible.

However, even in that highly charged and competitive community, it was impossible to ignore the impact this film had made, so a "special award" category was invented for the "pioneer outstanding talking picture which has revolutionized the industry."

The Academy's first president, Douglas Fairbanks, had asked all recipients to refrain from making remarks so that he could move the evening along briskly. All complied except one: Darryl F. Zanuck, accepting on behalf of the Warner brothers, made the very first Academy Award acceptance speech.

"This award is dedicated to the late Sam Warner, the man responsible for the successful usage of this medium."

And somewhere in a theater that very night, another audience was listening to a movie for the first time: "Wait a minute, I tell you. You ain't heard nothin' yet!"

For once, the movie had understated the truth.

The Jazz Singer had changed the world of film by giving it a voice.

19

THE BIG PARADE

1925

DIRECTOR: KING VIDOR
STARS: JOHN GILBERT, RENÉE ADORÉE
RUNNING TIME: 2 HOURS, 10 MINUTES

James Apperson is a small-town boy, the scion of a wealthy family. When the Great War breaks out, his father and his girlfriend convince him it is his duty to volunteer for the service.

Disillusion sets in as early as training camp, but that is nothing compared to what he encounters in France, where loneliness, filth, fear, and death are constant companions. Paradoxically, it is here that he finds his true love, Melisande.

He is terribly wounded and evacuated from France. He learns nothing will be the same. The last scenes find him back in France, looking for the French girl he left behind. He is hobbling on two wooden legs.

Note: Contrary to legend, actor John Gilbert's career did not come to an immediate end as soon as audiences heard his voice. Mr. Gilbert actually made ten sound movies before his death in 1936 at age forty-one.

MGM (Courtesy of The Kobal Collection)

I s it possible that one hugely successful silent film—*The Big Parade* (1925)—set in motion a series of events that, nearly a generation later, would make us deaf to the cries of the Holocaust?

Outlandish as the idea seems now, there is some empirical evidence it may be true.

This story begins on a steel-gray December day at the White House in Washington, D.C. It had been exactly one year since Pearl Harbor. President Franklin Roosevelt looked wearily at his visitor, the powerful Jewish leader Rabbi Stephen S. Wise. He hadn't caught the names of the others, but that didn't matter. It was Rabbi Wise who put the twenty-page paper firmly on his desk and did all the talking.

"Blue Print for Extermination," it read.

The president asked for a summary of its contents and Rabbi Wise accommodated him. It was brief, straightforward. He spoke of death camps and a reported decision by Nazi Germany to eradicate every Jew in Europe.

There had, in fact, been rumors about killings at the German concentration camps since 1940. A formal report on something called "The Final Solution" had been handed to the president in September.

Franklin Roosevelt did not believe it. He told Supreme Court Justice Felix Frankfurter that the deported Jews were being used on the Soviet border to build fortifications. The idea that they were being killed by the thousands was simply prepos-terous.

He was by no means alone in his skepticism. There were influential Jews in America who also doubted that such system-atic slaughter could be undertaken by a civilized nation in the twentieth century, among them the distinguished historian of the Jewish experience in Europe and America Jacob Rader Marcus.

Very few professionals in the State Department could be found who believed that a European nation would descend to mass murder. The attitude of the military was the same. The first OSS (Office of Strategic Services, predecessor of the CIA) assessment of the September report read "Wild rumor inspired by Jewish fears." Other military intelligence services called the charges "a simple revival of the old 'Hun' propaganda."

Yes, the "Hun" propaganda. Everyone of a certain age knew what that meant. The bold, graphic posters of the predatory "Hun" of World War I, the chilling reports of "Bleeding Belgium," the reported rapacity of occupying German troops, the mass shootings of innocent civilians who had been made hostages were still fresh in the minds of middle-aged Americans in 1942.

All who had come to maturity in the United States during the Great War were exposed to—and deeply angered by—the accounts that had been reprinted in every newspaper, told on every street corner. Then there were the U-boats, attacking while submerged, torpedoing unarmed merchant ships while half their crew slept, blowing them to eternity without a chance to defend themselves. Some of the victims were neutral Americans.

By the time the spring of 1917 arrived, surveys showed that most people in the United States had evolved from their attitude of strict neutrality in 1914 to a hardening belief that the Hun had to be taught a lesson. After all, hadn't Germany initiated the horrors of poison gas? Hadn't it begun the practice of bombing open cities from aeroplanes and airships, slaughtering women and children? Obviously, the Hun must be stopped.

Jeanette Rankin, the first and, at that moment, the only woman in Congress, might say, "You can't win a war any more than you can win an earthquake," but there were few listening to her.

America went to war. Hundreds of thousands of young men rushed to the colors. The American Expeditionary Force was ready in little more than a year. The English and French, perhaps just months away from signing a peace agreement early in 1917, hung on grimly while America got prepared.

For the Russians, it was too late. They signed a humiliating separate armistice, then continued their internal revolution with immeasurable consequences for the rest of the twentieth century.

The Americans smashed gamely into Axis fortifications at Château Thierry and Belleau Wood. If the German high command had hopes that young Americans wouldn't fight, those hopes were shattered in the trenches of devastated Europe. An admiring Winston Churchill said of the American efforts, "Courage and valour were all they had, but they gave them freely."

The infusion of fresh and willing troops was more than the Central Powers could take. They broke and ran, then called for an armistice.

The hated Hun of the posters was vanquished. The Allies were victorious and vindicated. Johnny came marching home to parades and speeches. Not all doughboys came back, of course. There were upwards of 100,000 American graves left in France.

Within a very few years, the graves began to speak louder than the parades and patriotic addresses. To many in the country, troubling questions began to emerge: What had it all been about, anyway, all that killing? A few reporters started telling of deliberate exaggerations engineered by British and French propagandists, beginning as early as 1914, in an attempt to inflame public opinion toward war with the Axis. Some of the horror stories, it appeared, had actually been made up out of whole cloth.

Who was this Hun we had so hated? Maybe he didn't look so different from us. Perhaps he didn't even exist. Wasn't it possible, on reflection, that the British, French, and Italians were just as guilty of starting the war as the Germans? In the end, wasn't it just another interminable European squabble with no point except a few changes in the national boundary lines? And, of course, the war profiteers, mostly arms manufacturers.

Profit. Perhaps we had been played for suckers and the Great War had been all about money. Armament makers on both sides got rich on the blood of young men.

Cynicism took root first with writers of the "Lost Generation." Articles and books with deep questions about America's involvement in the war began to appear.

On the other hand, Hollywood largely ignored the late war, except for a few slapstick comedies. In fact, from 1920 through 1924, only one top-ten moneymaker looked at the Great War at all. *The Four Horseman of the Apocalypse* in 1921 certainly had an antiwar theme, but its impact was diluted by the emergence of the decade's leading sex symbol, Rudolph Valentino.

Then came 1925.

This was the year of the Scopes "Monkey" Trial in Dayton, Tennessee. The year Nellie Ross of Wyoming became the nation's first female governor, and Ma Ferguson of Texas became the second. The Ku Klux Klan, 40,000 strong, marched in Washington, D.C., and radio's "Sam and Henry" changed their names to "Amos and Andy."

Most Americans seemed only vaguely aware of the intellectual debate about the Great War. The attitude continued to be that the Germans had started it, and we had finished it. We were the good guys and they were the bad guys. The Yanks didn't come back until it was over, over there. We and the Tommys and the poilus had made the world safe for democracy. The movies reflected that general mood.

Then into the land of celluloid and sunshine came a hard-eyed veteran named Laurence Stallings. He had returned from the war minus a leg. A talented writer, he became an editor and columnist for the *New York World*. Across the desk from him sat another editor and columnist, Maxwell Anderson. Together they wrote the brilliant antiwar play, *What Price Glory*.

First, however, Mr. Stallings had another story to tell. It was brought to the attention of the rising Hollywood director King Vidor, who had a screenplay written based on the Stallings tale and began shooting. He called it *The Big Parade*.

Vidor took a chance and gave the lead to John Gilbert, an actor who had only recently stopped billing himself as "Jack." Gilbert was a star, all right, but contemporary Hollywood didn't think him a very substantial one. He was known primarily for his mustache, his wardrobe, and his love scenes with assorted actresses. Vidor later said of him, "John Gilbert was an impressionable fellow, not too well established in a role of his own in life. The parts he followed in his daily life were greatly influenced by the parts some scriptwriter had written for him." If that was so, Mr. Gilbert had an austere stretch in his personal life in 1925. His beloved mustache was shaved off, he wore shapeless khakis for most of the film, and in his climatic scene, he walked with a graceless, decided limp.

The story was purely antiwar and it hit the country like a hurricane, sweeping deeply held beliefs before it. In a way, *The Big Parade* became a metaphor for the nation. Its first reels found young James Apperson, encouraged by his father and his girlfriend, in a rage to "join up." His accommodation to the soldier's life is slow, as reality creeps into his dreams of glory. Eventually he bonds strongly with the men in his squad.

In the fullness of time, he also bonds with a French girl, played admirably by Renée Adorée, who was—wonder of wonders—a French girl. The scene in which he teaches her to chew gum was used in film acting classes for years to come. In the end, the hero is changed profoundly, both emotionally and physically. Like his creator, Laurence Stallings, James Apperson loses a leg.

The scene that really caught the attention of the moviegoer, according to exit cards, was the one in which Apperson shared a cigarette with a dying German soldier. Millions of Americans looked carefully at that screen. The actor playing the German soldier didn't look like the posters of the Hun. He looked a lot like James Apperson, or, for that matter, like their brothers and sons who had gone off to war eight years before.

Director King Vidor pulled out all the stops. He could do that because the young genius of MGM, Irving Thalberg, had seen the early rushes and loved them. Thalberg was among those who had caught the emerging antiwar sentiment from the intellectual community and felt the time might be right to expose that point of view to the mainstream. Vidor was on the same wavelength.

The result was a well-crafted movie, some sequences filmed in color, some battle scenes shot in what appeared to be a sort of slow motion, very effective. In hundreds of cases, extras were actual veterans of the World War.

The Big Parade was a smash, the most successful picture of the decade to that point. It cost $380,000 to make and returned $3.5 million in its first weeks. Some reports put the final box office totals at $22 million.

Hollywood bookkeeping aside, the impact of *The Big Parade* on America was palpable. It brought antiwar sentiment to Main Street, made it a legitimate topic over the cracker barrel. To be sure, veterans were still honored every Fourth of July, but now sometimes as victims as much as heroes.

The floodgates opened, and wouldn't close in this country for nearly seventeen years, until World War II had actually started. The next year, *What Price Glory?* reached the movie theaters and it would do well, though not nearly as well as *The Big Parade.*

In 1927, the antiwar film was *Wings.* In 1930, director Lewis Milestone's all-talking masterpiece of Erich Maria-Remarque's *All Quiet on the Western Front,* hit the theaters, again with an antiwar message but that was by no means all. Major studios kept the drumbeat of antiwar films all through the 1930s. With *Calvacade, A Farewell to Arms, The Roaring Twenties,* and a dozen more.

It was as late as 1939, in fact, before major filmmakers in Hollywood began to address the possibility that war might, after all, be preferable to some things. In Ernest Hemingway's words in 1938, "There are worse things than war. Cowardice, treachery, and simple selfishness."

However, by that time, our most effective mass medium, strongly supported by much of our literary and arts community, had for fifteen years hammered home the view that a) We had been hoodwinked into war by Allied lies and propaganda, b) There wasn't a nickel's worth of difference between the British and French on the one hand and the Germans on the other, and c) We would be damned fools to get caught in the same European border squabbles again.

This is the backdrop against which the nation digested the news coming out of Germany after Adolf Hitler came to power. Most Americans only very slowly came to believe the stories they were hearing, mostly from British and French sources. Surely things could not be as bad as they were saying. Even those in the Roosevelt administration who supported efforts to keep Hitler in check were skeptical. They had heard it all before, back in 1915. It was just more exaggeration from those who wanted to draw us into the shooting war.

Against the flow of words from Europe, Americans had seen the graphic image of that young German soldier sharing a last cigarette with John Gilbert. They had seen another young German solider, this time played by Lew Ayres, die while reaching for a flower. Wasn't it once again an old man's war and a young man's fight? And, in the end, weren't the young men more alike than different?

Admirable sentiments in any age, but hardly preparation for the unique nightmare that was at that moment descending on the world.

We didn't—were not prepared to—believe the numbing magnitude of the atrocity until long after it was too late. It was the movies again, but not well-crafted screenplays, not actors, not dialogue with a message that finally convinced us. It was newsreels, grainy, flickering. Skeletal figures stacked like cordwood. Others, just as skeletal, staring at the camera, accusing us by their very presences. We knew those standing would die before anything could be done for them. We saw oven doors yawning, bones smoldering. We were shocked out of our disbelief.

In truth, we have never recovered.

Would a more accurate, more balanced view in the movies of the German military's role in World War I have made us more likely to believe the grim reports in World War II? Perhaps even in time to have raised an international clamor and make a difference?

Haunting as the conclusion is, a case could be made that it would.

Because there *was* a difference in the way the two sides waged war, even back in the First World War. Propaganda aside, it was, in 1914, Field Marshall Baron von der Goltz, the German military governor in Belgium, who wrote the following proclamation: "In future, villages in the vicinity of places where railway and telegraph lines are destroyed will be punished without pity whether they are guilty or not of the acts in question. With this in view, hostages have been taken in all villages near the railway lines which are threatened by such attacks. Upon the first attempt to destroy lines of railway, telegraph or telephone, they will be immediately shot."

That was 1914, not 1939. It was not the thoughtless act of some rogue commander in the heat of battle. It was the considered policy of the government of Kaiser Wilhelm. Innocent people would be summarily put to death for the crimes of the guilty.

The Nazi atrocities of the 1930s and 1940s did not arrive as a full-blown aberration after all. Seeds of the ultimate horror fell upon ground that been ploughed a generation before.

In our revulsion from the killing fields of Flanders in World War I, we chose to forget that. The ruthless culture of Prussian militarism receded from our memory or was sugar-coated, and the concept of "war guilt" dissipated apace.

The enormous popularity of *The Big Parade* began a process by which mainstream Americans could support unilateral disarmament, neglect even the most rudimentary military preparedness, applaud from the sidelines as Britain's Oxford Union passed the Joad resolution which read, "That this House will in no circumstances fight for its King and Country," support the Nye committee in the U.S. Senate, which in 1936 concluded that "The arms trade profoundly influenced the role the U.S. played in the Great War," to respond to a nationwide poll in 1937 by answering, 64 to 36 percent, that the U.S. made a mistake in taking part in World War I, to applaud that same year, the fourth annual—and largest—"peace demonstration" in New York with thousands pledging to "refuse to support the government of the United States in any war it may conduct," and even after World War II began and Great Britain was standing alone, to see our elected representatives pass an extension of the draft by only one vote. One vote.

On June 5, 1940, with France in its death throes, the commencement speaker at Xavier University in Cincinnati, a Dr. George Herman Derry, described as an educator and sociologist, told the graduates "Propagandists are pulling the same old bluff and blather about democracy that got us into the First World War. Only a 'Boobocracy' would swallow the poison gas that democracy is doomed if the Allies are defeated."

The brilliantly made series of movies beginning with *The Big Parade* lifted our eyes to a nobler vision of world peace and brotherhood among all people.

They also closed our ears to the agonized cries of those who were spirited away in the night, men, women, children, never to be seen or heard again.

We learned the bitter lesson that to be right at the wrong time is to be wrong.

Or did we? Are such lessons portable, generation to generation? The power of a bigger-than-life screen is seductive and, like all seducers, should be approached with caution.

Filmmaking has few eternal verities. The process has been revolutionized dozens of times since 1925. Today's technology will be considered quaint within a few years. Still, King Vidor's silver shadow shimmering from the long-ago 1920s has its lesson.

Even power wielded for the most altruistic reasons can, in an avalanche of unintended consequences, corrupt.

The Big Parade changed us, all right, but was it for the better or the worse? Your choice.

20

THE BIRTH OF A NATION

1915

DIRECTOR: D.W. GRIFFITH

STARS: LILLIAN GISH, MAE MARSH,
HENRY B. WALTHALL

RUNNING TIME: 2 HOURS, 5 MINUTES

Two families, the Camerons and the Stonemans, knew each other before the opening of hostilities in the Civil War. One's sympathies were with the South, the other's with the North.

In this first true epic film, we follow their fortunes in the war. We watch many of the great battles and we are present at other momentous events, including the assassination of Lincoln.

After the South's defeat, we see continuing bitterness and hardship. Many in the South applaud the rise of the "Clan" (really, the Ku Klux Klan) and the Invisible Empire over which it rules.

The closing scene is a triumphant ride of hooded "Clansmen," cast as protectors of civilization.

Note: Two future distinguished directors had small roles in *The Birth of a Nation*. Erich von Stroheim can be seen taking a spectacular fall from a roof, and Raoul Walsh portrayed Lincoln assassin John Wilkes Booth.

Biograph (Courtesy of The Kobal Collection)

ndrew Jones had never seen Massachusetts Avenue quite this way before. He was face down, head on the curb, the detritus of a Boston Saturday night there in the gutter, inches away from his nose. The taste of his blood was oddly metallic.

The small crowd around him murmured ominously. Andrew rolled over on his back, trying to focus his eyes. The policeman leaning over him had a florid face, with a nose that had obviously lost a round or two in street fights.

His voice was a hoarse whisper, but pleasant, almost conversational. "We don't want to bust up any more niggers, son. Just get up and go on home." He lightly swung the black billy club he had used on Andrew's face a few minutes earlier.

Andrew sat up slowly, his head throbbing. He looked down at the blood on his shirt—his best shirt—and his jacket—his only jacket. His mother would not be pleased.

He looked across the street. The men and women in the long line at the box office looked at him curiously. All their faces were white. The smaller knot of people closing protectively around him on this side of the street was made up, for the most part, of young men and women from Boston's black community.

Andrew looked past the policeman to the poster on the front of the theater. The glass in front of it had been smashed. Andrew smiled. That had been his contribution. Someone else had tried to rip down the poster, but had only half-succeeded. What remained was "D.W. . . . FIFTH'S . . . RTH OF A NATION." Worse, nearly all of the pictorial part of the poster remained. Andrew felt a cold grip in his chest as he looked. A man on a rearing horse, both covered and masked in white sheets. The sheets bore emblems of a round red circle and a white cross. The man held a burning torch high over his head.

Uncontrollable anger rose in Andrew's throat. He got painfully to his feet and started across the street again. Two friends grabbed his arms. Struggling against the restraint, Andrew spat in the direction of the poster. Instead, the spittle and blood landed on the policeman's badge, The officer's face turned red, and with practiced ease he flicked the billy club. For Andrew, things went black. As black as the night surrounding the red torch and the white sheets on the poster in front of the Boston movie house.

It was the first week of March 1915. *The Birth of a Nation* had exploded on the screens of America.

Nothing would ever be quite the same again.

By that year, movies had been around for nearly twenty years, but had been largely dismissed by the cognoscenti as "arcade attractions" and "flickering dreams for the masses." In fact, it was an article of faith among moviemakers themselves that the attention span of their audiences was one reel or two at the most. In other words, ten to twenty minutes.

It was a formula that had served David Wark Griffith well. An actor who wanted to be a writer, Griffith had little success with either. Then he found the infant medium of film—and his life's work. From the beginning, he exhibited a flair for moviemaking. He directed his first film in 1908 and the next year actually directed every film that Biograph Studios released.

He was just getting warmed up. In the next four years, he directed an astonishing 450 films. Though most were one-reelers, each was a complete story, and Griffith began to develop unique ways to tell them. He also experimented with longer forms; two reels, then four. From the outset he took the time to change camera angles, used the full shot, then close-up. He tried dramatic lighting, the intercut and the crosscut, iris shots, soft focus.

Within his very first year in films, he began to instruct his actors in restrained performance. This quality alone would set a D. W. Griffith film apart from the others. He was appalled at the histrionics and mugging that passed for film acting. He reminded his actors that the audience was not out beyond a proscenium arch. With a close-up, the viewers were as near as a lover's kiss.

The subject matter he chose was often unusual. He told stories of big-city gangs and small-town hypocrisies. He demonstrated what many associates thought of as a growing social conscience.

Unfortunately for the course of American history for the next quarter-century, that social conscience did not extend to the matter of race.

David W. Griffith was a product of his time and place. He was born in LaGrange, Kentucky, a small town not far from Louisville, in 1875. His father was not simply prominent, he was a genuine celebrity.

He had fought in the Mexican War, then stayed in the West for a time, escorting wagon trains to California. Then he studied medicine, interrupted his practice to serve in the Kentucky legislature, joined the Confederate forces at the outbreak of the Civil War, and became a Lieutenent Colonel of cavalry whose gallant exploits in battle were so well known that he became famous throughout the South as "Roaring Jake" Griffith.

When the war ended, so did the roaring. The hard reality of a small-town medical practice in a depressed economy left the Griffith family in reduced circumstances. By the time David was born in 1875, the Griffiths were impoverished, a fact they were always to attribute to the Reconstruction policies of the Republican Party.

The policies did not apply generally to Kentucky, of course, because the Bluegrass State did not secede from the Union. But "Roaring Jake," as a high-profile Confederate, did get his share of harassment from the politicians in power. Enough to implant a deep anger in the Griffiths that would far outlast the century.

The Southern view of American history became dogma to D. W. Griffith and a passionate subtext to his career. His racial bigotry was so ingrained that he did not recognize it and was genuinely shocked when it was called into question at the most important juncture of his professional life.

Reverend Thomas Dixon Jr. of North Carolina shared Griffith's view of the Civil War and its aftermath but, unlike Griffith, was able to get this opinion into print. He had two successful novels on the subject, *The Leopard's Spots* and *The Clansman.* The latter had also been dramatized for the stage, which is where Dixon and Griffith first met. Their careers then diverged, but they stayed in touch.

Through Griffith's rapid rise in the film industry, he kept Dixon's books in mind. He believed they held the makings of a great movie. Perhaps the nation would one day be ready for an epic film. A story so big it would elevate an entire industry to a position of respect, even of equality with the other arts.

It was a dangerous idea, every bit as daring as anything "Roaring Jake" undertook in the Civil War.

Not one reel, or two, or even four. Twelve full reels. A tale of two families at the critical moment of this nation's life.

The Stonemans of the North. The Camerons of the South. The sweep of the great war between the states. The arrogance of victory, the defiance of defeat. The creation of an Invisible Empire to win with midnight rope and fire what was lost on the battlefield. In short, terrorism.

To tell a story this big on celluloid would require thousands of extras with costumes and uniforms, hundreds of horses, the best actors in film. And money. More money than had ever been spent on a moving picture.

D. W. Griffith's demeanor changed dramatically as he approached what he hoped would be his masterpiece. The brilliant cinematographer G. W. "Billy" Bitzer, who had worked with Griffith on most of his early films, would be principal photographer on this great experiment. He noticed an immediate difference in his friend.

"He used to talk about the other films as 'grinding out another sausage,' but his entire attitude changed on this one. There was a glint in his eye and he got very serious . . . Personally, I did not share his enthusiasm. I read the book and figured that a Negro chasing a white girl was just another sausage, after all, and how could you show it in the South, anyway?"

Griffith faced down all doubters. His enormous early success gave him influence with backers and he used every bit of it. He set the budget at an unheard-of $100,000 for a single film. He would exceed it, borrowing from every source he could find.

His star, Lillian Gish, talked about the making of the film: "There was no script. He carried the ideas in his head, or, I should say, in his heart. As the son of 'Roaring Jake' Griffith, he firmly believed that the truth of the Civil War and Reconstruction had never been told and he was quite ready to tell, through this new medium of silent screen, the story he believed above all else in the world."

To dispel any doubt that this film was designed to revise the American view of history, Reverend Dixon was quoted as saying, "[We] sought to revolutionize Northern sentiments by a presentation of history that would transform every man in the audience to a good Democrat." "Democrat" in this context was synonymous with "Southerner."

Black Americans knew what was coming. They, of course,

had heard all about Reverend Dixon's novels. They understood him to be what was then called, euphemistically, a "Negrophobe." Now they knew D. W. Griffith shared Dixon's views.

In truth, up until now, this new medium had been something of a safe haven for African Americans. Early one- and two-reelers tended to portray blacks in fairly realistic terms for the times. Though all races and nationalities were caricatured, blacks were by no means limited to servile, comic, or villainous roles. *Birth of a Nation* would change all that. And much more.

There were rumblings in the film business on both coasts that something new was afoot. Newspaper reports described the massing of extras under the California sun, the booming of cannon, the thunder of hooves on a scale not seen before.

All through the months of filming, the shooting script retained the title *The Clansman*. Finally, Griffith was ready to show a rough cut to a few principals. One of them was the Reverend Dixon, who had sold the rights for his story to Griffith for $2,500 and 25 percent of any profits.

At the conclusion of the screening, a euphoric Dixon stood and exclaimed, "It's too big to be called *The Clansman!* It's nothing less than the birth of a nation!" Or, at least, of a new title.

It was time for Griffith to show his hand in the biggest gamble of his life. Every dime he had or could get, every favor he could call in, was in the pot. He had made the first epic film, using every ounce of know-how he had accumulated. Would an American audience sit still for a film that ran more than two hours?

The next step was the premiere and again, Griffith pulled out every stop. He hired Clune's Auditorium in Los Angeles. He commissioned Joseph Carl Breil to compose music especially for this film, and a forty-piece orchestra was engaged to play it. On the night of February 8, the theater was packed to see what

Griffith had been doing all these months. Everyone from the growing film industry was there.

They were stunned by what unfolded on the screen. A fully realized story on a grand scale. They didn't think much about the implications of the revisionist history flickering there before them. They were too caught up in the implications for their own industry. When the movie was over and the lights came on, they stood up and cheered, then went outside to begin considering how their world had changed in the last three hours. Young movie executive Samuel Goldfish—not yet Goldwyn—was quoted as saying, "It's a revolution." Smart as he was, he didn't know the half of it.

What was the U.S.A. of Andrew Jones of Boston and David Griffith of Kentucky like in 1915? It was the first year Americans had to pay income tax. The Panama Canal opened to commercial traffic, shrinking the world by thousands of miles. In religion, evangelist Billy Sunday, a former professional baseball player, was packing them in. On February 12, four days after the premiere of *Birth of a Nation*, construction began on the Lincoln Memorial in Washington, D.C.

A World War was raging in Europe, grinding up young lives like so many of Griffith's sausages. The United States, protesting it wanted to stay out of the conflict, edged closer to the Allies, pushed by Germany's U-boat war. German torpedoes sank the USS *William P. Frye*. President Wilson said, "Germany will be held to strict accountability for property or lost lives." A week later it was the British liner *Lusitania*. Aboard were 1,925 people; 1,198 died, including 114 Americans.

Still, one of the major song hits was "I Didn't Raise My Boy to Be a Soldier."

For Andrew Jones of Boston, there was a war closer to home, and if one wanted to use popular music to measure the temper of the times, he could point to any number of them that topped the hit parade just a few years earlier. How about "Coon! Coon!

Coon!" or "Every Race Has a Flag But the Coon," or "You'se Just a Little Nigger, But You'se Mine All Mine." This last ditty was written by Paul Dresser, older brother of a man who would become the great American novelist Theodore Dreiser.

Into this mix in March of 1915 came *The Birth of a Nation*, opening in virtually every city in the United States. It is impossible to exaggerate the reaction of moviegoers. It was a thunderbolt.

The first shock was economic. When the film opened at the Liberty Theater in New York on March 3, the admission was posted at $2.00 per person!

To give that price perspective, consider this. The previous December, Henry Ford had loosed a thunderbolt of his own. He raised the basic salary of his factory workers from $2.40 for a nine-hour day to $5.00 for an eight-hour day. These were, of course, top wages. Many in the nation still worked for $2.00 a day or even less. Mr. Griffith was asking—and getting—a full day's wages from many of those who came to see his movie.

Was it worth it? Most in the audience apparently thought so. What they saw was unique in their experience. It wasn't really that Mr. Griffith was using moviemaking tricks that had never been seen before. He wasn't. But no one had ever organized those various techniques into one epic film, and, it must be added, no one had ever done them so well.

Griffith was the American genius of film.

"It is the first great film spectacle." "At last, films are brought on a par with opera, literature, sculpture, and paintings as an art form." "The thundering climax had patrons standing and cheering." Critics who had been contemptuous of films for years became adulatory. President Woodrow Wilson, given a private showing, said "It's like writing history with lightning."

The Birth of a Nation ran forty-four consecutive weeks in New York, and, for a time, four additional theaters had to be booked to accommodate the overflow. Before the run was over, *one million* New Yorkers had paid to see it. There were identical runs in Boston and Chicago. There is a report that the movie ran for twelve consecutive *years* in a few Southern theaters, yielding only when sound came to the movies in 1927.

The process of filmmaking was changed overnight. Actress Ina Claire was there. "A new businesslike spirit was found on the sets of movies everywhere, as if a switch had been thrown. Summer camp was over. It was because of *Birth of a Nation.*" There were millions of dollars at stake now. Hard-eyed businessmen would take control.

There were other hard eyes taking a look at *Birth of a Nation.* At the moment of its enormous burst of success, black communities in every city saw through the tidal wave of money and popularity to the core message of the story. They also saw, as others did not, what the consequences would be.

The National Association for the Advancement of Colored People was only six years old in 1915. The board released a statement calling the movie "a flagrant incitement to racial antagonism." They, and every African American in the country, knew that the very genius of the film's portrayal of the Klan as "defender of civilized values" gave a cloak of respectability to racial prejudice—and gave it to the widest audience in history.

In Boston, the Monday after Saturday's attempt by protesters to keep the movie from opening, one thousand people, most of them black, gathered on the statehouse steps demanding that *Birth of a Nation* be banned. Governor Walsh was impressed. He promised a delegation that "the producers will be prosecuted."

The continuing pressure was evident when, on May 21, the Massachusetts legislature created a "board of censors," an act that would have its own unintended consequences in years to come.

In June, several black organizations presented Mayor Curley of Boston with petitions bearing six thousand signatures asking that the movie be banned.

The president of Harvard, Charles W. Elliot, chimed in. "I want to say that [this film] presents an extraordinary misrepresentation of the birth of this nation."

D. W. Griffith was stung by the criticism. "But I love the Negro," he protested. He reluctantly met with a few black leaders, but little came of it. Then, as now, economics swept all before it. There are no reliable figures, but at least one recent study indicates that *Birth of a Nation* might actually have grossed $50 million in its first release. The announced totals were, of course, much lower than that. Hollywood had already developed the "creative" bookkeeping for which it would become notorious.

It seemed that Reverend Dixon's dream had become true. In big cities and tiny hamlets all over the country, American attitudes about the Civil War period changed. One young girl in Atlanta was impressed. Already imbued with the same historical background as Griffith, she saw the national stage set for the success of her own epic story that would cover the same era and offer, in a slightly modified form, the same Southern "take" on the postwar Klan. One critic would call the 1939 movie version of Margaret Mitchell's 1936 novel *Gone With the Wind,* "Birth of a Nation with sex."

On the other hand, some believed sex was the most insidious and dangerous dark seam of *Birth of a Nation.* The scene depicting the black villain—actually a white actor in blackface, as were all the "Negroes"—stalking a white woman with rape on his mind and her subsequent suicide plunge drew angry responses from every audience, coast to coast.

Another Atlantan who went to see the movie was impressed by the film because it dovetailed with something he had on his mind. He went home and thought about things. He was well acquainted with the Ku Klux Klan, as were most Southerners. The Klan had been organized in the wake of the Civil War by the Southern hero Nathan Bedford Forrest. Forrest, a prewar slave trader, had developed into one of the most brilliant tacticians produced on either side of the conflict. However, his record was tarnished when men under his command committed the atrocity called the "Fort Pillow Massacre." African-American Union troops were among the defenders of Fort Pillow who surrendered to Forrest's troops. Some Southern soldiers, in rage and blood lust, slaughtered their unarmed black prisoners. It was an episode that would foreshadow hundreds of incidents to come.

After the war, when restrictive martial law came to the defeated states, Forrest organized the "Invisible Empire," which attempted to enslave by terror those who had been freed by law. Burnings, beatings, and lynchings became commonplace, all after dark, all committed by anonymous Southerners cloaked in white sheets.

The original Klan did not last long. Organized in 1866, it began to disband in 1869 as some of the North-South political tensions began to ease and some high Klan officials were called to account. By 1871, it was gone. There were occasional isolated reincarnations, which responded to local "incidents." Also, the threat of a revivified Klan was often held over the head of any rebellious leaders of minorities. However, the powerful, interstate, networked Klan was moribund.

Until Colonel William J. Simmons saw *Birth of a Nation* in Atlanta, a city that had seen a nasty "race riot" as recently as 1906. He pondered the heroic image of the "Clan" at the close of the film and the audience's thrilled response to masked men "saving womanhood" and "protecting civilized values." He spent the summer contacting like-minded men all over the South. He found an enthusiastic response.

On the twenty-fifth of November 1915, Colonel William Simmons announced the reorganization of the Ku Klux Klan. For the next ten years, it would be the fastest-growing "club" in the nation, and its influence would reach deep into traditionally Northern states. It would sponsor parades, dances, picnics, patriotic gatherings, and political candidates. It would also sponsor assaults, arson, and murder, mostly against African Americans, though other minorities were not completely ignored.

The Klan boasted 400,000 members by the mid-1920s and always claimed the moral support of D. W. Griffith, if not his public endorsement.

However that may have been, Mr. Griffith certainly vigorously defended his First Amendment rights under increasing attacks from civil rights activists and historians. He added a prologue to his film, which read:

A PLEA FOR THE ART OF THE MOTION PICTURE

We do not fear censorship, for we have no wish to offend with improprieties or obscenities, but we do demand, as a right, the liberty to show the dark side of wrong, that we may illuminate the bright side of virtue—the same liberty that is conceded to the art of the written word— that art to which we owe the Bible and the works of Shakespeare.

Still bedeviled, Griffith soon added a pamphlet, which he made available at later showings. Its title was *The Rise and Fall of Free Speech in America*.

He need not have worried. Though serious efforts to have the film banned continued in several states and Woodrow Wilson backed off from his earlier endorsement, millions continued to pay to see Mr. Griffith trumpet his version of the Civil War and Reconstruction for years to come.

As a direct result of this epic film, American movies were elevated from craft to art. They became the principal medium of popular entertainment and remained so for forty years. An uneasy confluence of art and business was born that would both lead and reflect American culture for the rest of the century. In another small breakthrough, one of Griffith's stars, Lillian Gish, with his early encouragement, became one of the first women to direct a major feature film.

But there was something else. A resurgent Ku Klux Klan, flourishing directly because of the protective coloration of this film's celebration of racial discrimination, scarred the nation's cultural landscape for a generation. Burnings, beatings, and death were the empirical result. In a footnote, there would be no realistic portrayal of the African American experience on the big screen as long as Mr. Griffith would live.

In the spring of 1930, D. W. Griffith filmed an interview conducted by his friend the fine actor Walter Huston—father of John Huston and grandfather of Angelica Huston.

The pace of the discussion was stately, the language elegant, two nineteenth-century men having a smoke and reminiscing. At one point Huston gave Griffith a sword, telling him it had been worn by a Confederate officer.

"My father wore a sword like that," said Griffith.

"When you made *Birth of a Nation*, were you telling your father's story?" asked Huston.

"Oh, no, I don't think so. Although now that you ask it like that, perhaps I did."

"How long did it take you to make it?"

"Oh, I suppose it began when I was a child. I'd get under the table and listen to my father and his friends talk about their battles and their struggles. . . ."

"Was the story true?"

"Yes, I think so," Griffith gestured toward the sword, "as true as that blade. Your father telling you of fighting day after day, night after night, eating only parched corn . . . And then, later, your mother staying up night after night, sewing robes for the Klan. The Klan at that time was needed and served a purpose. But then, in answer to your question, as Pontius Pilate said, 'What is truth?' "

Griffith continued. "It was a story about a tremendous struggle, people fighting against overwhelming odds, making great sacrifices, facing death, a great story . . . It's easy enough to tell that kind of story. Anyone can tell it. It tells itself."

Many would disagree with Mr. Griffith on that last point. To be effective—as effective as it undoubtedly was—the story would have to be told by a person of burning conviction, one who believed implicitly the stories of unequal battles told by his father. A person who could remember warmly his mother sewing robes that would then be used to hide the identities of men who would burn, beat, and kill on a thousand moonless nights.

No, this story would never have told *itself* to the world. It took the single-minded zeal of a gifted man who had mastered an emerging art form and could write his version of history with lightning.

D. W. Griffith is probably the most important person in the history of American film. But the masterwork that gave him immortality also marks him forever as a genius of racial prejudice, in twelve reels of shimmering nitrate.

Which leads the rest of us to ponder his next project. Had something of the enormity of what he had done penetrated his consciousness? The next D. W. Griffith film would be bigger in every way than *Birth of a Nation*. Bigger sets, bigger budget, more actors. The subject would have a larger historical sweep. Many critics, particularly those of other countries, would call this the greatest film he ever made, perhaps the greatest film *anyone* ever made. It would prove to be a commercial disappointment and lose Mr. Griffith a substantial amount of the fortune he had earned on *Birth of a Nation*.

The 1916 poster advertising this film at the same Boston theater doubtless brought a derisive smile to Andrew Jones's face, a face still bearing the scars of the previous year's protest. This time, the poster showed a frightened white woman holding a baby while a huge, menacing hand clawed toward her. At least, the young Mr. Jones might have thought, the hand was white. Small steps.

But it was the title, Griffith's one-word title, which he hoped would distill its whole message, that wrung bitter laughs from every African American who saw it. A monument to irony, it read: *Intolerance.*

The Birth of a Nation was the first movie to change us. It took many years for the nation born of this film to recover.

THE MOVIE THAT NEVER WAS

E ighteen months of a fairly intense regimen of watching films, reading about films, interviewing filmmakers, and talking to people in all walks of life about films has led me to some interesting paths. Along the way the exercise has, inevitably, shattered a number of preconceptions.

In the beginning of this project, for instance, it seemed that the easiest chapter to write would be the one about race relations in America. All that was required was for me to isolate the key movie, the brave film that was at least the precursor—and maybe the catalyst—of the civil rights upheaval of the 1950s, which led directly to historic national legislation in the 1960s.

This would, I presumed, require a trip or two, a few interviews, and a week or so of specific research, then it would be wrapped up. All I had to do was find the movie. That's all.

Let us dispense with the suspense and, in film parlance, cut to the chase.

I didn't find one.

Some argue that popular culture tells more about a people than they would like posterity to know. If so, this void in the center of one of the profound issues of our society tells us how dangerous we think *race* is. And, unfortunately, how ambivalent many of us remain on the subject.

Race. Even the word introduced into a conversation can still cause a wince and averted eyes in some quarters. And this, decades after *race* movies became ethnic movies, *race* and blues music became rhythm and blues and *race* riots became urban disturbances.

Movies have been all over the map on the issue of race from the very beginning. They often reflected whatever was the prevailing attitude. What they have never done in the mainstream business of movies is to lead. All that talent and power was never focused in any meaningful way on the issue of racial bigotry, particularly prejudice against blacks in America.

It can be argued with some justice that there were other issues of life and death that put everything else on the back burner: a Depression which threatened to sink our economic and political system; a world war we could actually have lost; nuclear annihilation the touch of one red button away.

Still, the question of race was one we were all too willing to put on that back burner. Perhaps it was too close to the bone. Perhaps there was too much guilt associated with it. Perhaps the enormity of the dichotomy of the institution of slavery—*slavery*—coexisting with the thunder and lightning and heart-stopping promise of the greatest words ever offered as a formula for representative government was still too hot to the touch: "We hold these truths to be self-evident, that all men are created equal . . ."

The words leave no place to hide. Ultimately, they must be lived up to, or the nation founded on them must perish and end up on the dust heap of history along with other failed hopes.

Popular culture tells us, if we know where to look, how we're measuring up, decade by decade. How do we feel about our government, our military, our legal system? What's our current take on women, on men, on children? What's our attitude on smoking, drinking, drugs, sex? What do we read, wear, eat? How do we treat the old, the ill, the poor, our pets? What makes us laugh, what do we feel about the rich and powerful?

And how about colored people who became Negroes, then blacks, then African Americans?

We saw the movies portray black Americans as arrogant and rapacious in *Birth of a Nation*. At least that had the virtue of giving them stature, a segment of the population to be feared. We have seen the consequences of that characterization in the previous chapter.

Black Americans knew they were going to be excluded from any meaningful participation in this revolutionary form of entertainment and communication. As early as 1916, actor Noble Johnson, along with members of his family and a few friends, formed the Lincoln Motion Picture Company with the purpose of making all-black films.

The hope was that blacks could be portrayed in the same way that whites were, and that blacks across the country could see black lawyers, doctors, judges, business people, housewives as well as the usual proportion of villains and vamps. Over the years, a small, always cash-starved independent black film industry struggled on, producing movies of all kinds. Their market was too small and the audience too poor to support much more than bare-bones productions, and establishment Hollywood was reluctant to help.

In the meantime, the big movies did just what black Americans knew they would. They cast black actors as servants or entertainers, usually for comic relief. In the earliest days, the black roles were often given to white actors in makeup, as in *Birth of a Nation*. By the 1920s, there was a growing cadre of black performers on hand to fill the roles. Seldom were the parts more than caricatures.

But nothing could extinguish the hope. Each time a black actor got national recognition, it seemed for a while that everything might change.

Some thought the children might lead them. In silent days, little Allen Hoskins was a standout in the *Our Gang* comedies as Farina. And earlier, "Sunshine Sammy," Ernest Morrison, got a lot of attention in Harold Lloyd comedies.

They were not, however, the opening wedge for blacks that many had hoped. And adult roles—rare in any case—remained those of villains or fools.

With the coming of sound, there was a resurgence of minstrel blackface in movies, with stars such as Al Jolson and Eddie Cantor topping the box-office lists. Blackface remained a feature of Hollywood musicals through the 1940s and even the 1950s, jarring the contemporary viewer of classic films such as 1942's *Holiday Inn*, which introduced Irving Berlin's great "White Christmas" but also presented a blackface production number, and 1951's *I'll See You in My Dreams*, where even all-American blonde Doris Day was seen briefly in blackface.

In 1929, there was an unusual amount of excitement in the black sections of Los Angeles. Word was out that a major, big-budget film was in the works with an all-black cast. It seemed too good to be true, but soon the rumors were confirmed.

The man responsible was no less an imposing figure than director King Vidor. His benchmark silents *The Big Parade* and *The Crowd*, among many others, put him in the forefront of top directors. Far from dreading the arrival of sound, he welcomed it and, in fact, would have blockbuster hits with *Stella Dallas, The Champ, Northwest Passage*, and *Duel in the Sun* in upcoming years.

But the very first sound project he wanted to do was a story he had written himself, *Hallelujah*, with an all-black cast. Everyone knew—or thought they knew—the problems. A movie like this was unlikely to make money because it would never be released in the Solid South, cutting out nearly a fourth of the potential markets.

Vidor was adamant. It was an important film and he was going to make it. As it turned out, he found a willing listener in the frail young chief of production at Metro-Goldwyn-Mayer,

Irving Thalberg. Thalberg had something of a social conscience himself and gave Vidor the go-ahead.

MGM did not scrimp. The entire cast was sent on location to Tennessee, the best technicians were assigned, and none other than Irving Berlin was hired to write original songs.

The cast was a mixture of veterans, newcomers, and a few amateurs. Even those with experience, of course, had never had starring roles in films. The adventure would be unique. Vidor decided, because of the overwhelming technical difficulties with sound on location in those early days, to shoot the movie as a silent, then add sound in post-production. It worked better than most thought it would.

Daniel L. Haynes and Nina Mae McKinney had the leads. The material is overly melodramatic by current standards but was right on target for contemporary films. It was an excellent production. Thalberg and MGM spent a great deal on advertising. *Hallelujah* had wide distribution in the North, the Midwest, and the West.

And audiences stayed away in droves.

The commercial failure was a terrible disappointment to the small community of black actors in Hollywood. They knew what a success would have meant for them. They also knew what a flop meant. It would be a long time before they would get another chance.

They were right. After this one glorious experiment, Hollywood fell back into its old ways.

In 1933, we saw the impressive Noble Johnson, a film pioneer, as the native leader in *King Kong*. Lost among the extras who portrayed the other aborigines was Jim Thorpe, the greatest athlete of his time—and a Native American.

The year 1934 saw what many believe was the most effective portrayal of a black-white relationship in the pre–civil rights era. The story was Fannie Hurst's soap opera tearjerker *Imitation of Life*, but, for once, black actors were in on the principal theme. Claudette Colbert and Louise Beavers had moments of actually speaking to each other, being in business together, talking about their daughters. They even touched on the explosive issue of sex with Louise's daughter, Fredi Washington, "passing" for white.

Consider this. In the coming years, painful lurches forward in the attack on institutional racism would be launched. Harry Truman's startling decision—with the stroke of his pen in an executive order—to desegregate the armed forces came shortly after World War II. At almost the same moment, America's most cherished sports institution, baseball, brought Jackie Robinson into the major leagues. Seven years later, the highest court in the land, with the *Brown vs. the Board of Education* decision, ruled that "separate" was by definition "unequal" and ordered schools coast-to-coast to be desegregated. And brave men and women throughout the South began challenging segregation everywhere, from buses to theaters to lunch counters.

And still, as we have seen, twenty-five years after the original, *Imitation of Life* was made again in 1959 with Lana Turner and Juanita Moore, and "passing" was considered just as shocking as it had been a quarter century before, across the divide of all those fundamental changes.

The same issue of "passing" was addressed in a more forthright way by director Elia Kazan in 1949 with *Pinky*, but the young actress doing the "passing" was the very white Jeanne Crain. It should also be noted that in all cases the person posing as white was a young female, never a male. Hollywood was nowhere near dealing with the implications of a black male and a white female in any sexually charged situation.

Prior to the 1960s, the only famous black-white couple was Shirley Temple and Bill "Bojangles" Robinson in their unforgettable dance routines through the mid-1930s.

Two more all-black feature films were made by major studios, *Green Pastures* in 1936, an adaptation of Marc Connelly's play starring Rex Ingram, and 1943's musical *Cabin in the Sky*, director Vincente Minnelli's first film, starring Eddie Anderson, Lena Horne, and Ethel Waters.

Again, these ambitious all-black productions proved not to be harbingers of things to come, but cut flowers in a vase, blooming beautifully in their time, only to wilt and be forgotten.

No African American stars were produced by the movies. Most who got substantial billing had made their names elsewhere; singer Ethel Waters, dancer Bill Robinson, stage actor Paul Robeson, radio comedian Eddie "Rochester" Anderson. Those who relied on Hollywood for their celebrity were leaning on a weak reed. The names Rex Ingram, Nina Mae McKinney, Oscar Polk, Daniel L. Haynes did not resonate through the decades, though they were stars of big-budget movies.

The names we remember are those of supporting players, always there for roles of servants or comedy relief. The formidable Hattie McDaniel, the first African American to win an Academy Award for performance, was Mammy in *Gone With the Wind*. She was in Hollywood to receive her award, but, significantly, was not invited to the premiere of the film in Atlanta, Georgia.

She would have been required to sit in the balcony.

Dooley Wilson provided the indelible soundtrack for *Casablanca* with "As Time Goes By." But Ingrid Bergman's character casually tossed off the line, "Have the boy sing 'As Time Goes By.'" The *boy*. Play it again, boy? Say it ain't so, Sam.

There were fits and starts. *Home of the Brave* (1949) touched on the problems faced by black GIs even before Korea threw minority foot soldiers into the thick of combat again. James Edwards had the lead and was remarkably effective, but he did not become the first black star.

In 1962, Brock Peters played an all-too-real role opposite

Gregory Peck's Atticus Finch in *To Kill a Mockingbird*, but he did not become a star.

That mantle was still to come and it would be worn by an intense, intelligent man born in 1924 in Miami, Florida, to a Bahamian family. His name was Sidney Poitier.

The timing for once was good. Hollywood, trailing the widening civil rights movement by several steps, as usual, was on the lookout for an African American leading man. And, at long last, the wider audience was ready to accept that kind of phenomenon on the big screen.

Poitier paid his dues with menial jobs, U.S. Army service, the American Negro Theater, and small roles in New York. He made his first film in 1950, but it was his role in *The Defiant Ones* (1958) that fired the long-delayed shot across the bow of movie stardom. The successful film costarred Tony Curtis and got Mr. Poitier his first Best Actor nomination from the Academy.

Five years later he would stand at the podium and accept the first Best Actor Oscar for an African American. He received it for his role in *Lillies of the Field* in 1963. But it was in 1967 that he would pull what hockey fans would recognize as "the hat trick." In that one year, he starred in three box-office blockbusters, all of which were also distinguished films. *In the Heat of the Night* costarred Rod Steiger; *To Sir with Love* addressed growing problems with youth; and, above all, *Guess Who's Coming to Dinner* dealt with the long-taboo question of interracial marriage. How important was the film? For young black Americans in 1967, it apparently was very important.

Ed Rigaud, now the director of the mammoth Underground Railroad Museum and Freedom Center on the riverfront in Cincinnati, Ohio, was born in New Orleans and was a teenager when he saw *Guess Who's Coming to Dinner.*

"You must understand that, like all young men, I was

struggling for self-esteem," he said, " but I was still trying to sort out what was the right kind of self-esteem. I had been going to movies all of my life, and the only successful, interesting people I saw up on that screen were white. It seemed the only way to get ahead in the world was to emulate whites. I wasn't comfortable with that, but I couldn't see any other way.

"Then, that day in 1967, I saw an articulate, confident, successful man who was also uncompromisingly black.

"I knew that most people were fascinated by the unusual treatment of interracial marriage, but that held only passing interest for me.

"Here was a black man standing on equal footing with the best Hollywood had to offer. He had found self-esteem on his own terms.

"For a kid from New Orleans who used to be marched off by the Blessed Sacrament nuns to a Mario Lanza movie to get 'culture,' this was a revelation.

"If you want to know the truth, I believe it changed things for me."

Did movies change things for other African Americans? Black friends have told me they sat in dark balconies during *Tarzan* movies and cheered for the natives. Yes, and cheered for the Indians in the Westerns, too.

Blanche Chambers is ramrod straight, slim, quite beautiful. She has lived in the Ohio River town of Maysville, Kentucky, all of her life, which began February 3, 1924, just a few weeks before the birth of Sidney Poitier.

As a child, Blanche was a self-taught tap dancer and a good one. Her mother, known in Maysville as "Miss Lizzie," was "in service." One of her jobs was as a maid at the elegant New Central Hotel on Market Street.

Just across the street was a shop with a sign hand-painted on the window: "A. Clooney, Jeweler." Over the shop lived

Blanche's best friend, Mr. Clooney's granddaughter Rosemary. As much as Blanche loved to dance, Rosemary loved to sing. The connection extended to younger siblings, so Blanche's sister "Pud," a dancer, was best friends with Rosemary's sister Betty, a singer.

For a time, they were nearly inseparable. They would perform with any encouragement—or none at all. Sometimes they would do a show on a street corner, drawing a small crowd, whom Mr. Andrew Clooney would then inform that he was running for mayor in the next election and would appreciate their vote.

The Chambers children were black, the Clooneys white. They could play together, perform together, but they could not go to school together, or drink from the same public fountain, or go to the movies together. For Blanche, there was always the balcony.

"For me, it was not a big thing. I could see the movies just fine from the balcony, and that's what I went there for.

"Mama told me not to worry about what I couldn't change, and I never have. She told me some people would treat me mean but most would treat me just fine, and it turned out she was right."

Blanche never married. For many years she was companion to an elderly lady. She is active in the Episcopal Church as a lay reader, a chalice bearer, and a leader of morning and evening prayer. She lives modestly and in great dignity in the same house that has been her home most of her life. When she was younger, she loved the movies.

"I liked the same people everyone else did. I loved Fred Astaire. The dancing, you know. And Bill Robinson. I wouldn't miss a Tyrone Power movie.

"I know it will seem stupid to many people now, but I never paid any attention to the fact there were so few on the screen who looked like me. Folks look at me like I'm crazy when I tell them that when I saw Willie Best or Stepin Fetchit [Lincoln Perry] in the movies, I laughed just as hard as anyone. They were funny. Besides, they were doing exactly the same routines that Ed Garden and Skitch Howell and 'Navy' Davis were doing right here in Maysville. Why, they'd put on burnt cork, just like those old minstrels. Didn't you know that black people were the ones who started that 'blackface' makeup? It was show business, that's all. They entertained.

"A lot of my friends and all the young people I know are really upset by what used to be on the screen. But you know what? In the end, it's just a movie. It doesn't mean anything; it's just there to entertain.

"Do I think a movie can change anything important? No, I don't. It's just a picture show. Nothing will ever get any better until people actually feel it in their hearts, and that has to come from real people, not a picture show.

"Mama said things were going to get better because people would be better to each other, and I think I've seen that in my life.

"Come to think of it, one example of it—people treating each other better—did happen in a movie house. Rosemary came home [to Maysville] for the premiere of her first movie [*The Stars Are Singing*]. It was in January 1953, and everything was still segregated, you know. The show was going to be at the Russell.

"Let me tell you, thousands of people were in town and they had big shows up at the tobacco warehouse and the biggest parade I've ever seen in town. She had her Grandmother Guilfoyle in the convertible with her, and she went out of her way to find me, too.

"Well, finally I got to the Russell, up in the balcony, of course, and Rosemary got up on stage and made a nice little speech. Then the lights went off and the movie started.

"Don't you know, in a few minutes there was a commotion

in the back and here came Rosemary, up into the colored balcony, her mink coat and her pretty dress and all, and she came and sat next to me, and we watched that movie and giggled like schoolgirls.

"Now, don't you think that caused plenty of talk in Maysville from then on? And it wasn't long before there *wasn't* any colored balcony anymore.

"Yes, laws have to be changed if they discriminate against people. But the real change, the real respect, will only come, like Mama said, in the heart. Not in movies.

"I love all people. I live for the Lord and for people. I'm very happy."

Blanche paused for a moment, then smiled.

"But now that I can sit anywhere I want, I can't find many picture shows I *want* to see."

Individual movies or individual incidents have, apparently, made a difference in individual lives. Only an African American can assess the impact of a film with a racial theme on his or her heart—and I am not African American.

But a researcher can—must—look for smoking guns, blazed trails, tangible evidence, laws changed, in order to see whether or not a business working in the public interest mounted a concerted effort to make things better for one group or another.

In the matter of race, sports changed things, the highest court in the land changed things, the military changed things, and, eventually, the federal government changed things. The movies changed nothing. They stayed safe behind the curve of one of the great movements of the twentieth century.

Here's the film that could have changed things. The Movie That Never Was.

But the story of film is far from over.

There are still many troubling subtexts to our evolving society, that need telling, segments left behind when we move forward, scapegoats when we fail, the powerless and voiceless, all waiting for the still-potent medium of film to take up their cause and join them at the barricade—*now*, when it can still make a difference.

When will it arrive on our screens—troubling, challenging? Where is the next movie that will change us?

ABOUT THE AUTHOR

NICK CLOONEY would sit in the Saturday darkness of the Russell Theater in Maysville, Kentucky, with his older sisters Rosemary and Betty. Hours later, they would be the characters they had just seen.

His legendary broadcasting career spanned the end of the age of radio and the golden age of television. He has received more than three hundred awards in broadcasting and writing, including an Emmy, the Freedoms Foundation George Washington Medal, and an honorary doctor of fine arts degree from Northern Kentucky University.

Nick writes a column for *The Cincinnati Post* every Monday, Wednesday, and Friday and does a morning radio show on radio station WSAI. He and his wife, Nina, live in Augusta, Kentucky. Their daughter, Ada, graced them with a granddaughter, Allison, and a grandson, Nick; and their son, George, is a television and film star and a producer and director.

APPENDIX

1

SAVING PRIVATE RYAN (1998)

CAST: Tom Hanks, Edward Burns, Matt Damon, Tom Sizemore, Jeremy Davis, Vin Diesel, Ted Danson, Harve Presnell

DIRECTOR: Steven Spielberg

PRODUCERS: Steven Spielberg, Ian Bryce, Mark Gordon, Gary Levinsohn

WRITER: Robert Rodat

CINEMATOGRAPHER: Janusz Kaminski

MUSIC: John Williams

EDITOR: Michael Kahn

PRODUCTION DESIGNER: Tom Sanders

COSTUMES: Joanna Johnston

2
STAR WARS (1977)

CAST: Mark Hamill, Harrison Ford, Carrie Fisher, Peter Cushing, Alec Guinness, Anthony Daniels, Kenny Baker

DIRECTOR: George Lucas

PRODUCER: Gary Kurtz

WRITER: George Lucas

CINEMATOGRAPHER: Gilbert Taylor

MUSIC: John T. Williams

EDITORS: Paul Hirsh, Marcia Lucas, Richard Chew

PRODUCTION DIRECTOR: John Barry

ART DIRECTORS: Norman Reynolds, Leslie Dilley

SET DIRECTOR: Roger Christian

COSTUMES: John Mollo, Ron Beck

SPECIAL EFFECTS: John Dykstra

ANIMATION: Adam Beckett

MAKE-UP: Stuart Freeborn, Rick Baker, Doug Beswick

MECHANICAL EFFECTS: John Stears

SOUND EFFECTS: Benn Burtt

SOUND EDITING: Sam Shaw, Robert Rutledge, Gordon Davidson, Gene Corso

VISUAL EFFECTS: John Dykstra, Grant McCune, Robert Blalack, Richard Edlund

3

TAXI DRIVER (1976)

CAST: Robert DeNiro, Cybill Shepherd, Jodie Foster, Peter Boyle, Harvey Keitel, Albert Brooks, Leonard Harris

DIRECTOR: Martin Scorsese

PRODUCERS: Michael Phillips, Julia Phillips

WRITER: Paul Schrader

CINEMATOGRAPHER: Michael Chapman

MUSIC: Bernard Herrmann

EDITORS: Marcia Lucas, Tom Rolf, Melvin Shapiro

ART DIRECTOR: Charles Rosen

SET DECORATION: Herbert Mulligan

COSTUMES: Ruth Morley

SPECIAL EFFECTS: Tony Parmelee

4

THE GRADUATE (1967)

CAST: Anne Bancroft, Dustin Hoffman, Katharine Ross, William Daniels, Murray Hamilton, Elizabeth Wilson

DIRECTOR: Mike Nichols

PRODUCER: Lawrence Turman

WRITERS: Calder Willingham, Buck Henry

CINEMATOGRAPHER: Robert Surtees

MUSIC: Dave Grusin

EDITOR: Sam O'Steen

PRODUCTION
DIRECTOR: Richard Sylbert

SET DECORATOR: George R. Nelson

COSTUMES: Patricia Zipprodt

MUSIC AND LYRICS: Paul Simon

5

WHO'S ARAID OF VIRGINIA WOOLF (1966)

CAST: Elizabeth Taylor, Richard Burton, George
Segal, Sandy Dennis

DIRECTOR: Mike Nichols

PRODUCER: Ernest Lehman

WRITER: Ernest Lehman, based on Edward Albee
play

CINEMATOGRAPHERS: Haskell Wexler, Harry Stradling

MUSIC: Alex North

EDITOR: Sam O'Steen

PRODUCTION
DIRECTOR: Richard Sylbert

SET DECORATOR: George James Hopkins

COSTUMES: Irene Sharaff

6

DR. STRANGELOVE: OR HOW I LEARNED TO STOP WORRYING AND LOVE THE BOMB (1964)

CAST: Peter Sellers, George C. Scott, Sterling Hayden, Keenan Wynn, Slim Pickens, Peter Bull, Tracy Reed, James Earl Jones

DIRECTOR: Stanley Kubrick

PRODUCER: Stanley Kubrick

WRITERS: Stanley Kubrick, Terry Southern, Peter George, based on novel *Red Alert* by Peter George

CINEMATOGRAPHER: Melvin Pike

MUSIC: Laurie Johnson

EDITOR: Anthony Harvey

PRODUCTION DIRECTOR: Ken Adams

ART DIRECTOR: Peter Murton

COSTUMES: Bridget Sellers

SPECIAL EFFECTS: Wally Veevers

7

MARTY (1955)

CAST: Ernest Borgnine, Betsy Blair, Esther Minciotti, Karen Steele, Jerry Paris, Frank Sutton, Walter Kelley

DIRECTOR: Delbert Mann

PRODUCER: Harold Hecht

WRITER: Paddy Chayefsky, based on his own television play

CINEMATOGRAPHER: Joseph La Shelle

MUSIC: Roy Webb

EDITOR: Alan Grosland, Jr.

ART DIRECTORS: Edward S. Haworth, Walter Simonds

COSTUMES: Norma

8

ON THE WATERFRONT (1954)

CAST: Marlon Brando, Karl Malden, Lee J. Cobb,
Rod Steiger, Pat Henning, Eva Marie
Saint, Leif Erickson, James Westerfield

DIRECTOR: Elia Kazan

PRODUCER: Sam Spiegel

WRITER: Budd Schulberg, based on newspaper articles by Malcolm Johnson

CINEMATOGRAPHER: Boris Kaufman

MUSIC: Leonard Bernstein

EDITOR: Gene Milford

ART DIRECTOR: Richard Day

9

THE SNAKE PIT (1948)

CAST: Olivia de Havilland, Mark Stevens, Leo Genn, Celeste Holm, Glenn Langan, Helen Craig, Leif Erickson, Beulah Bondi

DIRECTOR: Anatole Litvak

PRODUCERS: Anatole Litvak, Robert Bassler

WRITERS: Frank Partos, Millen Brand, based on a novel by Mary Jane Ward

CINEMATOGRAPHER: Leo Tover

MUSIC: Alfred Newman

EDITOR: Dorothy Spencer

ART DIRECTORS: Lyle Wheeler, Joseph C. Wright

SET DECORATION: Thomas Little, Ernest Lansing

COSTUMES: Bonnie Cashin

10

THE BEST YEARS OF OUR LIVES (1946)

CAST: Myrna Loy, Fredric March, Dana Andres, Teresa Wright, Virginia Mayo, Cathy O'Donnell, Hoagy Carmichael, Harold Russell

DIRECTOR: William Wyler

PRODUCER: Samuel Goldwyn

WRITER: Robert E. Sherwood, from a novella by MacKinlay Kantor

CINEMATOGRAPHER: Gregg Toland

MUSIC: Hugo Friedhofer

ART DIRECTORS: Geroge Jenkins, Perry Ferguson

SET DECORATOR: Julia Heron

COSTUMES: Sharaff

11

THE MIRACLE OF MORGAN'S CREEK (1944)

CAST: Eddie Bracken, Betty Hutton, Diana Lynn, Brian Donlevy, Akim Tamiroff, Porter Hall, Emory Parnell, William Demarest

DIRECTOR: Preston Sturges

PRODUCER: Preston Sturges

WRITER: Preston Sturges

CINEMATOGRAPHER: John F. Seitz

MUSIC: Leo Shuken, Charles Bradshaw

EDITOR: Stuart Gilmore

ART DIRECTORS: Hans Dreier, Ernst Fegte

SET DECORATOR: Stephen Seymour

COSTUMES: Edith Head

12
THE GREAT DICTATOR (1940)

CAST: Charles Chaplin, Paulette Goddard, Jack Oakie, Reginald Gardiner, Henry Daniell, Billy Gilbert, Carter de Haven

DIRECTOR: Charles Chaplin

PRODUCER: Charles Chaplin

WRITER: Charles Chaplin

CINEMATOGRAPHERS: Roland Totheroh, Karl Struss

MUSIC: Meredith Willson

EDITOR: Willard Nico

ART DIRECTOR: J. Russell Spencer

13
STAGECOACH (1939)

CAST: Claire Trevor, John Wayne, John Carradine, Thomas Mitchell, Andy Devine, Donald Meek, Louise Platt, George Bancroft

DIRECTOR: John Ford

PRODUCER: Walter Wanger

WRITER: Dudley Nichols, based on short story by Ernest Haycox

CINEMATOGRAPHER: Bert Glennon

MUSIC: Richard Hageman, W. Frank Harling, Louis Gruenberg, Leo Shuken, John

Leipold, based on 17 folk tunes from the
19th Century

EDITORS: Dorothy Spencer, Walter Reynolds

ART DIRECTOR: Alexander Toluboff

SET DECORATOR: Wiard B. Ihnen

COSTUMES: Walter Plunkett

SPECIAL EFFECTS: Ray Binger

14
BOYS TOWN (1938)

CAST: Spencer Tracy, Mickey Rooney, Henry
Hull, Leslie Fenton, Addison Richards,
Edward Norris, Gene Reynolds, Minor
Watson

DIRECTOR: Norman Taurog

PRODUCER: John W. Considine, Jr.

WRITERS: John Meehan, Dore Schary, based on a
story by Dore Schary and Eleanor Griffin

CINEMATOGRAPHER: Sidney Wagner

MUSIC: Edward Ward

EDITOR: Elmo Vernon

SPECIAL EFFECTS: Slavko Vorkapich

15

TRIUMPH OF THE WILL (1935)

CAST: Adolf Hitler, Rudolf Hess, Nazi Party
Rally Participants

DIRECTOR: Leni Riefenstahl

PRODUCER: The Nazi Party

CINEMATOGRAPHERS: Leni Riefenstahl, Sepp Allgeier

MUSIC: Herbert Windt

EDITOR: Leni Riefenstahl

16

LOVE ME TONIGHT (1932)

CAST: Maurice Chevalier, Jeanette MacDonald,
Charles Ruggles, Charles Butterworth,
Myrna Loy, C. Aubrey Smith, George
Hayes

DIRECTOR: Rouben Mamoulian

PRODUCER: Rouben Mamoulian

WRITERS: Samuel Hoffenstein, Waldemar Young,
George Marion, Jr., based on play *Tailor
in the Chateau* by Leopold Marchand and
Paul Armont

CINEMATOGRAPHER: Victor Milner

MUSIC AND LYRICS: Richard Rodgers and Lorenz Hart

EDITOR: Billy Shea

ART DIRECTOR: Hans Dreier

SET DIRECTOR: A. E. Frendeman

COSTUMES: Edith Head, Travis Banton

17
MOROCCO (1930)

CAST: Gary Cooper, Marlene Dietrich, Adolphe Menjou, Ullrich Haupt, Juliette Compton, Francis McDonald, Albert Conti

DIRECTOR: Joseph von Sternberg

PRODUCER: Hector Turnbull

WRITER: Jules Furthman, based on novel *Amy Jolly* by Benno Vigny

CINEMATOGRAPHERS: Lee Garmes, Lucien Ballard

MUSIC: Karl Hajos

EDITOR: Sam Winston

ART DIRECTOR: Hans Dreier

COSTUMES: Travis Banton

18
THE JAZZ SINGER (1927)

CAST: Al Jolson, May McAvoy, Warner Oland, Eugenie Besserer, Bobby Gordon, Otto Lederer, Richard Tucker, William Demarest, Myrna Loy

DIRECTOR: Alan Crosland

PRODUCERS: The Warner Brothers

WRITER: Alfred A. Cohn, titles; and Jack Jarmuth, based on play *Day of Atonement* by Samson Raphaelson

CINEMATOGRAPHER: Hal Mohr

MUSIC: Louis Silvers

EDITOR: Harold McCord

19

THE BIG PARADE (1925)

CAST: John Gilbert, Renee Adoree, Hobart Bosworth, Claire McDowell, Claire Adams, Robert Ober, Tom O'Brien, Karl Dane

DIRECTOR: King Vidor

PRODUCER: Irving Thalberg, uncredited

WRITER: Harry Behn, based on a story by Lawrence Stallings; titles, Joseph W. Farnham

CINEMATOGRAPHER: John Arnold

MUSIC: William Axt, David Mendoza

EDITOR: Hugh Wynn

ART DIRECTORS: Cedric Gibbons, James Basevi

20

THE BIRTH OF A NATION (1915)

CAST: Lillian Gish, Mae Marsh, Henry B. Walthall, Miriam Cooper, Mary Alden, Ralph Lewis, George Siegmann, Walter Long, Wallace Reid, Raoul Walsh, Erich von Stroheim

DIRECTOR: D. W. Griffith

PRODUCER: D. W. Griffith

WRITERS: D. W. Griffith, Frank E. Woods, based on novel and play *The Clansman* by Thomas Dixon, Jr.

CINEMATOGRAPHER: G. W. Bitzer

MUSIC: Joseph Carl Breil, D. W. Griffith

EDITOR: James Smith

COSTUMES: Robert Goldstein